Designed for executives, managers and entrepreneurs in all sized companies, this practical, comprehensive guide provides you with the tools you need to keep your organization running as efficiently and profitably as possible. Here you'll see specific strategies and techniques you can use to:

Move your company from a sales to a profit orientation by restructuring its goals and reward systems

Identify and evaluate those risks that may pay off big, and those that may threaten the corporation's survival

Set up and maintain a decentralized management structure that encourages employees to initiate decisions as well as implement them

Develop budgets that reflect the *real* capabilities of the organization and the *real* opportunities of the marketplace

Revamp your administrative systems to encourage creativity and strengthen your company's ability to react (or pro-act) to a rapidly changing environment

And that's just the beginning. You'll also see how to spot the indicators that reveal an organization's true potential for success...evaluate the organizational climate to see if it encourages short-term profitability at the expense of long-term goals...distinguish between problems that can be treated internally and those that require external intervention...and much more.

Nowhere else has such a simple but comprehensive means been made available for business professionals to assess and improve the health of their corporation. This is one book that should be on every executive's desk.

Corporations, like living organisms, experience predictable patterns of behavior as they grow and develop. And, like living organisms, they are faced with specific transitional problems as they progress through the various stages of their lifecycle. According to Dr. Ichak Adizes, the success or failure of any organization depends on its ability to meet the challenges presented by this growth, and make healthy transitions from one stage of development to the next.

And if there's anyone who really understands organizational behavior and what keeps a corporation vital and growing, it's Ichak Adizes. Regarded as one of the world's foremost management theorists, Dr. Adizes has spent more than 22 years successfully helping to increase the effectiveness and efficiency of hundreds of companies around the world.

In this revolutionary new guide, Dr. Adizes gives you a close look at how corporations develop — and how to keep yours a dynamic and vital entity. He shows you step-by-step how to assess your organization's strengths and weaknesses and how to determine where your company is located on the lifecycle curve. He offers tested strategies which can be used to change the organizational climate and remove obstacles that prevent growth. Adizes also provides innovative forecasting methods that will help you predict what problems lie ahead for your company and specific preventive measures you can take to avoid them.

Corporate Lifecycles: How and Why Corporations Grow and Die and What to do About It

Ichak Adizes, Ph.D.

Professional Director
Adizes Institute, Santa Monica
and
Adjunct Associate Professor,
Anderson School of Management, UCLA

AN ADIZES INSTITUTE BOOK

PRENTICE HALL
Englewood Cliffs, New Jersey 07632

Prentice-Hall International (UK) Limited, *London*
Prentice-Hall of Australia, Pty. Limited, *Sydney*
Prentice-Hall Canada Inc., *Toronto*
Prentice-Hall Hispanoamericana, S.A., *Mexico*
Prentice-Hall of India Private Limited, *New Delhi*
Prentice-Hall of Japan, Inc., *Tokyo*
Simon & Schuster Asia Pte Ltd., *Singapore*
Editora Prentice-Hall do Brasil, Ltda., *Rio de Janeiro*

© 1988 by
Prentice-Hall, Inc.
Englewood Cliffs, New Jersey

Printed in the United States of America

10 9 8 7 6 5 4 3 2 1

Library of Congress Cataloging-in Publication Data

Adizes, Ichak.
  Corporate lifecycles: how and why corporations grow and die and
what to do about it / Ichak Adizes.
    p. cm.
  Includes index.
  ISBN 0-13-174400-3
  1. Organizational change. 2. Corporate culture.
  3. Organizational behavior. I. Title. II. Title: Corporate life
cycles.
  HD58.8.A34 1989
  658.4'06—dc19   88-28665
                                                              CIP

ISBN 0-13-174400-3

PRENTICE HALL
BUSINESS & PROFESSIONAL DIVISION
A division of Simon & Schuster
Englewood Cliffs, New Jersey 07632

This book is dedicated to the memory of my best friend, Marco Naiman.

Acknowledgments

This book grew out of 20 years of experience working with several hundred companies around the world. It grew out of working and lecturing to several thousand top executives in business and government, internationally. Everyone contributed something. I listened, noted, remembered, analyzed, conceptualized, and represented it in this book. The list of people to whom I owe recognition is endless. To all of them, my thanks.

I especially want to thank Dr. Ivan Gabor of the Adizes Institute, Professor William Newman, and Dean Kirby Warren of Columbia University, Joel Schiavone, President of Schiavone Corporation, and Martin F. Saarinen, Director of the Lutheran Theological Seminary, Columbia, South Carolina for their comments and support. Lyn Castorina, Elaine Barber, and Janet Kirkland edited the book. Clark Wigley put the material together and did the charts. Rosemary Sostarich typed endless drafts. My sons, Topaz and Shoham, had to give up their daddy on many sunny days.

To all of them, my deepest thanks.

About the Author

Dr. Ichak Adizes is the founder of the Adizes Institute in Santa Monica, California. He is the developer of the diagnostic and therapeutic methodology for organizational and cultural change which bears his name. In the process of developing and applying the Adizes methodology, he has worked with organizations with as few as 30 and as many as 90,000 employees. Adizes^{SM} has been applied for increasing the effectiveness and efficiency of organizations in 10 countries as diverse as the U.S., Greenland, Malaysia, Israel, Spain, Mexico and Norway, and in different technologies ranging from the banking industry to food services, and from churches to government bureaucracies. Twelve hundred pages of manuals and 100 hours of video and audio tapes document the methodology. Among the companies which practice Adizes are Domino's Pizza (went from $150 million in annual sales to $1.5 billion in seven years), the Franklin Mint and 400 other companies around the world. Seventy-five certified Adizes Associates apply the methodology worldwide.

A noted lecturer and author, Dr. Adizes speaks four languages and has worked with and addressed audiences in more than 35 countries. He has been the keynote speaker for the Young President's Organization, Columbia University Executive Development Programs, the American Association of Advertising Agencies and the Direct Marketing Association. His work has been featured in magazines and newspapers including *Fortune, Business Week*, the *New York Times*, and the *London Financial Times*.

Dr. Adizes is the author of *Industrial Democracy Yugoslav Style* (1971), Free Press and Columbia University); *Self Management* (with Elisabeth Man Borgese) (1975, ABC Clio Press and the Center for the Study of Democratic Institutions); *How to Solve the Mismanagement Crisis* (1979, Dow Jones Irwin); all presently available from Adizes Institute; and he has written more than 40 journal and magazine articles. He is an Adjunct Associate Professor at the Anderson Graduate School of Management, UCLA and has held appointments as a Visiting Professor at Stanford University, Tel Aviv University and Hebrew University, Jerusalem.

Contents

Introduction

We know that living organisms—whether they are plants, animals or people—are subject to a phenomenon called *Lifecycles*. Organisms are born, grow, age, and die. As they change along the lifecycle, these organic systems have predictable patterns of behavior. At each stage, the behavioral patterns manifest themselves as a certain struggle, as difficulties or transitional problems which the system must overcome. Sometimes the system does not succeed in resolving those problems by itself; it develops diseases or abnormalities which require external intervention for resolution.

Medicine has been developing the diagnostic and therapeutic tools for treating organic systems over several thousand years. The tools for diagnosing and treating an individual's psyche have a more recent history. The tools for diagnosing and treating organizational behavior—to change culture and consciousness—are in infancy. *Corporate Lifecycles* is an attempt to contribute to this emerging field.

Working as a consultant to top management, I realized that the Lifecycle concept applies to organizations as well as living organisms. After spending a number of years working with several organizations simultaneously, I experienced déjà vu, a sense of having been there before. Similar problems occurred with many different clients. It seemed that I could predict how a certain type of client's boardroom would look before I ever stepped into it. I began to anticipate the problems that would be presented to me. Reading newspapers and organizational case studies, I had a strong sensation that I knew how each story would end.

Organizations have lifecycles just as living organisms do; they go through the normal struggles and difficulties accompanying each stage of the Organizational Lifecycle and are faced with the transitional problems of moving to the next phase of development. Organizations learn to deal with these problems by themselves or they develop abnormal "diseases" which stymie growth—problems that usually cannot be resolved without external, professional intervention.

Over the years, I constructed a theory that predicted change in organizational cultures, explained why change occurs and provided a prescriptive theory and tested practice on to how to manage that change. This theory and practice provided clients with several distinct advantages. It enabled them to discriminate between the normal problems that could be treated internally and abnormal problems which required intervention from outside. Because the stages in the organization's lifecycle are predictable and repetitive, knowing where the organization was in the lifecycle enabled management to take proactive, preventive measures and deal with future problems earlier or avoid them altogether.

When an organization makes the transition from one stage of the lifecycle to the next, difficulties that generate certain kinds of energy occur. Further, it became evident that when energy was directed to stimulate transition, the organization would experience specific, normal transitional problems. However, in some cases, that energy, instead of being directed toward solving external problems, is sometimes turned inward.

An explanation which distinguishes between external and internal marketing can be helpful here. *External marketing* is the resources an organization spends selling its services to its clients. *Internal marketing* is the time and energy people in the organization spend "selling" their ideas to each other so that something can happen. It soon became obvious that when internal marketing significantly exceeds external marketing, the organization becomes both ineffective and inefficient; it gets stuck in a certain mode. If this phenomenon is very prolonged, it becomes an abnormality which requires external treatment—new energy must be imported to make a change.

The Adizes[SM] methodology, outlined in *Corporate Lifecycles*, tells how to convert internally-spent energy to externally-directed energy, and it tells how to make the change from the inside out. The ability to change an organization from the inside is the primary reason that this method of intervention has been able to show a significant amount of change in organizations, consequently the methodology focuses on that conversion of internally-spent energy to externally-spent energy. The more energy that has been spent internally that can be turned toward the external client, the higher the potential for change once the energy is redirected.

Changes resulting from Adizes interventions have had profound impact in changing organization climates—that is, in how an organization perceives itself, how people relate to each other, how they work as a team, and how they make decisions and react to problems. It has had external impact on organizations as well, specifically on how well these organizations subsequently perform in the marketplace. That impact can be reflected in market share, profit margins, profitability, quality of service, brand loyalty and turnover of personnel.

Applicability

This methodology for changing corporate cultures is applicable to organizations in different technologies and of different sizes, as measured by volume of sales or number of employees.

The methodology has also been applied to approximately 400 organizations so far, with profit or not-for-profit goals. These organizations range in size from 30 to 90,000 employees, and have varying technologies, including construction, heavy manufacturing, religious organizations, governments, fast food, and banking. The methodology has been applied in 20 countries: Australia, Brazil, Denmark, England, Germany, Ghana, Greece, Greenland, Iceland, India, Israel, Malaysia, Mexico, Norway, South Africa, Spain, Sweden, the United States, Venezuela, and Zimbabwe.

Among the companies that have practiced this theory of management is Domino's Pizza, a company that went from $150 million to $1.5 billion in sales in seven years. Another organization I worked with intensively to de-bureaucratize and change its location on the Lifecycle, is the second largest bank in the world, the Bank of America with $120 billion in assets and 90,000 employees. The theory also applies to not-for-profit organizations including the largest children's welfare organization in the world—the Los Angeles Department of Children's Services. In the Ghana Ministry of Health I facilitated the establishment of the Health Delivery Planning Unit considered by the World Health Organization as a model for Third World Countries. I have consulted with the Swedish Prime Minister's office on how to rejuvenate the governmental machinery and bureaucracy. (Unfortunately, in Sweden, the therapeutic part was never carried out because the government of Prime Minister Felding, who had invited me as a consultant, lost its plurality in the parliament and the project ended.) Among the smaller companies this system was applied to a food broker in Chicago with 80 employees, a church in Downey, California, and a chain of food stores.

The real test of the validity of any technique or methodology is if others can use the concepts and tools to achieve results and success comparable to those of the developer. The theories described in *Corporate Lifecycles* have been tested by others and demonstrated by more than 75 Certified Adizes Associates in ten countries. They have been further tested over the last 10 years in lectures and other materials to several thousand chief executive officers from organizations around the world. Their experience and feedback on my ideas have been an invaluable addition to this book.

Corporate Lifecycles is organized into four parts. Part I provides a description of the behavior of an organization throughout various stages so that identification of where an organization is on the Lifecycle can be done. Chapters 1, 2 and 3 describe the normal and abnormal problems which arise during each stage of growth and aging. Chapter 4 discusses how goals and leadership styles have to change as the organization moves along the Lifecycle and how to diagnose where an organization is located on the Lifecycle curve.

Part II of *Corporate Lifecycles* provides the tools for analyzing the changes in behavior during an organization's growth. Those tools introduce the reader to a management theory I have developed over the years to understand the process needed to change the location of an organization on the Lifecycle. These analytic tools are used in Part III to predict how organizational cultures change.

In Part IV, we go beyond description and analysis and into *prescription*, and here we will introduce the practice of how to change organizational behavior, as well as how to change organizational cultures and their performance.

While this book focuses primarily on corporations, it also points out similarities to marriages, the personal process of growth and aging, to the process of change in civilizations, to biological systems, and to religion. Those similarities have been used only in order to explain the points and stimulate thinking on the similarities.

This book does not survey the current management literature or present a finding on a limited point. Rather, it tests concepts, analyzes experiences, and notes the difference the application of the methodology makes to clients. The proof of the theory is its applicability and the fact that others could reproduce the same achievements.

Ichak Adizes
August 1988
Adizes Institute
Santa Monica California

Part I

THE LIFECYCLE OF A CORPORATION

Introduction to Part I:
The Nature of Growth and Aging in Organizations

As with living organisms, growth and aging of organizations are primarily manifested in the interrelationship between two factors: flexibility and controllability. When organizations are young, they are very flexible; but they are not always controllable. As organizations age, the relationship changes. Controllability increases and flexibility decreases. It is like the difference between a baby and an older person. The baby is very flexible and can put his foot in his mouth, but his movements and behavior are not very controllable. As we age, eventually an older person will lose controllability too.

Young organizations are very flexible. "We used to commit 80 percent of our resources during breakfast, sitting on the stairs of the shop," one of the founders of Logicon, a large high-tech company in Southern California, told me. "Now that we have grown, even a small investment takes months and reams of paper to approve."

A word of caution: Size and time are not causes of growth and aging, as if large companies with long traditions are old and small companies with no tradition are young. What causes growing and aging in organizations is neither size nor time. I have diagnosed 100-year-*young* and 10-year-*old* corporations. Phillip Morris for instance appears behaviorally to be a very young company even though it had sales at the time I looked at it of $8.5 billion. There are many companies which can be considered "old", even though their size is not particularly large or their existence has not been particularly long.

"Young" means the organization can change relatively easily, although what it will do because it has a low level of control, is fairly unpredictable. "Old" means there is controllable behavior, but the organization is inflexible; it has little propensity for change.

When an organization is both flexible and controllable, the organization is neither too young or too old. It has the advantages of both youth and maturity, it is both flexible and controllable. This stage I call Prime. This organization can change direction and make that change occur as desired. The organization can control

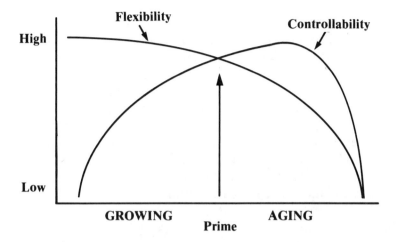

Figure 1: The Nature of Growing and Aging

what it wants to do. The purpose of this book is to analyze what affects flexibility and self control, and how to manage those factors so the organization will arrive at and stay in Prime.

THE NATURE OF PROBLEMS

As companies grow and age, the relative deficiency in either flexibility or self-control creates predictable and repetitive difficulties which managers typically label "problems." The job of management is not to create a situation where there are no problems at all, but to lead the organization to Prime, and in doing so, to exchange one set of problems for another.

Growing means the ability to deal with bigger, more complex problems. The function of leadership, then, is to manage the organization in such a way that it is able to move to the next, more demanding stage of the Lifecycle. I learned this from my mother when I was a child. I would come home and complain about my problems, and she would say: "If you can't handle these problems now, how are you going to handle bigger problems as an adult? This is nothing in comparison to what is ahead of you."

There is a Sephardic saying which I believe exists in other cultures. "Little children—little problems. Big children—big problems." You can tell the "size" of a person by the "size" of the problems that preoccupy him. *Small* people spend their lives worrying about small problems: what the neighbor did or did not do, who wears what makeup or drives what car. *Big* people worry about big problems, those which are more complex to analyze and difficult to resolve. They seek insight about their own lives—about the nature of the environment, the quality of life, the political system, the education of their children, and the next generation. A person must grow out of small problems to free up the energy to deal with bigger problems. That is the process of growing and maturing. The same applies to organizations.

Aging means there is a decreasing ability to deal with problems. The same problems an organization has been dealing with for years begin to seem increasingly insurmountable as the organization ages. This process of aging can be reversed, however. The purpose of management is to provide for balanced growth or rejuvenation and to bring the organization to Prime and keep it there.

The key to success in management then, is not to eliminate all problems, but to focus on the problems of the present stage of the organization's Lifecycle so it can grow and mature to deal with the problems of the next stage. When the organization reaches Prime, the key to success is to deal with the *causes* of aging so the organization does not age. Aging is a process that does *not have* to occur in organizations. An organization can remain in Prime forever, if it can continuously rejuvenate itself, a subject we cover in this book.

To live means to continuously solve problems. The fuller a life is, the more complex the problems are that must be resolved. The same applies to organizations. To manage an organization, one must continuously solve problems. An organization is without problems only when there is no change. This happens only when the organization is dead. To solve problems and have no new and more complex ones emerge, is equivalent to dying.

One of the liberating experiences managers seem to get in my lectures on the Lifecycle theory is the realization that they are not alone with the problems they face. Having problems is normal. They come with the territory called living, or in this case, managing. What causes a person to feel inadequate is the belief that only he or she has problems. That can have a debilitating effect. Knowing which of your problems are normal and shared by others in the same situation helps you realize that the problems you are experiencing are not caused by you but by the situation.

One day, an executive who had been listening to my lectures for a long time came to me for some personal managerial advice. He had many seemingly overwhelming problems that he wanted to talk about. As he drove me to a neighboring city, I listened to his crises and noted they were not all that severe. I even volunteered to tell him about my managerial problems so that he would have a point of reference. He was surprised.

"You, of all people, have problems? You look like you have it all together."

It was my turn to be surprised. Why would he think that I did not have problems? I realized that he had placed me on a "no problems" pedestal just as I had done to others. I realized then that *we all have problems*. Some people may make it look easy, but they are like ducks—calm on the surface while they paddle frantically underneath.

Not all problems are normal, however. What are the *right* problems to have? I can illustrate this with an example. Suppose I describe a person with the following characteristics. This person cries a lot, sleeps a lot, and drinks a lot of milk. "Is this behavior a problem?" The typical response is no, because the assumption is that I am referring to a baby. If I told you this individual is a 45-year-old and the chairman of the board of an organization, what would you say?

Whether a set of behavioral patterns is a problem or not depends on whether the behavior is normal or abnormal for that particular stage in the Lifecycle. This is true for either an individual or a company. In other words, to be successful in management, we must be able to differentiate between normal problems, which emerge in an organization at a particular stage of development, and abnormal or pathological problems that can lead to the demise of the company.

NORMAL VERSUS ABNORMAL PROBLEMS

Normal problems are those the organization can solve with its own internal energy; it can set processes in motion and make decisions that will overcome the problems. If these problems are predict-

able for that stage in the Lifecylce—if every organization at that
stage has them, although with different intensity and duration—I
call them *sensations*. If they are not expected, I call them *transitional*
problems; they will disappear once the transition to the next stage
of the Lifecycle is completed.

Abnormal problems, on the other hand, require external, professional intervention. The organization is stymied. The same problems
repeat themselves for a longer than expected period of time, and
management's attempts to resolve them only produce other undesirable side effects. Abnormal problems that are frequently encountered at a particular place in the organization's Lifecycle, I call
complexities. If the abnormal problems are rare I call them *pathologies*.

When we look at the lifecycle theory, we notice there are many
problems which are normal for any given stage. They are predictable
and should be controllable within the organization itself. These
problems should be regarded as sensations rather than problems
that syphon energy. Management can deal with them and still keep
functioning and growing. A problem is pathological if management
should not have the problem to begin with, and if they are not
capable of promptly dealing with the situation. The organization

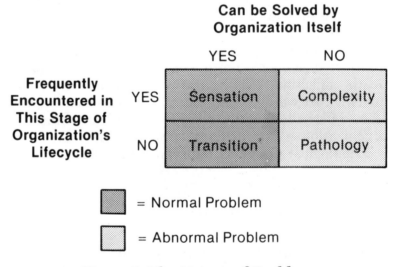

Figure 2: The Nature of Problems

needs help from the outside because it has difficulty harnessing the energy to solve the problems by *itself*.

Pathological problems retard the organization's ability to develop. They stymie and entrap the organization in a particular stage of the lifecycle. The organization gets "stuck" like a person might. A person might be middle-aged, but instead of having the problems of middle-age, that person might still be suffering the problems of adolescence.

Let us take three examples from organizations:

1) An example of sensation is a shortage of cash. This is frequently encountered in infant organizations; however well-managed organizations can handle it promptly. But the magnitude of this shortage can be bigger than expected. As long as management can handle an expected shortage of cash in a fast growing company, it is a transitional problem. If management cannot handle it, this same problem becomes a complexity, and if the shortage is vast and management is incapable of solving it, it is a pathological problem which can produce infant mortality.

2) An example of a complexity that can turn into pathology is an extremely autocratic management style. This is frequently encountered in the early stages of growth, but the organization might not be able to solve it by itself. Management might be caught in its own web. There is no internal source of energy to change the style of management; even the board of directors is practically nominated and controlled by this manager. This complexity can deteriorate into a pathology—unexpected problems might emerge that are even less controllable by the organization. For example, a pathological problem is *the founder's trap* syndrome in which the founder excessively dominates the organization and the organization's success is almost exclusively dependent on the founder's availability. The founder is the biggest asset and liability the company has. Frequently, when this person dies, the company dies, or the family that owns it loses control. This usually happens within three generations. The trap or pathology generally is that the organization cannot free itself *by itself* from this predicament.

3) In the aging phases, bureaucratization—the decreasing ability of an organization to deal with clients' needs—is the repetitive problem that must be resolved. Since Prime is the most desired place to be on the Lifecycle, and it is not necessary to depart from

this stage, whenever the organization cannot reverse this deterioration by itself, aging can be diagnosed as an abnormal phenomenon that should be treated as well.

Curative treatment would be to remove the organization's pathological problems so that it can move on to the next stage of the Lifecycle and experience a new set of normal problems. *Preventive treatment* would be to develop the organization's capabilities to avoid abnormal problems in future stages of the Lifecycle, so that no new complexities or pathologies evolve.

Adizes is a diagnostic methodology for discriminating between the different types of problems. It is also an *intervention methodology,* curative, and preventive. Its purpose is to overcome complexities and pathological problems of growing and aging, to bring an organization to Prime and to develop the organization's internal abilities to remain there.

The focus of this book is on how to change and treat abnormal organizational problems whether they are complexities or pathologies. These are the problems which stymie and delay corporate growth, as well as the organization's ability to deal with future problems. Furthermore, as a preventive tool, the purpose of this book is to prevent a deterioration of problems where sensations become transitional or worse, transitional problems and complexities become pathologies.

In Part I, we will describe the problems an organization encounters at each stage of the Lifecycle. Whether those problems are sensations or complexities depends on how long the problems have gone unresolved. Whether the problems are transitional rather than

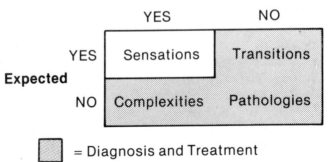

Figure 3: The Adizes Intervention Methodology

sensations differs from one organization to another, depending on the internal political make-up of the organization (see Chapter 5). In both cases, however, if they are not treated in time, they may develop into pathologies. This book will present a diagnostic, therapeutic, and preventive theory of how to prevent that from happening.

1

Description of Organizational Lifecycles: The Growing Stages ⸺⸺⸺⸺

COURTSHIP

The first stage in the development of an organization is called **Courtship**. The organization is not yet born. It exists only as an idea.

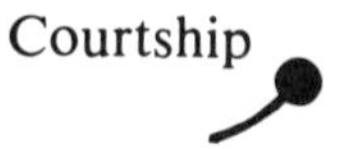

Courtship

Figure 4: The Courtship Stage

Building Commitment

In Courtship, the emphasis is on ideas and the possibilities the future offers. Although the company does not physically exist yet, and some may question what the excitement and enthusiasm are all about, there is something very important taking place. During this time, the company can be compared to a jet sitting at the end of the runway preparing for take-off. The pilot is revving up the engines and creating a lot of noise. Although nothing of substance appears to be happening, something very crucial is taking place. Thrust and momentum are building so that once the brakes are released, the jet will take off quickly and smoothly. An analogous phenomenon happens in the Courtship stage of an organization's development. During this time of much talk and no action, the founder is building commitment. He is "selling" his idea of "how great it is going to be."

To whom is he selling his idea? To himself. Commitment to the idea is building internally, and at the same time, the idea is being tested on others. What do they think? Is this viable? The more he sells his idea to others, the greater the build-up of his own commitment becomes.

This same phenomenon of building commitment also occurs in a courtship before a marriage. We call it falling in love. It seems as if falling in love is a necessary prelude to getting married; it builds a commitment which is necessary to sustain the marriage.

For a plane to fly and perform the function for which it was designed, it must first take off. To become airborne, it needs a forward thrust—the momentum that was built during the engine-revving stage. Similarly, for an organization to start performing the function for which it was designed, it needs to undertake risks. And no risk is taken without the commensurate commitment that is built during the Courtship stage.

Plane	Organization	Marriage
build forward thrust; momen-tum	build commitment	fall in love
take-off	undertake the risk	tie the knot
fly	sell footwear (for instance)	build a family

This process of building commitment is accompanied by excitement, enthusiasm and emotion—or "heat," as if energy is coalescing to one point to be released.

The process of building commitment can generate abnormal problems, complexities or pathologies. In a marriage, for instance, while building the commitment of falling in love, unrealistic promises can be made which one or both of the partners may come to regret later on.

Similarly, in the Courtship stage of the organizational Lifecycle, an identical phenomenon may occur. While building commitment, the founder could be making promises, which in retrospect, he may regret. Promises made during the Courtship seem to be part of the process of building commitment. Founders will frequently promise and give away shares of the future company to family members, lawyers or friends. It seems as if in order to get a piece of the action, all these beneficiaries need to do is make some vague promises of supporting the founder in some way. This can happen because at this stage of the Lifecycle, the company has no tangible worth. The inexperienced founder does not believe he is giving away anything significant. Later on, this lavishness will return to haunt the founder.

In marriage, a love relationship is necessary for establishing commitment. In the corporate Lifecycle, the founder must *fall in love* with the idea of the company being conceived. Later on when the company comes into being, it is his love for his baby that is going to sustain the founder's motivation during the difficult times of Infancy.

An organization is born when commitment is successfully tested—when risk is undertaken. Conversely, an organization dies when no one shares the commitment for its operation. Thus, the degree of commitment needed in an organization is a function of the degree of risk the organization is going to take once it is born. If we know the size of the jet, we can tell the pilot how much thrust it will take to get it off the ground. If we can predict the bumps on the road map of a marriage, we should be able to predict how much commitment is needed to avoid divorce. If we know the size of the risk the fledgling company will face, we can tell the founder how much of his and other people's commitment will be required to have a successful launching of the organization.

When innovators come to me with a new product wanting to start a company, at first I do not listen to *what* they say. I listen to *who* says it and *how* it is said. To create a successful company, one needs more than just a good idea, a market and the money to back it up. What the new company needs is a *product champion*, someone who is not going to sleep at night once the company is born.

I ask these potential company founders, "Who is going to head the company?" and if the answer is "We are looking for someone," my response is "When you find that person, come back. Let's not talk about market research in a vacuum. We need to examine the commitment of the person who is going to turn the findings of the market research into reality."

When people present ideas for establishing a new organization, their "noise level," or "revved up motor" must be tested. How really committed are they? Do they have a significant financial commitment to the endeavor? The bigger the task, the more zealous the commitment must be; it should be commensurate with the difficulty of making such an organization work in the long run. The difficulty of establishing an organization can be evaluated by the complexity of putting it together; by the promptness of positive feedback (How long will it take before positive results will come in?), and by the degree of innovation necessary (How many existing "sacred cows" must be slaughtered?). If the commitment is not commensurate with the difficulties to come, it is expended on "labor pains" and a stillborn organization is delivered.

The relationship of commitment to risk can also be seen on a macro-level. For example, the success or failure of a revolution can be predicted by looking at the commitment of the revolutionaries. To have a revolution, the commitment must be commensurate with the difficulty of the task. The task of changing a society is immense. To bring about a significant change (which a revolution is by definition) the revolutionaries must be willing to die for their cause. In the early 1980s, it was popular in parts of the United States for Iranian exiles to protest against the rule of the Ayatollah Khomeini. Although there were many angry threats and banners, very few of the protestors were prepared to die for their cause. Their degree of commitment was a clear indication of the movement's long term potential for success.

As Conrad Hilton said: "If you want to launch big ships go where the water is deep." Too many people want to launch carriers in shallow waters.

Building a high level of commitment is the key to success, because when the organization is born, this commitment—or lack of it—is what will keep the company alive or kill it. If the commitment is not substantial, the organization will often break up at the first signs of rough times.

Product Orientation of the Founder: Prophet or Profit?

When we talk about commitment to undertake risk, the question should be asked: Why is a person committed? What motivates the founder or the product champion? If the motivation is only to make money, it is an insufficient commitment at this stage of the Lifecycle. No one really knows for sure what a company will produce in terms of profits. When a baby is in the cradle, is it his parent's motivation to feed and change him so he will be a doctor or a lawyer when he grows up and support them in their old age? It better not be.

The motivation of a founder has to be transcendental; it must exceed the narrow limits of immediate gain. The commitment cannot be only rational. First and above all, it must be an emotional commitment to the idea and its functionality in the marketplace. The founder should be responding to a perceived need; the idea should obsess him—he can't help but satisfy that need. The profits or money the product or service will produce are merely a validation of the founder's evaluation of the situation.

In Courtship, the founder's motivating goal should be to satisfy a market need, to create value added. The founder should be excited about the needs the product will satisfy and when challenged, he should defend the functionality of his product and its service. If we were to ask the founder to describe the company five years hence, he should describe a company that is servicing clients increasingly well—one that is satisfying needs more effectively. If he speaks about the return on investment *exclusively,* his commitment is not sufficient to sustain the newborn company when difficulties arise in the future. Of course, without profits the company will die. While return on investment can kill a deal, it won't make a deal. What will successfully make the deal is the founder's belief that there is a real need, that there are live clients who will appreciate what the founder has done.

This commitment to client needs is independent of whether the client perceives the need or not. This is an important point to make. A founder, like a prophet, is making prophecies about the needs as he perceives them—not necessarily as expressed by potential clients. Thus, the founder talks about what the market *should* buy, not necessarily what it *is* buying. If market needs were known, and if the market already expressed its wishes in high sales volume of the product or service, the innovation and risks are lower and the necessary commitment can be lower. This is not a prophet who gives birth to a movement, but a "me too" founder.

The more I think about it, the more the analogy of motherhood comes to mind. The founder must give birth; he must respond to a crying need—the cry of a baby not born yet. He is like the prophet Jonah, who can't contain his prophecy. It is a fire in his bones. If, like Jonah, he tries to escape, a whale will carry him to his destiny.

If a founder gives birth to a company because of his anticipated return on investment, it is analogous to a prophet who makes prophecies because he wants to go to heaven, or a mother who gives birth because she wants to have a doctor for a daughter. The prophet does not want to go to hell; the mother does not want to have a child who can't hold a job; and the founder does not want to go bankrupt. Return on investment (ROI) is a limiting, not a driving factor. ROI does not give birth to an organization, although lack of it can eventually kill the company.

People who are exclusively interested in money or return on investment will get discouraged and quit before profits are realized, because profits will not always be coming in. Ideas must be made operational and in the process of doing so, mistakes can be made which might mean losing money. Those seeking money exclusively will get discouraged, while those who are motivated by the idea of satisfying needs will continue experimenting and searching for the right solution to satisfy those needs—even if profits are not yet there. Having a baby requires that you be willing to take care of him through all the childhood diseases and illnesses. It is not all smiles all the time.

Look at profits as a scoreboard in a tennis match. You can't win by watching the scoreboard. It only tells you *if* you are winning. To actually win a game, you must watch the ball. Each volley is an opportunity to do better than the previous one. The same is true with Infant organizations. The founder must be determined to hit the ball—satisfy his clients' needs as measured by sales. The player might not hit each ball, but each volley is like a new game, starting from zero. When he is learning to play there is little need to look at the scoreboard. It is meaningless. It takes on meaning only when most of the learning has been done and he is testing to see what he has learned and what else there is to learn. A person who must win every game can never afford to learn a new game. A person must be committed to the idea of *learning* the game first and to *winning* it later.

The entrepreneur who starts a company for needs that have not been satisfied or expressed yet, is product-oriented rather than market-oriented. He is committed to a product that *should* satisfy a need he has difficulty in articulating. He does not *respond* to an expected market need, but instead, he tries to educate and change the behavior of the market. He, in a sense, expresses that need *for* the market. Through his actions, he makes that need articulated and operationalized. In truth, he is more a business prophet than a business entrepreneur. And like other prophets, he can be put on the cross, because, in the short run, the power structure will reject him. No one understands his message, because until the product works, no one else understands the need.

This makes him highly vulnerable to those who come and promise help in selling the product. In promising to produce a marketing capability, these newcomers might take a significant share of ownership. Frequently, the prophet who is dedicated more to the product than to control and return on investment, ends up losing control of the company to a marketeer. The only reward the founder gets is that his product will survive and be accepted. It is the marketeer who gets to enjoy the fruits of the innovation which is measured in money and recognition.

Why is the prophet-type of founder not market-oriented, regardless of how many marketing courses he has had? The prophet-type of founder focuses on what the market *should* want, and that necessarily orients him toward the product or service which *should* satisfy that need. Since that service or product must be developed, the founder must be product-oriented until the qualities, capabilities, and functionality of the product are accepted. If the founder overlistens to the market, he will accommodate the perceived need prematurely. The founder will fight dilution of his dream, always speaking of the reality he is trying to change.

Many founders are accused of being ignorant of marketing strategies and realities. At this stage of the Lifecycle it is a normal problem, a sensation. It is not a pathological problem. The phenomena is normal and desirable. To quote George Bernard Shaw: "Reasonable men adapt to their environment; unreasonable men try to adapt their environment to themselves. Thus all progress is the result of the efforts of unreasonable men."

As we will see in the next section, this characteristic of a founder's committment to client needs as *he perceives the market should have* (rather than commitment to a product the market wants) and his relatively low commitment to profit (which is essential for the future healthy growth of the company), can become a pathological problem for the organization later on. The founder might not know when to let go of his exclusive dream. He will be too product-oriented for too long. He does not compromise to look at the marketing strategies necessary to place the product or service in the market. He acts according *to* his perception of what *should* be for too long, rather than accept what is and provide the market with what it wants.

Even when the founder goes beyond product-orientation, he might still develop difficulties in making the transition to profit-orientation. This change will require attention not only to technology and client interface, but also to financial and human factors, elements of management in which the founder might not excel. Since the founder usually insists on making strategic decisions by himself, and since he does not always excell in all of them, those elements get mismanaged.

What is normal at one stage of the Lifecycle can become abnormal in another stage. Fanatic commitment is necessary for Courtship and Infancy, but it can become pathological later on. An example would be a company that is chronically losing money because it is in a declining industry. However, the founder is fighting that reality. In some cases, the more he fights it, the deeper into trouble the company sinks. The founder clings to how things *should be*, holding on to the dream. This is an important paradox to understand. In order for the birth of the organization to be a healthy one, we need the commitment of the founder; the more committed he is, the better. However, the time will come when he needs to be realistic and know how to let go. This paradox makes it difficult to appraise the qualities of a good founder. If he is committed, can he let go? If he is capable of letting go, is he committed enough?

Healthy founders are highly committed, and at the same time, have an eye on reality. They are committed, but flexible. They can learn from experience. A founder is a reasonably unreasonable person—someone who has fanatically strong beliefs, but one who will also listen to reason.

A normal Courtship is one in which reason can be applied to the dream without destroying it. The commitment is "dry-tested" to reflect future reality and it still survives. The difference between normal and pathological Courtship concerns whether such a test of reality is conducted or not.

Figure 5: The Affair

Is It Real Or Just An Affair?

It is normal to have doubts during the Courtship stage of organizational Lifecycle. Conversely, it is pathological to have no doubts whatsoever. The normal doubts and questions the founder should answer are:

- *What exactly* are we going to do?
- *How* is it going to be done?
- *When* should it be done?
- *Who* is going to do it and *why?*

This is reality testing. A Courtship which has no reality testing is an *affair;* at the first sign of obstacles, the commitment evaporates. It is a Courtship with pathological problems—there are fantasies of how things *should be because we want them to be that way,* whether it is realistic to expect them to be that way or not. No hard-nosed questions are asked. The idea remains at the fantasy level; it is not operationalized.

Pathological problems do not look like problems during Courtship because they do not appear problematic or painful. Everything is rosy. That is precisely why Courtship's pathology is so dangerous. It can give birth to an Infant organization, but since the idea was not tested, the Infant organization is not ready to deal with reality and might collapse. The organization moves from no pain at conception, to all pain after birth. There is no real test for how much pain the founder(s) and company can tolerate. There is no simulated test of commitment.

The same principles apply to a marriage. The transition from rosy courtship to the reality of a marriage can be quite devastating to some people. Let us simulate the reality of being in a marriage. Ask the hard questions that need to be asked at an early stage. I believe that in the process of writing a pre-marital contract, many couples will decide not to get married. The same thing happens in business negotiations. We become excited with an idea and start negotiations to form a partnership, but when the details are worked out and put *into writing*, it does not look as exciting anymore.

COURTSHIPS

Normal	Abnormal
excitement, reality tested	no reality testing of commitment
realistically committed founder	unrealistically fanatic founder
product orientation—commitment to its value added	exclusive ROI—profit orientation
commitment commensurate to risk	commitment not commensurate to risk
founder keeps control	founder's control is vulnerable

What finally sparks the birth of the company? It is not when the articles of incorporation are signed. It is when there is some tangible expression of commitment made, when some risk is undertaken. The risk can have different manifestations—someone quits his old job, signs the rent check for the new office, or promises to deliver a product on a certain date. When substantial risk is incurred and undertaken, the organization moves to the next stage of development, called Infancy.

INFANCY

Once risk has been undertaken, the nature of the organization changes dramatically. The risk must be covered. Cash is needed to pay bills. The focus shifts from ideas and possibilities to the production of results—the satisfaction of needs for which the company was established. In a business organization, it is expressed in terms of sales, sales and more sales. Now that there is risk, we don't need more ideas, we need sales. "Don't tell me about more

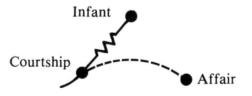

Figure 6: The Infant Organization

new product ideas, tell me how much of our current products you have sold."

For many fledgling companies, this switch from ideas to results is a trying time. This stage is analogous to the period before and immediately after a marriage. An oftenheard spousal complaint is, "The romance has gone out of our lives. Before we were married, you used to talk to me all the time, but now that we're married I hardly see you." This is usually rebutted with something like, "I know, but when we got married we agreed that we wanted to have a family and buy a home and that takes money. We have to earn it too."

The same thing happens in Infant companies. In Courtship, there was time to talk and dream. With the undertaking of risk, there is no time to talk—only time to act. This switch can be seen on a social/political level as well. Once a revolution succeeds, the first people to get thrown into prison are the ideologists who started the movement in the first place. Why? Because the new social order does not need more new dreams, it needs to fulfill the ones it already has.

At this stage of the organization's life, it is not what someone *thinks* that counts, but what he does. The question the founder is asked, or the question he asks his employees is, "What have you *done? Did you sell, produce, or get anything *done?*" The dreamers of yesterday are shunned and discouraged. "I have no time to think," will be the typical complaint of the manager of an Infant organization. "There is just too much I have to *do.*"

There is a major paradox facing Infant companies. The higher the risk it faces, the higher the commitment needed to ensure success is. This means that in Courtship, the founders must be dreamers who can build commitment to the dream. Once the company is born, however, the risk is large, and the organization will need a very hard-working, results-oriented founder who is not a dreamer. The higher the risk in a venture, the greater the *wake-up* shock when the organization is actually born. It takes a very special person to make the transition from a prophet to an action leader who makes the prophecy come true. If the transaction involves two leaders, there will be conflict between them (because the first will cling to the ideal while the second one needs to compromise the ideal if he has to operationalize it and put it into action).

A company in Infancy has few policies, systems, procedures,

or budgets. The whole administrative system might be written on the back of an old envelope in the founder's vest pocket. Most people in this organization, including the president, are out, selling—*doing*. There are few staff meetings. The organization is highly centralized and is best described as a one-person show. It rushes ahead at full-speed, without knowledge of its strengths and weaknesses. It's like a baby who hits instead of touching because he does not know how much pressure to exert. Similarly, the Infant organization makes excessive commitments in the mistaken belief that it can keep them. Schedules are overbooked and delivery dates postponed. If a product does arrive on time, parts may be missing, or the service manual may be unavailable. However, the organization is responsive to client complaints. Its members try to meet clients' needs, usually by working on weekends and holidays.

The Infant organization is very personal. Everybody is on a first-name basis and there is very little hierarchy. The organization has no system for hiring or for evaluating performance. People are hired when needed, because they impress those who hire them. They are usually asked to start working right away, because the Infant organization is late in hiring the help it needs. Tomorrow it wants the people it needed yesterday. People get promoted if they produce results or if they know how to exert pressure on the boss.

At this stage in the Lifecycle, the organization is like an infant. It requires its "milk" (operating capital) often; and if it does not get it, it is very vulnerable. Usually, it has no managerial depth—no one else is capable of leading if the founder dies. It has no track record or experience, so a mistake in product design, sales, service or financial planning can have fatal repercussions. Such mistakes have a high probability of occurring because the organization is usually a shoestring operation with no capital for establishing the complementary team that is necessary to make well-balanced business decisions.

The organization cannot remain an Infant forever. The time and emotions necessary to keep an Infant organization alive are often far beyond the immediate economic returns it offers. If Infancy is prolonged, the pride of ownership wanes. The founder/owner becomes exhausted and gives up. In this case, the death of the organization is not imminent and sudden, as in previous cases; it is a prolonged process with an everdecreasing level of emotional commitment to the enterprise manifested by constantly increasing complaints about "how bad it is."

Problems of Infant Organizations

The characteristic behavioral patterns of Infant organizations are:

- Action-oriented, opportunity-driven

thus

- Few systems, rules, or policies

thus

- Inconsistent performance

thus

- Vulnerability; a problem can become a crisis on short notice

thus

- Management is by crisis

thus

- There is little delegation; management is a one-man show

thus

- Commitment of the founder is constantly tested and crucial for survival

In many ways, Infant organizations are like real infants. In order to survive, they need two things.

1. Periodic infusion of milk (cash). If they don't get enough they will die.
2. Parent's love (founder's commitment). If this drops the organization may also die.

These are the two most critical factors that cause pathological problems in Infant organizations.

The Problem of Undercapitalization

We have to fully understand this need for periodic infusion of cash. Frequently, I encounter businesspeople who, like inexperienced parents, have planned for the room, toys and cradle but not for the milk. The *milk* that the company needs is working capital for such purposes as financing increases in inventory and accounts receivable.

There is a tendency to underestimate the need for cash and working capital. It stems from the enthusiasm typical of the founder during the Courtship stage. Since enthusiasm is functional and indispensable for building commitment, a realistic view of cash needs is incompatible with such a fanatical buildup of enthusiasm.

The tendency is to project high success and low capital needs. Founders hope that "a crying baby" will somehow get the milk it needs. So they "give birth" and worry about the "baby's" needs later. As a result, there is the danger of undercapitalization and the more the new company sells, the higher the probability of developing the problem called undercapitalization will be. A company with 35 percent or more average sales growth per year will generally experience difficulties in financing this growth from its own internal sources.

The pains of undercapitalization during Infancy can be avoided if the founder takes a hard look during Courtship at *what* will be done, *how* it will be done and *who* will do it—for both the short and long term. For a healthy Infancy, there must be a realistic business plan, and cash flow must be monitored on a weekly basis. Recordkeeping focus should be on *cash flow*. Accrual accounting is good for tax purposes and profitability analysis, but not for monitoring the immediate survivability of the company. Monitoring the turnover of accounts receivables and inventory is also essential to avoid unnecessary increases in working capital that can drain the Infant company's liquidity.

Infant organizations complain of being undercapitalized. To generate cash they make several basic mistakes:

1. They take short-term loans for investments that yield results only in the long run.
2. They start selling at discount prices to generate cash. The discounts could be so large, that they do not even cover the variable costs. As a result, the more they sell, the more they lose.
3. They sell stock to venture capitalists who are not sympathetic to "the cause."

The first two mistakes may bankrupt the company. They relieve the symptoms, but aggravate the disease over the long run—the company will end up in even deeper trouble. The third solution, with the venture capitalists, can be like the wolf in the children's story "Little Red Riding Hood." They come in with great big smiles. "All we want to do is help," they say. However, their real intent might be a rapid and substantial return on their investment. Such traders can put a clamp on a company's growth by squeezing profits in the short run and eventually destroying the company.

The founder should watch the organization's cash flow, its loan structure, its cost accounting and, if he brings in venture capital, it better be from those who are there for the long haul.

The Founder's Commitment

The second variable that can cause Infant mortality is the loss of the founder's commitment. Why is this founder's commitment so important?

Infant organizations usually have negative cash flow in the beginning (cash needed for operating is higher than cash revenues). This creates a pressure to be action-oriented, opportunity-driven, highly responsive and flexible—to get cash at any cost. This means little space for rules and policies. The organization is experimenting and trying to define success. Once success is articulated, rules and policies can be developed to control the repetition of that success later on. Rules and policies at this stage would suffocate the chances of satisfying client needs. With a lack of rules and policies, being very flexible and expedient to get to cash, the organization develops *bad habits*. It makes decisions that set precedents and continuance into the future.

For an infant, the cost of such bad habits is low while the value is high. As the organization grows in people and clients, the value of bad habits declines and the cost can skyrocket. Examples abound. To get a sale, all kinds of adaptations are made to meet clients' demands. Later, it can cause the founder to lose control. Big contracts with high risk can be signed and a big loss could be the result.

With few policies and rules, there is inconsistent performance. Although this is normal for an Infant organization, it makes the organization vulnerable, and problems can become crises which turn management into a fire brigade.

In an environment of management by crisis, it is not unusual to find very little delegation. It tends to be a one-person show, and it has to be the founder's show. If the founder is not committed, problems will go unresolved and become crises that can annihilate a company. But why be committed?

The founder of an Infant organization typically reaps the following "benefits":

- The "reward" of working 12 to 14 hours a day, seven days a week for a lower takehome income than if he was an employee somewhere else. The opportunity to make a million dollars is a distant dream in the face of the current reality of lots of hard work.
- The "reward" of struggling to make payroll every week for a group of employees who don't act as grateful as they might.
- The "reward" of working very hard, only to get home and be attacked by his spouse and family for neglect.

Why do it?

There are very few tangible rewards to be had from the company at this stage. Often, the only thing that keeps it together is the founder's love and commitment to what the company can and should be—to the idea and commitment created at Courtship. The founder cannot let the dream die, it is his own self-esteem that is on the line. This fledgling organization is the founder's *ticket to immortality*. This is his creation, his footsteps on a virgin beach. This is the monument that will be there after the founder dies.

An infant requires a lot of work and many sleepless nights. What does he give in return? Even when a new baby smiles, it is not because it recognizes anyone, but because it has gas. Why are the parents so committed in spite of no evident return? Because it is *their* baby. The same is true for the company founder. In Infancy, there is no tangible return. Talk about potential future profits is like talk about what the baby will be when it grows up. It is just talk. What keeps the founder going is the commitment he made during Courtship. If that commitment disappears, the company dies. This focused commitment to the organization might be so strong that it puts a strain on the founder's personal life. Founders are often given a choice—the company or the family. In the case of revolutions and starting a new country, people have to sacrifice more than their families—they should be willing to die for the cause.

Taking care of an Infant organization requires constant attention. The founder is continuously faced with problems for which he is not prepared: a complaining customer, an unsatisfactory supplier, a reluctant banker, or an unproductive employee. There are no precedents, rules, policies, stability, or organizational memory to rely on. Each decision is a new precedent, and making decisions from scratch requires an abundance of energy. Getting the cash necessary to make ends meet requires more sales, and more sales creates the need for more resources that require more cash, which requires even more sales. This endless circle requires working long days and having many sleepless nights.

The founder of Banco de Commercio, Mexico, once told a gathering that his wife asked him why was he going to start a bank. "To start a business," she said, "is like going to sleep young and waking up old." It requires full attention, total dedication and total commitment. It is like a long dream. To many, it is a nightmare.

For a successful marriage, we need an understanding husband who is supportive of the mother after a child is born. By the same token, for the successful birth of a company, we need an understanding and supportive spouse. Thus, in checking whether the birth of a company is going to be a healthy one, we have to check the supportiveness of the family. If this support is not present, starting a new company might produce a family divorce or a mortality of the Infant organization. A prudent founder should enlist the cooperation of his or her spouse and encourage him or her to share the joy and pain of creation.

However, the founder's commitment, which is crucial, can be lost not just because of a non-supportive spouse. One of the most prevalent causes is the interference of outside influences. There is an analogous situation in the animal kingdom which describes this situation. What can happen to a wolf cub that will cause the mother to reject the cub and let it die? If the cub is touched by human hands, the mother will reject it because her smell is no longer on the cub. If an Infant organization is touched by external hands to the extent that the founder no longer identifies with the company, this same phenomenon can occur. Founders often give away shares during Courtship or sell off pieces of their companies to venture capitalists and other external groups to secure an adequate supply of capital. If there is continuous alien intervention from these hands, to the point where the founder does not identify with his creation, he might reject the "baby" as no longer being his own. Then the organization dies.

This rejection syndrome can occur in a larger organization as well. New departments or spin-offs are like new organizations which need high excitement and activity. However, every time "the baby" wants to do something new, corporate headquarters requires the completion of dozens of forms and formal budget requests. Any action requires excessive time to get through the proper channels. With so much aggravation and interference from the corporate parent, the founder of the unit may walk away from the new unit saying "You make the rules—you run the show." In some corporations, there are so many rules and regulations controlling new ventures that the environment creates infertility.

This external intervention can come from government which, through rules, laws and requirements, can create an environment in which only large and well-established companies can compete. For start-up companies, the cost for lawyers and accountants, as well as the time necessary to identify and comply with all the regulations is so overwhelming that the founder may become alienated and quit.

When government intervention is minimal, the social climate is one of *if it is not forbidden, it is apparently permitted.* With intense external control and intervention by government, the climate is the opposite. *If it is not permitted, it is apparently forbidden.* Thus, in societies where the government is deeply involved in regulating economic affairs, the entrepreneur might perceive that he will have to ask permission for everything because it appears as if everything is forbidden. Asking permission stifles entrepreneurship. Added to the normal risk of starting a business, this factor can destroy initiative.

For example, in Sweden, the law requires that the board of directors include elected employees. Furthermore, it is very difficult to fire anyone. A company that is already established, can afford the cost of compliance. For a start-up company that needs to change direction frequently and is constantly experimenting to define success, this can be prohibitive. Because, as it redefines its strategies to achieve success, it might have to change its structure and its people. The founder can perceive a loss of control even before he starts the company.

For a company to succeed in Infancy the founder must be enthusiastic, passionate, even jealous of anyone else interfering with his creation. This type of zeal is universal. Have you ever seen movies about the animal kingdom? All animals protect their young zealously, no stranger is allowed to approach. The founder is a human animal and behaves in the same manner when it concerns *his* baby— the new organization. Here the zeal takes the form of a one-person show, a highly-centralized organization. He is extremely protective and is the only boss—the king or queen of the mountain. According to my theory, this is not a problem. It is a sensation and it is a desirable one.

Many consultants, spouses and people in general accuse founders of Infant organizations of not delegating, of working too hard, of being too opinionated. I suggest this behavior comes with the territory of starting an organization, and it should. It only becomes pathological if it continues after the organization has gone beyond Infancy in the Lifecycle.

Action-Orientation and Lack of Planning and Systems

Because an Infant organization is fighting for survival, decisions must be made promptly. However, since there is no significant experience track record, there is little organizational memory, and few, if any rules or policies. Thus, many decisions are first time precedents—the company is managed from crisis-to-crisis. As a result, the prevailing attitude is "If it's not a crisis, we have no time for it." In such an environment it is normal to have only very task-oriented people working for the organization, "managerial cowboys" who say something like "shoot first—ask questions later." The desired image is that of the hard-working, reactive, short-attentioned "railroad engineer," who says something akin to "show me the tracks and get out of the way." There is no time to plan or think because everyone is busy *doing*. The hard work and dedication required to survive is personally exciting and fulfilling to these railroad engineers. Their lights burn late into the night. Their families go days without seeing them. If the people are single, they often marry their co-workers. This is guerilla time. Only the strong survive, and those who do, establish close friendships in this high-stress situation.

There are no titles, organization charts, or hierarchy in this environment. MBAs often have a difficult time functioning in this work setting. Their questions about job descriptions, structure, strategies, goals, compensation, benefit plans, and career succession ladders are met with dumbfounded amazement. Asking for a job description, they could be told: "Let's see. Your job is to do anything and everything that needs to be done. As far as career succession, you are starting at the top. The harder you work, the higher you go. Any more questions—just ask the one and only boss."

When I started the Adizes Institute, I was fortunate to get one of my brightest MBA students as my first employee. Sitting in my kitchen, he asked me about his career succession ladder. That was a reasonable question. I remember teaching him that well-run organizations must have long-range goals and objectives, and they must translate these goals into specific plans of action, one of which was career development for managers. But sitting in my kitchen, with a company that consisted of just him, me, $5,000 in the bank and no experience in how the idea would work out, the question was ludicrous. My response to his question was "Henrick! You are standing at the top of the ladder, except that the ladder is underground. You want to climb the ladder? Great! Start pumping it up yourself."

For an MBA who is taught to make decisions of a strategic and policy nature, who is taught to think like a boss, to have "a one and only boss" can be quite discouraging and depressing. Furthermore, many of the skills taught in business school can cause unrealistic expectations and be useless to an Infant organization. An MBA's request to know what the long-term goal and strategy is cannot be answered. Infant organizations cannot prepare long-range plans and strategies. The Infant does not have the necessary experience with the product and its markets to make realistic long-range goals, plans and strategies. It has a vision, a dream, an intent— but not plans and measurable goals. This is all very vague and certainly not definite enough for a *numbers* person. However, it is all that can realistically be expected from an Infant.

"If we knew what to do, we would do it; we're still trying to find out what we actually have to do," a founder once told me. Out of the new experiences, patterns will emerge that can be used later for projecting the future and for making long-term goals and strategies. Without real experience as to what works, a detailed, long-range planning process can be a frustrating practice in futility.

What is needed is short-term planning to test ideas and gain experience.

In Infancy, there is no delegation of authority or responsibility. The company has no organizational memory as yet, and what works and what does not work has not been established. This is something that has to be learned at the "university of hard knocks." Experience must be gained first-hand. It is difficult at this stage to articulate experiences and transfer them secondhand. To do this, we need a pattern of recurring experience from which to draw. Since the organization is short on cash, it cannot afford to let people learn from mistakes. Thus, the founder must keep a very close eye on the organization if it is going to survive. Thus, there is no real delegation of authority and should not be. The subordinates are errand boys or "gofers" who assist the founder. This is normal. If there is delegation, the founder might lose control and the company would suffer. This reminds me of a cartoon I saw once in the *Wall Street Journal*. Two unshaven winos with torn clothes are sitting on a park bench drinking from bottles and talking. The caption underneath says, ". . . and then my consultant told me to delegate."

There is an additional reason why the founder *should not* delegate. The people working for him are usually not as good at the job as he is. If they were outstanding entrepreneurs who could make the same quality decisions as the founder, they would be starting their own companies. Employees of Infant companies often are people who were looking for a temporary position and then decided to stay. They probably were not hired as the result of a search, but instead wandered in or just happened to be available.

It is normal and desirable that an Infant organization be led by an individual who conducts a one-man show—the founder who works seven days a week, 15 hours a day. Only in the next stage of the Lifecycle, where there is some stability, time to breathe and an experience track record, will the founder be able to delegate. And he should do so.

It should be apparent by now, that what is functional behavior at one stage of the Lifecycle, often becomes dysfunctional at another stage. Normal problems can become abnormal and then pathological. Zealous commitment is mandatory for a successful Courtship, but it can become a pathological problem in Infancy if the founder does not let go of a bad idea and adapt to reality. During Infancy,

Figure 7: Infant Mortality

the founder's hard work, lack of delegation and a short-term result orientation are crucial for the survival of the organization. These same traits, however, could turn into a pathologic stranglehold for Go-Go, the next stage in the organization's Lifecycle.

If an organization is to grow, its management must also grow. Note that to grow does *not* mean more of the same. It means to *change*. The growth is qualitative not just quantitative. If this does not happen, a change in leadership is called for. At the end of Chapter 3, we will take an in-depth look at the styles of leadership that are appropriate for each stage in the Lifecycle.

Infant Mortality

A healthy Infancy is one which has a balanced growth reflecting cash availability. It is where the founder feels he is in control of the operation, there is support at home, and none of the daily crises are fatal. It is normal that the founder is working long hours, does not delegate and makes all the decisions.

Infant mortality will occur when the founder suffers from ennui; when he becomes alienated from his creation or loses control of the organization. It also occurs if the company irreparably loses liquidity.

INFANCY

Normal	Abnormal
Risk does not evaporate commitment	Risk evaporates the commitment
Negative cash flow	Chronic negative cash flow
Hardwork nourishes commitment	Loss of commitment
No managerial depth	Premature delegation

Normal	**Abnormal**
No systems	Premature rules, systems, procedures
No delegation	Founder's loss of control
"One-man show"—but willing to listen	No listening—arrogance
Make mistakes	No room for mistakes
Supportive home life	Non-supportive home life
Supportive external intervention	Founder alienated by external intervention

An organization cannot remain an Infant forever. The energy required for takeoff is greater than the energy necessary for maintenance. One cannot long sustain the energy level required for the takeoff of an Infant organization. The founder and people in the organization lose their enthusiasm, lose their commitment, and the company dies. Time is of the essence. A prolonged Infancy is a sign of pathology.

An organization will emerge from Infancy and move into the next stage of the organizational Lifecycle when cash and activities become somewhat stabilized. The negative cash flow and the need for cash infusions cease to be a problem. Customers start bringing in repeat business, there is some brand loyalty, suppliers stabilize and production problems are no longer a daily crisis. The founder finally has time to breathe. This is analogous to the time when a baby's digestive system is stabilized and he starts sleeping through the night. Once this stabilization occurs, the Infant organization moves into the next stage which is called Go-Go.

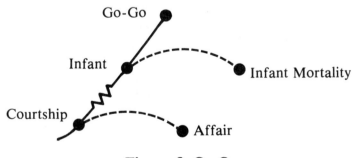

Figure 8: Go-Go

GO-GO

What is a Go-Go organization? In Courtship, we had an idea. In
Infancy, the idea was put to work. We have now reached a stage
where the idea is working, the company has overcome negative
cash flow and sales are up. It appears that the company is not
only surviving, it is even flourishing. This makes the founder and
the organization arrogant, and arrogant with a capital "A."

Opportunities As Priorities

The greater the organization's success, the more arrogant the
founder becomes. Sometimes he feels he is invincible. As a result,
Go-Gos usually will get into trouble by going in too many directions
at the same time. Go-Go companies are like babies when they begin
to crawl—they're into everything. They see no problems, only opportunities. Everything they touch they either eat or break. Go-Go
companies act in the same way: everything is an opportunity. On
Friday night, the founder of a Go-Go company, a shoe business,
goes away for the weekend. On Monday morning, he walks into
the office and announces, "I just bought a shopping center." This
does not surprise the employees. It has happened before.

"The real estate business? How did we get into that?"

"Well, I got a deal that was too good to pass up. Besides,
what we did for the shoe business we can do for real estate!"

Present success has made the founder forget the difficulties
of the Infancy era. The success of the Go-Go is the realization of
the founder's dreams, and if one dream can be realized, why not
other dreams too?

Pathologic Go-Gos are like mini-conglomerates; they tend to
be involved in many related and unrelated businesses. Unfortunately, this diversification usually means that Go-Gos are spread
much too thin. They inevitably make the mistake of being in a
business about which they know nothing. The company can lose
more money overnight on a shopping center, than they made in a
whole year selling shoes.

Almost every opportunity seems to be a priority. At one meeting
of a Go-Go organization, the managers were each asked to list the
organizational priorities as they perceived them. When these percep-
tions were put together, there were 173 different priorities. Too
many priorities means that they have no priorities.

When I reorganize Go-Gos, I sometimes feel I am watching a cat give birth. Just when I think that the last kitten has been born, another head emerges. I typically ask a Go-Go organization—"How many businesses are you in?" After they have finished giving me *all* the details—they invariably remember just one more deal, one more business, one more opportunity they are exploring or already committed to. As the founder of the International House of Pancakes used to say: "The world is on sale." They have so many irons in the fire, they cannot and do not give attention to each one.

In the Go-Go stage, sales are up fast and easy, so the founder becomes sloppy in his investments. He does not plan for results— he just expects them. Frequently he will have to pay the price.

Reactive Sales Orientation

If in Infancy the organization is product-oriented, in Go-Go it turns to its market. However, this turning to the market does not mean a marketing organization; it is only a selling orientation. This distinction needs further explanation.

Marketing is the *thinking* part of selling—deciding what products to sell at what price, with what channels of distribution and how to promote them. It is a planning, positioning function. Selling is a producing, *doing* function. It involves carrying out the plans and providing information on how well the plans work or do not work in the marketplace; this in turn could require that a new marketing (strategic) decision be made.

Since the Infant organization had to survive by selling, the selling orientation becomes addictive, with *more* meaning *better*. The organization equates sales with success, and it exploits opportunities rather than plans for them. It is an opportunity-*driven* organization, rather than an opportunity-*driving* organization. The attitude is, "If there is an opportunity to make a buck, we go and make it. Who knows if there will be another opportunity tomorrow?" The organization *responds* to the environment, rather than *planning* the environment it wants.

A proactive marketing orientation means identifying new client needs and designing services and products to satisfy them. In Go-Go, it is too early to do this because the organization is still captive of and wants to capitalize on the needs already identified in Courtship.

In the Courtship stage, there is a vision. In Infancy, there is an experimentation with the vision, thus a product orientation. Once the experimentation is completed, in Go-Go the organization moves to a sales orientation.

This sales orientation can have abnormal outcomes. Go-Gos assume a fixed profit margin on sales, thus believing more sales automatically mean more profits. However, as they expand uncontrollably, their cost accounting becomes useless. Eventually, they might be selling more, but instead of making more profits, they might be losing money. To maximize sales, they give discounts to the channels of distribution, commissions to salesmen, and rebates to clients. Due to their fast growth and rate of change, their cost accounting is ineffective. As a result, they usually do not know the costs of goods sold, and the net price of the product could be lower than the total cost of the product sold. As a result, the more they sell, the more they lose.

I have witnessed this phenomenon frequently.

Rapid Growth

Overnight success can breed arrogance. The change from difficulty and pain in Infancy to even limited success in Go-Go yields arrogance. The results of this arrogance are that the organization becomes involved in ventures with which it has no business being involved.

If Infancy is management by crisis, in Go-Go, it is crisis by management. The parents of a 2-year-old cannot let the toddler out of sight. Following him around, the parents constantly have to say: "NO! NO! NO!". The toddler is constantly getting into trouble. The Go-Go company needs the same kind of attention. In making the transition from Infancy to Go-Go, the company's vision changes from a very narrow, nose-to-the-grindstone perspective, to a panorama of endless possibilities.

In the Go-Go organization, space is scarce because the organization is growing so fast. New offices are acquired as they're needed, or after they're needed. So, it's normal for a Go-Go organization to be scattered all over town—or all over the country.

The rapid growth the company experiences has organizational manifestations. In Infant organizations, there is no organizational chart or job descriptions. There is hardly a salary administration system. It is like a good family—everybody does whatever needs to be done. Salary increases are given when there is money and the founder is in a good mood. There are no performance appraisals. Since everybody knows what everybody else is doing, such formal appraisal systems are not needed. For an Infant organization, this is normal, it is a sensation. For the Go-Go, it can be transitional. At the next developmental stage, if this behavior continues, it becomes pathological.

Lack Of Consistency and Focus

At this stage of development, the organization may have a whole array of people with different capabilities and incentive systems. It is a random patchwork of decisions on who does what and for how much remuneration. There is little training, performance appraisals, or salary administration systems. Since it has no systems or established policies, the employees are hired at different times, under different agreements. Some are highly-qualified and some are not. The Go-Go organization doesn't have the time or the focus to weed out the incompetents.

Success and arrogance, reactive sales orientation, ambiguity about tasks and responsibilities cause the Go-Go organization's interest span to be a short one. Managers jump from task to task, trying to cover all bases simultaneously. Both the organization and its managers lack focus. If this lack of focus continues, the organization may go bankrupt. In order to survive, the organization must develop policies about what *not* to do, rather than on what *else* to do.

The Company Is Organized Around People

In the Go-Go organization, people share responsibilities and tasks overlap. For example, in one such organization the president was the chief buyer, the top salesperson and the designer. The salespeople also did some buying, and the accountant was the part time office manager. In the Go-Go stage, there might be an organization chart, but it will look like a piece of paper a chicken has walked all over—dotted lines, straight lines and broken lines drawn in all directions. If you ask an employee, or even an executive, "Who do you report to?" you'll probably get a vague, confusing answer. "I mostly report to Sam, but sometimes to Lee. However, when there is a quality problem, I report to Bob, and come to think of it, to Al as well." And so on.

The company is organized around people, not around tasks. It grows in a non-planned way. The organization *reacts* to opportunities. It does not plan, organize or position itself to exploit future opportunities which it creates. The organization is not controlling its environment, but being controlled by it. It is *driven* by the opportunities, not *driving* them.

Behavior is reactive, not proactive, and as a result, people are assigned tasks by their availability, not necessarily their competence. For instance, in one organization, Canada Sales reported to Engineering, because the head of Engineering was from Canada; in another company, Region A reported to Mr. Z, solely because Mr. Z had some free time. This management by expedience works for a while, but as the company continues to grow, the organization can become a tangled ball of string that is very difficult to unravel.

A normal problem of a Go-Go is that everything is a priority. As the company grows up, it learns what not to do by making mistakes which are inevitable for a Go-Go. It is a trial-and-error learning process, and when the Go-Go makes major mistakes—and loses market share, a major client, or money—the organization is thrown into the next phase of its lifecycle. When there is a major crisis, the organization is cured of its arrogance. The bigger the success and arrogance is in the Go-Go stage, the bigger the crisis to occur and push the organization to change. The organization realizes that it needs a set of rules and policies on what and how to do or not to do. The development of rules and policies indicates the emergence of an emphasis on the company's administrative subsystem, and the transition to the next stage of development— Adolescence. If this emphasis on the administrative systems does not occur, the company slips into a pathology called the Founder's or Family Trap.

In Courtship, organizations which have insufficient commitment to pass the test of reality slip into a premature death called an Affair. What is an Affair but lots of enthusiasm with no real commitment. An Infant organization that makes a fatal mistake doesn't receive enough "milk," or the love and commitment of the founder is killed, slips into Infant Mortality. Go-Go organizations that cannot develop their administrative systems, that cannot institutionalize their leadership, fall into the Founder's or Family Trap.

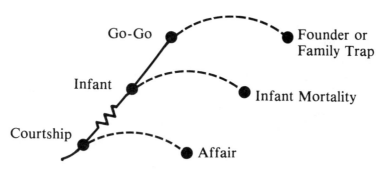

Figure 9: The Founder's Trap

The Founder's Trap

What is the Founder's Trap? In the Courtship through Go-Go stages of the Lifecycle, the founder is basically the company, and the company is the founder. They are one and the same. For example, if the company needs a bank loan, the founder must pledge his personal assets in addition to the company's, because the bank sees the two entities as one. The founder is the driving force the bank is relying on to get the loan repaid. He is both the biggest asset and the biggest risk. With the emergence of administrative subsystems, the organization moves toward institutionalizing the guiding leadership of the founder. Because the company is now sufficiently established, the founder can no longer act as a one-man show. He cannot reach deeply enough into the company to personally implant his leadership style and philosophy. Therefore, a system must be designed to do it. But how? The founder tries to decentralize by delegating authority and responsibility. It usually does not work well.

Delegation Versus Decentralization

A Go-Go will get into trouble and lose more money in a week in real estate than it made all year in the shoe business. The typical reaction to this calamity is to implement controls. The founder[1] recognizes that he is losing control and says something like "We need to get organized. We need better controls around here." The

---

[1] The *founder* should not be thought of literally. By the time a company is in Go-Go, the original founder might be long gone. By founder, I mean the top manager of the organization who behaves as if he founded and owns the company.

company then creates a set of rules and policies, but who's the first to violate them? The founder. As an alternate scenario, the founder might call management together and say, "As you all know, and have constantly reminded me for the past few months, this company is just too big for one person to call all the shots, so I'm starting to delegate authority around here. You each have your own areas of responsibility and you're free to start making decisions as of today. *However*, ask me first before you make any big decisions, and don't make any decisions I wouldn't make."

In both instances, the founder is trying to delegate authority, but he does not want to lose control. Although he only wants to delegate, he ends up decentralizing. Let me explain the difference.

Delegation is the process of transferring tasks down the organization hierarchy and creating a sense of commitment for carrying them out. The task can be to make decisions or to implement the decisions. When the task is to implement a decision that has already been made, and the authority given is only tactical in nature, it is called delegation. If the task is to initiate decisions, that is, to make decisions as to what *should* be implemented, it is *decentralization*.

A Go-Go organization cannot decentralize. To have workable decentralization, there must be a system of control in existence. Decentralization provides a centrifugal force, for which the organization needs a counter—a centripetal force—otherwise management will lose control. This centripetal force is provided by policies which describe what the decentralized units can and cannot do, thereby maintaining unity in spite of decentralization. The administrative subsystem (rules and regulations) act as the centripetal force. In Go-Go, this administrative subsystem has not been fully developed yet.

Thus the founder, in trying to delegate, without the control system, ends up unintentionally decentralizing. People begin to take initiative, something which the founder finds threatening because it does not always reflect his own judgments, values, needs and preferences. Let us not forget that there was no delegation whatsoever during Infancy. The sudden jump from autocratic centralization to decentralization is justifiably frightening to the founder. He feels he is losing control. So, in fact, he is saying "You make only those decisions I would have made myself." When his subordinates fail to do this, and that is inevitable, since only through trial and error can they learn the founder's mind, he recentralizes authority. Then, once again, there is too much to do, and the founder cannot embrace and control the total organization; so, back to delegation, which ends up as decentralization, and back to the founder's sense of betrayal and of losing control. The relationship between the founder and the company is like a yo-yo. "You are in charge. No I am in charge." In the process, the organization is in high turbulence, with much pain and mental anguish. At a certain point, people say "Nothing is going to happen here until the old man dies."

Founder's Remote Control

What began in Infancy and Go-Go as a founder's loving embrace is now a stranglehold that is stifling the continued growth and development of the company. The company is trapped by the embrace of its founder. But the founder is frustrated too. The company is successful as measured by sales—the proof that the product works. Because of the Go-Go's perceived incredible economic success, the founder feels he has made it—gone from rags to riches. The founder feels he has made his imprint. Now he wants to do other things— he wants out of the day-to-day operation of the company. So the founder starts to become interested in the community, politics, health, travel, or anything that provides a more meaningful outlet for his energies. Making pizzas becomes boring, although pizzas are the source of his success. If he has experienced substantial financial gain from the company, he might prematurely cash in on the fruits of his labor, doing the things he really wants to do, but could not afford in the past. The chairman of Wells Fargo Bank told me that they watch out for this problem in banking. First, the founder gets a loan for the business. With success, he starts to carry himself differently and dress differently. Later, he comes in for a loan for a fancy car, then a boat and then a plane. Finally, he comes in for financing on the most expensive luxury of all, his paramour, and eventually—his divorce.

There is a complication that should be noted. The founder wants to delegate, but without losing control. The incremental distancing of the founder along with the difficulties of delegation, creates a remote control embrace, which is the worst possible situation. The founder is gone, but no one else has the right, the chutzpah or the courage to make decisions. The founder believes that with delegation of authority, his subordinates will begin running the show. However, he's always watching from the sidelines, and when they overrun the show because he unwillingly decentralized, he is back with a vengeance.

On a visit to the company the founder may hear or notice a decision which was made that displeases him, and all hell breaks loose. In one afternoon, power is again recentralized. Then he disappears once again for a month or more. The people cannot decide what to do and they get very anxious. They try to imagine how the founder would have decided, but this is risky at best. The founder is usually too creative, and by this stage, too arrogant, to second-guess. His greatness encompasses his ability to run the business by intuition. However, this intuition has not been institutionalized and transferred to someone else who can act in his stead. When the subordinates do not act, paralysis reigns. The cycle begins again when the founder reappears and becomes upset because no one took action, no one dealt with the problems. However, if someone does make a decision that the founder subsequently determines was poor judgment, heads roll. People begin to dread the founder's appearance and take on a fearful "damned if you do, damned if you don't" attitude. The founder, on the other hand, feels trapped by his creation. A frustrated founder told me a joke that illustrates this point.

"When do you stop making love to a 200-pound gorilla?"

"I don't know," I said.

"Not when you want to, but when the gorilla wants to!" he said.

In Infancy, what started out as a good idea and a nice little company, got away from the founder during the Go-Go stage. What started out as a cute, little monkey is now a huge ape demanding the founder's attentions, but the founder cannot, does not know how to, and does not want to, give those attentions any more.

The Founder's Trap means that when the founder dies, the company might die as well. The Founder's Trap can also develop into a *Family Trap*. The company may experience this when a family member takes over the company on the basis of ownership, rather than competence and experience. If this happens, the company has not separated ownership from management. It has not depersonalized the leadership role to an extent that it is capable of selecting the most competent person for the job. Instead, the person with the most ownership takes over. This nepotistic behavior is poison to many companies. The new leader is not always the most competent one. The action causes the competent managers to leave the ship. How many generations does it take to kill a company in a Family Trap? In the countries in which I have lectured, I always get the same answer: three. In Mexico, the folk saying is "Father—Merchant; Son—Playboy; Grandson—Beggar." In China, the saying is "From peasant shoes to peasant shoes in three generations." In the United States, the expression is, "From sleeveless to sleeveless in three generations."

One of the big innovations of capitalism is the separation of ownership from professional management. If the company is not going to lose its hard-won gains, it must make the change from management by intuition (as in Go-Go) to a more professional orientation. This should happen in Adolescence. If the organization cannot make this transition, it falls into the founder's or Family Trap.

The transition to Adolescence occurs usually with a major crisis. It is caused by the mistakes of the arrogant Go-Go. The causes for the transition have been present for a long time: the arrogance, the fast uncontrollable growth, the lack of systems, budgets, and policies, the lack of structure, the centralized decision making. It is a company primed for crisis.

I have had the experience of warning CEOs of Go-Go companies that the makings of a crisis were present. What was missing was the spark, the straw which inevitably broke the camel's back. Usually the warning is ignored. "Do you realize that we have had 180 percent growth in sales per year? We are at the top of the *INC.* magazine chart for the fastest growing small companies in the United States. Do you realize our stock has gone from $2 to $12 a share?"

Then it happens. They sell a product that has no quality assurance and they are sued; or they invest in a deal that "goes South" fast. The classic, textbook crisis frequently encountered is the result of planning by wishful thinking. For the arrogant founder, wishing is a reality as good as having that reality. That is what made a Go-Go a successful endeavor, making dreams come true, proving the doubters wrong, being successful by being unreasonable, not listening to others. Now that the company is successful, the founder becomes even bolder. He projects growth exponentially and starts spending money to prepare for that growth. It can be in fixed expenses that are difficult to cut like computers, buildings for offices, plants, and so on. Then the dream does not come true. Expanding to a new market was not as easy as expanding in the first market they penetrated; but cutting costs means admitting that the dream was not reasonable. It means accepting defeat even if it is temporary; and being unreasonable. Fighting defeat was what initially made the founder successful. So he fights, and the more he fights, the more the organization loses. The point is, it must be a major crisis to awaken the arrogant. That is the beginning of Adolescence.[2]

---

[2] In making analogies to human behavior, we should note that what is described in this book as Go-Go behavior, in human behavior is referred to as early adolescence—the arrogance, the feeling of omnipotence. Thus, the names given to each stage are not exactly parallel.

2

The Second Birth and Coming of Age ━━━━

ADOLESCENCE

In this stage of the organizational Lifecycle, the company is reborn.

In Infancy, the company was born for the first time. That was a physical birth. Now in Adolescence, the organization is being reborn apart from its founder—an emotional birth. In many ways, the company is like a teenager trying to establish independence from family. This rebirth is more painful and prolonged than the physical birth of Infancy.

The most distinctive characteristic behavior of Adolescent organizations is conflict and inconsistency. Some of them are:

- An "us versus them" mentality, old timers against new people
- Inconsistency in organizational goals
- Inconsistency in compensation and incentive systems

All of these traits result in many unproductive meetings and can cause departure of entrepreneurial leadership and the demise of the organization. The Z symbol on the curve in Figure 10 between the Go-Go and the Adolescent stages pinpoints this transitional stage.

Why is this transition such a difficult time? There are three principle reasons:

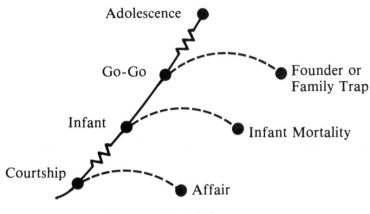

Figure 10: Adolescence

- Delegation of authority
- Change of leadership
- Goal displacement

Delegation of Authority

The move to Adolescence requires *delegation of authority*. In a society, this is analogous to making the move from an absolute monarchy to a constitutional monarchy where the king is willing to abide by a constitution. The founder must be willing to say, "I am willing to subject myself to the company rather than have the company be subject to me. I will be bound by the same policies that bind everyone else." It is rare that a king subjects himself to a constitution, giving up his absolute powers voluntarily. This change is usually accompanied by a revolution. This revolution erupts not just because the king loves power and does not want to relinquish it, but also because the king has developed a behavior based on one set of circumstances that may no longer be relevant. He has trouble changing his behavior to fit the new environment.

In the Adizes Institute, I have experienced this phenomena, even though I know that this should not happen, but being a doctor does not make one invulnerable to illness. At the Institute, we spend a lot of time developing rules and policies which I am often the first to break. Why? Because when the circumstances for which a decision was made change, I find myself changing the policy there and then rather than requesting that someone who has that particular responsibility attend to the problem. This behavior on my part stems from our Infancy days when *I had* to make decisions on the spot and by myself. I am allowing the same behavioral pattern control my actions in Adolescence. This behavior has a price. Since I violate policies, others follow my example. We end up with a set of policies that no one follows, causing the organization to continually behave unpredictably and accentuates the founder's feel that he is losing control.

A founder with a Lone Ranger style of management, with powers of a president who acts also as the chief salesperson, bill collector, product innovator and financier, needs to change his style. Specialization is required now that the business has outgrown the founder's individual capabilities. There are not enough hours in the day to manage the organization as a one-man show. He must delegate. The trick is to do it without losing control. Delegation of authority is not easy. The founder wants to do it, he just does not know how and is fearful of the potential results.

In Infancy, the founder did not and should not have delegated responsibility for major decisions. As a result, he became the major depository of critical information on company decision-making. This, however, is a double-edged sword. The employees probably do not have enough information to make decisions of the same quality as the founder. Since they do not have all the necessary information and insight, he must step in at crucial points and make decisions. The longer the founder holds on, the longer the process is for others to learn how to make and implement their own good decisions. Thus, lack of delegation creates an environment which prohibits further delegation.

From crisis to crisis, the founder begins to learn how to delegate. He starts to give the troops a chance to prove themselves. Typically, he starts out being as incompetent at delegating as his subordinates appear to be at making decisions. With the first signs of a potential mistake, he quickly recentralizes authority. This behavior is normal up to a point. It becomes pathologic if the founder continues to repeat the behavior, no matter how competent his people are—which means falling back into the founder's trap. In despair, the founder will often resolve to find a professional manager who can lead them through the nightmare of decentralization. This step can happen either by hiring an individual or selling the company to a more professional "parent." Let us focus on the difficulties that stem from bringing in a professional manager. The difficulties associated with selling out will be discussed later in the section on acquisitions and takeovers.

Change in Leadership—From Entrepreneurship to Professional Management

Bringing in a professional manager changes the leadership of the company. Leadership in this context means the process of changing organizational culture—taking the company from one stage of the Lifecycle to the next. In reality, it means taking the organization from one set of problems to another. Leadership is resolving the problems of today, which are normal and desirable, and preparing the company for the problems it will be facing tomorrow. The new manager must be a leader. He is not another gofer brought in to carry out the founder's decisions. This new person is a chief executive officer, a chief operating officer, or an executive vice president, whose purpose is to take over for the founder. He is there to get the gorilla off the founder's back and solve the problems of the Go-Go organization. The company must become more professional. This means being less intuitive in its decision-making and becoming opportunity-*driving*, rather than opportunity-*driven*. This new leader should create systems, design compensation packages, redefine roles and responsibilities, and institutionalize a set of rules and policies. He will be saying "No! No! No!" when the company is used to hearing only "Go! Go! Go!" from its founder.

What type of leadership is needed? In an Infant organization, we needed someone who was oriented toward risk-taking and results. We needed someone who was willing to step forward and make the commitment: "Here is my $10,000. Who else is in?"—a very results-oriented *doer*. For a Go-Go company, where the organization had achieved success with the original idea and began exploring new options, we needed to get past the one-product myopia. In addition to a short-term results orientation, the organization needed visions. These were not impossible requirements since the typical profile of a business entrepreneur is to be creative and results-oriented. The difficulty arises going into Adolescence. In this stage, the emphasis necessarily switches to systems, policies and administration; *this is an area which requires a totally different set of skills.* Founders usually recognize this need as well as their own lack of skills or interest in this area. They try to satisfy the need by hiring a professional manager from the outside to do the job. What they quickly find is that these "hired guns" are not like them. They come to work on time, and heaven forbid, they leave on time. They sit in their offices all day long with their computers and paper-work. They don't talk much, but when they do, all they say is what *not* to do. They're not particularly open or friendly. It gradually dawns on the founder that "This person is not like me. If I ran a company like this person manages, we would have never gotten this far." This logic starts the revolving door syndrome for hired managers. They get fired over and over "because they don't fit in." The founder may then hire another type of administrator, someone who "is like us and doesn't sit in his office all day."

This doesn't seem to work either. Everyone may like the new administrator, but the job doesn't get done because he is not getting the company organized and systemized, and most importantly, he is not controlling the founder. "We need someone stronger than that person," the people say. However, when a stronger person is brought in, it is too upsetting to the organization's culture, the founder feels threatened, and the revolving door turns once again. The paradox is that the founder is looking for "someone like us," who will "do the things we do not do."

The founder is looking for someone who can fly a submarine. What he must realize is that the leadership style required for Adolescence is not like that for the previous stages. Adolescence is a critical transition point. The company does not need someone like the founder. It needs an administrator who is a totally different animal, someone who can complement the founder's style, knowing these two orientations will conflict.

The founder must pass the baton to the administrator at the right time to ensure the healthy transition into Adolescence. Good management is not a marathon race. It is a relay race in which you pass the baton to the next runner at precisely the right time.

What is the right time? The right time occurs when the company is doing well, so there are no excessive pressures to go out and sell; this means that the situation does not force the wrong style of leadership. Who changes leadership when everything is fine? The founder is happy now! The transfer occurs when there is crisis, and at that time, inwardly turned leadership is not popular.

There are other difficulties in passing the baton to another person. At this stage of the Lifecycle, the organization is disorganized and to an outsider, everything appears confused and confusing. The company's organization chart could not possibly fit on one piece of paper. "Everyone and his brother" reports to the founder for one reason or another. The compensation system is a patchwork of special deals that have turned into policies through default. There is no management depth. The organizational behavior is a mirror of the founders and usually has a guerilla (partisan) culture. Employees talk about the old days and have their own rituals and pecking order. Seniority is often rewarded by a founder desperate for stability. Since the organization has no extensively documented policies, these senior people serve as the organizational memory, and if they leave, they can throw the organization into chaos until someone else figures out how to do their jobs. Because of their indispensability, these senior people have immense political power.

The founder also remembers that the senior people stuck with him through infancy. He values loyalty. They carry the same scars. They were loyal to him through the difficulties of the past. The founder listens to them, the old timers.

Into this environment comes the new manager who is going to "professionalize" the company. The manager's efforts at developing rules and policies are seen as direct attacks on partisan seats of power. Long-time employees will generally try to resist his efforts. When he tries to get his hands on the levers of power, the real battle begins. The old power structure bypasses the new chain of command, and goes directly to the founder to complain about the new boss.

"He is ruining morale." "He doesn't understand how this company works." "He is going to kill this company." And the final blow: "He doesn't do it the way you do it."

Whom does the founder support? The new administrator? Probably not. So, the new person is forced to resort to hiring his own supporters to outflank the "old boys" in the organization. Sides are chosen and guerilla tactics prevail. Cliques are created and an *us versus them* culture is created.

The administrator may try to establish a new incentive system that removes personal bias in favor of objective rewards based strictly on performance. This new system encounters opposition from the old-timers since they will lose their special deals. The new boss may also want to restructure jobs and reassign responsibilities, which of course, is attacked by the old-timers, who fear losing their power bases. The new manager faces opposition everywhere he turns.

However, the biggest source of problems usually comes from the founder who hired the manager in the first place. It is the founder who supplies all the priorities for new projects and products; and, in his usual style, these ideas are poorly thought through. The new manager is requested to develop a budget, and goes to great lengths to prepare it. It's probably the first budget the organization ever has had, but the new activities the founder wants or has already started, are not included. The founder changes his mind faster than the professional manager can change budgets.

The founder is the first to violate the administrator's newly-established policies and procedures. The old-timers watch the game. When the founder sets the example with the first violation, they assume the professional manager is a lame duck and that all the other rules can be violated too, and they proceed to do so. Guess who gets called on the carpet to explain why the new budgets, rules and policies are being violated? The new manager. This treatment is enough to cause the manager to develop a strong persecution complex, as well as intense dislike for the founder and his old buddies. The manager sees himself in a no-win situation and begins to wonder how he ever accepted the job in the first place. He feels impotent, exhausted, disliked and totally unrewarded for his attempts to make a contribution to the organization.

Goal Displacement

What further complicates the transition of authority is that the company must undergo a displacement of goals. The company must switch goals from *more is better* to *better is more*, from working harder to working smarter. If you ask a Go-Go how it is doing, the typical response is "Great! Sales are up 35 percent." If you ask about profits, the next response is "Gee, I don't know, go ask accounting." The orientation of a Go-Go is toward more sales, on the assumption that they necessarily mean more profit; it acts as if the profit margin on sales are fixed. However, this attitude can get a Go-Go into trouble. It may actually be losing money with more sales. When someone finally adds up the total direct and indirect costs necessary to get the sales growth, he often finds that the company is losing money. Why didn't he already know this?

Often, it is because the company has so many products, in so many markets, with so many special price deals that are continuously changing that it is an impossible task to keep up with all the data. This is typical for a Go-Go. The accountants can usually figure it out—about six months too late to do anything about it.

Due to this turbulence, morale starts going down, some good people leave or show signs that they might leave. The founder, desperate to keep the show together, tries to buy their commitment and offers them stock and/or profit sharing. This creates a new set of problems. It creates a political problem. If in the past they wanted but could not control the founder's behavior; now, they want to and believe they should be able to, because they own a piece of the action, and it is their assets that he is endangering. So they start fighting the founder more which causes internal marketing energy to increase. Attempts to do profit sharing has its own problems. To create a new incentive system, the organization must develop a clear responsibility, authority structure and information systems which will tell how well an individual is doing, otherwise, profit sharing is like a windfall. It does not create higher commitment and it does not control turnover of management unless the windfall is very high. Functionally, it is like a bribe.

Although everyone wants to be better organized, the response for attempts to do it are often met with: "My department's fine. Go work on sales, that's where the problems are." In order to make the transition, everyone must participate in the restructuring. This transition is comprehensive, and in order to carry it out, trust and respect throughout the organization is needed. The transition must be made with the right sequence of events.

Those changes require time, lots of thinking time in the office, away from the firing line, where the action has been traditionally. But the Adolescent organization does not want to spend the time in the office. They are still really Go-Gos at heart. The company wants to get organized *and* keep the same rate of growth. These two requirements are mutually exclusive. The company must relax its hectic sales pace to allow systematization to take place. A typical Go-Go solution to this problem is "Fine, we'll just have to get organized faster." So they buy a computer to speed up the process. Since they did not devote the time and energy to really think through the organizational needs, they merely computerize their ignorance. Now they have the ability to make their mistakes faster.

The end result of these three factors—delegation of authority, change in leadership and goal displacement—is conflict with a capital "C." This conflict has many dimensions. It is conflict between:

- the old-timers and the newcomers.
- the founder and the professional manager.
- the founder and the company.
- corporate and individual goals.

Normal Versus Pathological—The Divorce

The conflict in Figure 11 manifests itself in cliquish behavior. Cliques form out of those for and those against any particular project, system or individual. This conflict and resultant pain causes a turnover of personnel, especially of the entrepreneurial types.

"It is not fun anymore."

"We are not dealing with clients or with the products."

"We have forgotten why we are here. We are only fighting."

The energy which was dedicated solely to the market and promulgation of service, now turns almost totally inward. It is spent on internal fighting and on regulating conflicts that are feeding, or being fed, by the rumor machine.

If the company was established by a partnership or co-founders, the partner who is the more creative risk taker is often seen as

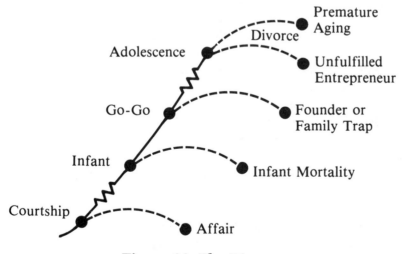

Figure 11: The Divorce

the principal threat to the stabilization of the company. The partner that is more stable and better organized will start to resist his creative partner and fight to oust him.

If the administrator has been brought from the outside, the fight for control becomes even more acute. The battle will depend on who has the most control. If control is with the entrepreneurial founder, he will fire the administrator and the revolving door for administrators will turn once again. If an external board of directors has control, the dynamics of the "revolution" change; the professional manager and the board will develop an alliance. If this happens, there is a good chance that the entrepreneurial founder will be squeezed out and the administrator will get the job of Chief Executive Officer.

The alliance develops because the board realizes this is a power struggle not only between the administrator and the entrepreneurial manager, who by then may not be the original founder. He is the one who built the company up. The conflict is also between the board and the entrepreneurial manager. As long as the entrepreneur was successful, he could call the shots and the board's authority was limited. Now that the entrepreneur's results are not favorable and the mistakes of the Go-Go organization are pouring in, the board wants control of the company. By the time the administrator is installed as chief executive officer or president, the board gets the authority it wants. The new president accepts that authority, something the entrepreneurial type did not and would not do.

The most painful transition occurs if the partnership is in the family. Spouses get involved along with parents, children and other relatives. Then the lawyers are called in.

Conflict in the three dimensions stated above is normal in the Adolescent organization. Pathology occurs when the conflict results in a critical loss of mutual respect and trust among those who have formal and informal control of the decision-making process in the company. They leave feeling they have many other ideas and opportunities to realize, so why should they put up with the nonsense? They liked the company when it was small and flexible. When it became too inflexible or political, it stopped being fun. They are the ones to get paid off and leave the company. This exit can produce a pathological phenomenon—the organization ages prematurely. It loses the principal entrepreneurial component that gave it flexibility, and the environmental awareness that provided vision and the driving force for the company. As a result of the entrepreneurs leaving, the organization falls into premature aging. When the numbers people take over, the system becomes efficient but it loses effectiveness. Profits might go up, but sales are down. (This is not necessarily bad, depending on which sales are eliminated.) The *organization man* becomes the behavioral model; *work with the system, follow the rules* becomes the motto. The organization ages prematurely and starts behaving like an Aristocracy in the aging stages of the Lifecycle.

It is referred to as *premature* aging because the organization benefits from the momentum and entrepreneurship of Go-Go for a while, but never arrives at its full potential: Prime.

ADOLESCENCE

Normal	Abnormal
Conflict between partners or decision makers, between the administrative and entrepreneurial types	Back to Go-Go and the founder's trap
Temporary loss of vision	Entrepreneurs leave, administrators take over
Founder accepts organizational sovereignty	Founder is squeezed out
Incentive systems reward the wrong behavior	Individuals get bonuses for individual performance while the company is losing money
Yo-yo delegation of authority	Paralysis while power shifts back and forth
Policies made, but not adhered to	Rapid decline in mutual trust and respect
Board of directors exercises new controls over management	The board fires the entrepreneurial types

If the administrative systemization succeeds and leadership is institutionalized (we will see how this should be done later in the book), the organization moves to the next stage of development and enters Prime.

PRIME

What is Prime? It is the optimum point on the Lifecycle curve, where the organization achieves a balance of self control and flexibility. The characteristics of Prime organizations are:

- Functional systems and organizational structure
- Institutionalized vision and creativity
- Results orientation; the organization satisfies customer needs
- The organization makes plans and then follows upon those plans
- The organization *predictably* excels in performance
- The organization can afford growth in both sales and profitability
- The organization spins off new Infant organizations

Prime organizations know what they're doing, where they're going and how to get there. They make money and are similar in growth characteristics to the Go-Go with one major difference. A Go-Go can tell you why they *made money*. A Prime can tell you why they *are going to make money*. And they do. The variance be-

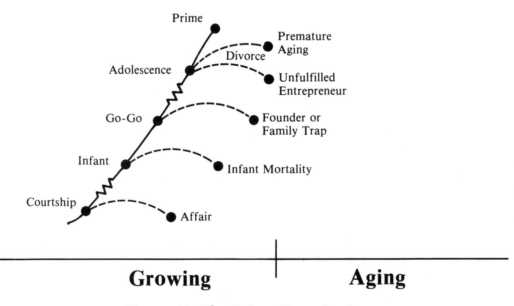

Figure 12: The Prime Organization

tween actuals and the budget is significant in a Go-Go—that is if they have any budgets at all.

In Prime, a company has an aggressive budget, and the variance of actual over budget is tolerable. A Prime organization has the vision and aggressiveness of a Go-Go, with the controllability and predictability of implementation acquired during Adolescence.

What is the typical problem of a Prime organization? Well, what are the problems in the other growing stages?

STAGE	TYPICAL COMPLAINT	
	Normal	**Abnormal**
Infant	No delegation	Prolonged under-capitalization
Go-Go	Too many priorities	Arrogant, central-ized leadership
Adolescent	Too many meetings	Too much in-fight-ing
Prime	Not enough well-trained people	Complacency

If we identify the typical problems we can tell where an organization is on the Lifecycle curve. The fact that an Infant organization does not complain about management training does not mean that it necessarily has well-trained managers. Neither do the Go-Go or Adolescent organizations. The problems that pertain to their places in the Lifecycle (cash flow for an Infant and in-fighting for an Adolescent) are so overbearing that the issue of management quality never surfaces.

At each stage in the Lifecycle there are problems. Some are remnants of previous stages and some are the tip of the iceberg of future stages. In healthy development, the problems that have the highest priority to the company are those which pertain to where the organization is currently located on the Lifecycle. Which problems are of secondary importance depend on how far the company is into a particular stage of the Lifecycle. It is like the moon. We can have a new moon, a full moon or a waning moon. Thus, we can have a rising Go-Go, full Go-Go or a waning Go-Go. In the rising phase, the secondary problems are from the previous stage and the tertiary problems are those of the next stage. In waning, the priorities shift. The priority is still with the current stage, but the secondary emphasis is placed on the next stage and the problems of the prior stage are tertiary in importance. It is like shifting weight when you walk. In the beginning your weight is mostly back, some in the middle, less forward. Then the weight moves to the middle with more forward, less in the back. Finally most of your weight moves forward, some is in the middle, and the least is in the back. You have moved forward and the process will repeat itself with the other leg.

That is a healthy forward movement. In the waning stages of pathological movement instead of future problems increasing in importance, unresolved past problems pull the organization back to previous stages in the Lifecycle. Some subsystems move forward, but some are underdeveloped and stay back, retarding the total development of the company. The organization should not have these problems. If it does have them, they must be resolved or they are pathological problems which impede the company's development.

The following are examples of how problems change in significance on the healthy part of the Lifecycle as the organization grows.

If we list the problems of Infancy, the importance of problems, as measured by how frequently people mention them will be: 1) a cash shortage and 2) too much to do.

There will be no mention of in-fighting. Infants do not tolerate in-fighting because there is too much to do. There will be little if any mention of the quality and training of people. Infants do not train. They have no time to invest in people. They hope and pray that the person they just hired is already trained.

In Go-Go, the importance of problems changes.

A rising Go-Go will have:

frequently	1) too much to do
	2) lack of delegation
sometimes	3) in-fighting
	4) not enough well trained people

Waning Go-Go will have:

frequently	1) too much to do
	2) infighting
sometimes	3) leadership crisis
	4) not enough well trained people

Early Adolescence will have:

frequently   1) in-fighting
                     2) leadership crisis

sometimes   3) market loss
                     4) not enough well trained people

Late Adolescence will have:

frequently   1) leadership crisis
                     2) not enough well trained people

sometimes   3) too much to do
                     4) some in-fighting

Early Prime will have:

                     1) not enough well trained people
                     2) some in-fighting

Usually, a company in Prime does not complain about being short on cash. That does not mean that they have plenty of it. Cash shortage for Prime is an expected and controlled event. It is a sensation, not a problem. The same applies to having too much to do. Prime has no less to do than Go-Go, but it is expected, planned for and controllable.

It should be noted that on the bell-shaped curve of the Lifecycle, Prime is not on the zenith of the curve, because as they say in the fruit business, "If it's green it's growing, if it's ripe it's rotting." If a Prime organization is at the top of the mountain, there is only one way to go—down. Prime does not mean that you have arrived, but that you are still growing. It is a process, not a destination.

Why is the curve still going up and what is going up? The curve depicts the vitality of the organization, its ability to achieve effective and efficient results in the short and the long run. The vitality is going up even after an organization moves out of Prime. This increase in viability comes from the organizational momentum that was generated in Courtship, tested in Infancy, refueled in Go-Go, institutionalized and channeled in Adolescence, and is being fully capitalized on in Prime. If the Prime organization does not refuel this momentum, if they lose entrepreneurship, if they keep capitalizing on the momentum rather than nourishing it, they will lose the rate of growth and eventually the organizational vitality will level off. The organization will proceed to the phase called Stable, which is the end of growth and the beginning of decline.

The challenge of Prime is to stay in Prime. What causes an organization to move out of Prime will be discussed in the analytical part of this book. What must be done in order to keep an organization in Prime or to rejuvenate it to Prime is discussed in the prescriptive part of the book.

PRIME

Normal	Pathological
Insufficient managerial training	Complacency

3

Description of Organizational Lifecycles: Aging Organizations ═══════════════

THE STABLE ORGANIZATION

The Stable phase is the first of the aging stages of the organizational Lifecycle. The company is still strong, but it is starting to lose its flexibility. It is at the end of growth and the beginning of decline. Organizationally, it suffers from an attitude that says, "If it ain't broke, don't fix it." The company is beginning to lose the spirit of creativity, innovation and encouragement of change that made it into a Prime organization.

As flexibility declines, the organization mellows. It is still results-oriented and well-organized, but there is less conflict than in the previous stages. There is less to fight about and less threat from aggressive colleagues. In such an organization, there is increasing adherence to precedence and reliance on what has worked in the past. By this time, the organization has usually achieved a stable position in the marketplace. It has developed a sense of security that may be unfounded in the long run. Creativity and a sense of urgency still occurs from time to time, but they are short-lived. Orderliness prevails and conservative approaches are adopted so past achievements are not endangered.

In the Stable organization, people spend more time in the office with each other than with clients or salespeople, as they did in

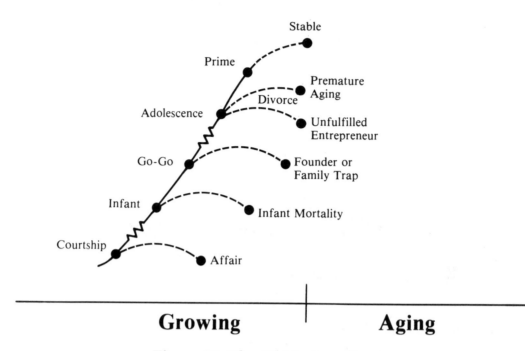

Figure 13: The Stable Organization

the past. Disagreements that were quite vocal before are expressed with a sheepish grin, as if to say "it's not really *that* important." The sense of urgency has disappeared. People are willing to prolong meetings. When a new meeting is announced, the protests that were loud and clear before—"Where the hell do I find time for another meeting?"—are few and rare. The climate becomes more formal; new ideas are heard, but the excitement is not there.

Several changes take place during the Stable stage. One such change occurs in budgets. Resources for research are reduced in favor of developmental spending. Similarly, budgets for marketing research are reduced to boost the profitability of the company. Management development is substituted with management training. Short-range profitability considerations start taking over.

The second change that occurs is a power shift within the organization. Finance people become more important than marketing or engineering or research and development people. Return on investment becomes a dominant performance indicator; measurements replace the conceptual soft thinking. The organization takes fewer risks and has less incentive to maintain its vision. The organization is still growing, as measured by sales, but the underlying causes of decline are already present: entrepreneurial spirit has dwindled.

The following are characteristics of the Stable organization:

- Has lower expectations for growth
- Has fewer expectations to conquer new markets, technologies, and frontiers
- Starts to focus on past achievements instead of future visions
- Suspicious of change
- Rewards those who do what they are told to do
- More interested in interpersonal relationships than risks

In this stage, interaction between people within the organization becomes important. The growing stages required change, which produced conflict. Thus, in the growing stages, interpersonal relations were not of major significance. In the Stable stage, where there is not much change, conflict diminishes. There are fewer disagreements and an important "old buddy" network emerges. This lack of conflict does not produce any noticeable dysfunctional results at this stage of the Lifecycle; only the negative investment is made— the results will appear later.

If creativity is dormant long enough, it begins to effect the company's ability to meet customer needs. The slide into the next phase of the Lifecycle, Aristocracy, is subtle. There are no major transitional events as in the growing stages. From Prime on, the movement along the Lifecycle is a *process* of deterioration.

When organizations grow, you can see the transition points, bud and then flower. When they age, there are no distinct points, just the process of continuous incremental rotting.

In organizations, the decline of entrepreneurial spirit leads to Stable and then to Aristocracy. It is a process of increasing self-preservation and distancing from the clients. This stage can often be mistaken for Prime, particularly by those in the organization. It has the purpose, activity, integration and administrative competence of an organization in Prime. However the energetic activity of entrepreneurship, proaction is not there. The seeds of decline are not on the surface.

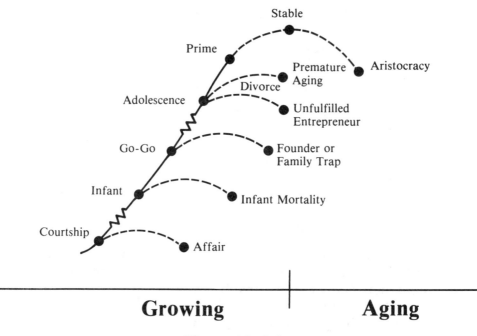

Figure 14: Aristocracy

ARISTOCRACY

This stage is identified by the following behavioral patterns:

- Money is spent on control systems, benefits and facilities.
- Emphasis is on *how* things are done rather than *what* and *why* it is done
- There is formality in dress, address and tradition
- Individuals are concerned about the company's vitality, but as a group, the operating motto is "Don't make waves." It's business as usual.
- There is low internal innovation. The corporation may buy other companies to acquire new products and markets, or in an attempt to buy entrepreneurship.
- The organization is cash rich—a potential takeover target.

The decline in flexibility which began in Prime, has a long-range effect: eventually the capability to achieve and produce results must also decline. As the organization is less proactive in dealing with long-run opportunities, its capability to respond to short-run needs also suffers. The company produces results, but it is not proactive. Goals with short-term, relatively assured results become the norm, and the seeds of mediocrity are sown.

The decline in long-term results orientation creates a new style of organizational behavior; the climate in the Aristocratic organization is relatively stale. What counts in this organization is not *what* you did, but *how* you did it. As long as you lie low long enough, and make no waves, you can survive and even get promoted, regardless of what you have produced.

The Aristocratic organization can be distinguished from other organizations on the Lifecycle by how its members dress, where they meet, how they utilize space, how they address each other, how they communicate with each other, and how they handle conflict.

Dress Code

In Infancy, if you can sell, you can wear your clothes inside out. No one will care as long as you produce results. By the time the company is in the Go-Go stage, suits and sportcoats with ties are expected, but the dress code is not uniform. In Prime, the professional look is required. The suits are neither too expensive nor too cheap; white or baby blue shirts are expected. The tie has a certain look to it. The uniform look is practically demanded. It is a functional uniformity that communicates a premeditated image. By the time the organization is an Aristocracy, only the uniformity remains. It is not necessarily functional to present a desired image. The uniform, for the sake of uniformity, is a three-piece suit—the darker the better. Management is dressed as if they are going to a wedding or a funeral. Conservative uniformity of dress reflects the conservative uniformity of their thinking mode. Form dominates function in the organizational climate and expresses itself in their furniture, dress code, memos, and the space they utilize.

Meeting Rooms

Where do Infant organizations meet? They don't have time for meetings, so there is no formal meeting place. Meetings occur in taxis on the way to airports, in restaurants during meals, in corridors and elevators. Go-Go companies, if they meet at all, usually do so in the founder's office where the center of power is. Working breakfasts, lunches, and dinners are a way of life. Decisions are made quickly and usually by the founder—discussion of a problem is short. People wander from topic to topic, and it is often difficult to understand how the discussion led to the decision.

In pathologic Adolescence, the real meetings take place outside the official meetings, usually in hallways, or at people's homes in the middle of the night. The rumor mill reigns over these unofficial meetings. The formal meetings are dull, filled with tension and restrained anger. Behavior is cliquish. Who you are seen with has tremendous significance and is interpreted by people who closely follow the power shifts in the organization. Additionally, at this stage of the Lifecycle, there are many power shifts. In normal Adolescence there are many meetings. Instead of being on the road, people are in meetings deciding responsibilities, rules, policies, information needs and reward systems.

By the time the company is in Prime, it will have an official meeting room that is highly functional and used for committee work. There will be sturdy chairs and tables designed for utility over comfort. It will be well-lit and have lots of writing pads and wall space. Contrast each of these characteristics with the boardroom typical of an Aristocracy, as follows.

A highly polished, dark wood table surrounded by matching plush chairs dominates the room. The carpet is thick. The lighting is dim and the windows are heavily draped. From the panelled walls, a larger-than-life portrait of the unsmiling founder stares down at the participants, as if to say "Don't forget where you stand." The room can be empty, but the roar of silence is overwhelming. When you walk in, the dim lights, the silence, the dark uniforms and the founder's portrait make a person feel uncomfortable and out of place. It becomes almost impossible to say, "Hey, guys, we're losing market share." Industrial psychologists point out that space, lights and color impact workers' behavior. Executives are influenced the same. The formal board room decor shouts, "Don't make waves!"

Use of Space

An Infant organization has no space. People share tables, typewriters and telephones. The organization is very cost-conscious; it is a shoestring operation. In a Go-Go company, people are typically spread all over town, or the country. The sales department is on Main Street, accounting is several miles away in another building, and the headquarters are in another town. Why? The Go-Go is an opportunity-driven company. It does not plan, it reacts. If there is a significant increase in sales, they just get some space somewhere and hire some people.

In Adolescent companies, the dispersion of offices inherited from Go-Go aggravates further the inherent culture of gossip to feed the rumor machine. During the Prime stage, consolidation of space occurs. The company moves into a new building capable of housing all related operations. In Prime, people are proud of the space utilization. The office space is well-planned and facilities support the function for which they were designed. There is no excessive opulence, luxury or showmanship.

By the time the organization reaches Aristocracy, form has overtaken function. The empty corridor alone could adequately serve the needs of several Infant companies. The president's office, with its private bathroom, dining room and secretary's office, probably cost as much to rent as the entire company facilities when the organization was a Go-Go. One such company spent a cool million dollars on the president's office, furniture and decor alone. It had the most lavish bathroom I have ever seen.[1]

How They Address Each Other

In Infant and Go-Go organizations, people usually address each other by their first names. The names used in Adolescent companies are not fit for print. In Prime, people begin using first and last names. By the time the organization has reached Aristocracy, people address each other in meetings almost exclusively by last name. They become very formal. It's Mr. Smith and Ms. Jones. They may be Bob and Mary inside their offices, but in those meeting rooms, the address is formal. In certain countries, the formality is accentuated by military, educational, and social titles like Colonel Shwart-

---

[1] This preoccupation with form is probably true for civilizations as well. When a society starts to worry about architecture, form and decoration, I wonder if it is aging.

zer (retired), Dr. Alexburg (although he has a PhD in medieval literature, which is irrelevant to the job he is doing for the company), and "Don" Alexandro, in Mexico. In Italy, one is called "doctor" for completing an undergraduate degree; in Brazil, one is called "doctor" because the person is an executive.

Communication

In the Courtship stage, people speak vaguely about what they think and feel. They repeat and contradict themselves, are easily annoyed and show their sensitivities. In Infancy, it is short and straightforward—less talk, more action. *Action speaks for itself*, and *action speaks louder than words*, are the mottos of an Infant organization. The mode of speech is short, direct, and sometimes offensive in its honesty. It is a sharp departure from the romantic era of Courtship.

In a Go-Go company, the communication is confusing. Demands are made whether or not people can meet them. They are expected to do the best they can. Usually, no matter what they do, it is still less than what is expected. In the Go-Go organization, four-letter words are used as a normal style of expression. Aggressive arrogance shows in the use of language.

In Adolescence, paranoia reigns. People give endless interpretations of what someone said and why he said it. In Prime, the communication is clear. You know what, why, when, how and who. Tasks are demanding, but achievable. People measure what they say, and they speak in a measured way, as if verifying the weight and importance of what is being said.

By the time the organization is Aristocratic, the mode of delivery is the essence—the medium is the message. People speak slowly . . . period. It has nothing to do with the content. Managers overuse visual aids and written communications. During meetings, people hedge when they talk, using endless double negatives and qualifiers. Listening to such a meeting, one wonders what was really said. The transcript of an Aristocratic organization's meeting is often a maze of hints, insinuations and veiled suggestions. Unless you are part of the culture and know all that is really going on, it is hard to understand what is being said at a meeting.

"It seems that, under certain circumstances, it may be assumed that . . . however, on the other hand, not necessarily so, we might conclude that . . ."[2]

If you ask someone privately what the person said, you might be told, "He said we're losing our market share." Why doesn't the person come right out and say it like he would have in the Infant or Go-Go company? Because the problem being communicated is not yet acute; while making waves might be politically dangerous. So he makes waves hoping that no one really gets rocked. Furthermore, the company might weather the storm. It is successful. Enchanted with its past, the Aristocratic organization is paralyzed to deal with the future. We can understand this phenomenon once we discuss how the organization deals with conflict and cash.

Conflict and Crisis Handling

A fourth distinguishing characteristic of Aristocracies is how people deal with conflict as a group. This characteristic has been well-illustrated by a movie called *Garden of the Finzi Continis*.[3] The behavior of an aristocratic Italian-Jewish family is depicted just prior to World War II. When the Fascists started to persecute Jews, the Finzi-Continis refused to believe that anything serious was going to happen.

> "We've been here for a long time," they said. "We are one of the most distinguished families in Italy."

And so they continued to play tennis behind the high walls of their castle and they ate in their chandeliered dining rooms, and continued business as usual. While each person in the family was deeply worried *individually*, as a group they would not express their worries. As a group enchanted with their past, they were paralyzed to deal with their future. The group dynamics were stronger than the individual fears.

The Aristocratic corporation behaves in a similar fashion. It usually has its own beautiful and expensive "castle", with space wasted as though it costs nothing. The people are individually wor-

---

[2] I noted massive hedging in communications in communist countries. In meetings, people say things in a way that is very very difficult to understand unequivocably.

[3] "Garden of The Finzi Continis": (Warner Brothers: Italian, 1971).

ried about the company and its future, but in formal meetings, they express none of these doubts. When a consultant faces managers collectively and points to threats from the competition, they are prone to reply, "Don't worry, we've been here long enough. They need us. We have a name, a tradition, a know-how." But *individually*, the managers agree with the consultant. The situation is bad and *someone* (usually someone other than the complainer) should do something. In one organization, managers explicitly said, "We don't like to compete. We'd rather serve." This results in repeating tomorrow what they did yesterday.

The Aristocratic company denies the present reality. While it is losing its market share and is increasingly unable to compete in terms of products or marketing skills, its members maintain a "business as usual" attitude. They also have a track record of historical performance that must be maintained. "Dividends must be distributed. We cannot afford to let the widows and orphans who invested in us be disappointed." So they distribute X dollars per share every year even though it is becoming a larger share of their profits.

One company I worked with declared dividends that amounted to 93 percent of the year's earnings, even though its product was becoming obsolete and no new products were being developed. This was suicide. I asked "How come?" The answer was typically Aristocratic. They planned top-down teleologically and structurally. Top management decided how much return they wanted to give to the shareholders. Then they determined how much profit they needed to show. Then they derived how much profit each unit *had* to contribute, and thus the amount of sales they *should* have, and what expenses they could have.

Please note. These factors had nothing to do with what was happening in the marketplace. This is self-centered, arrogant, aristocratic, detached, thinking-in-a-vacuum type of behavior. It is *should*, not *is* oriented.

In reality, the units could not produce the sales and thus the profits, but since top management committed to the board to declare a certain amount of dividends, the result was that 93 percent of the earnings were declared while the company was going stale.

The business as usual behavior (although it is anything but usual), is even more accentuated if the organization is an industry where one of its assets is clients' confidence in the organization.

Take for example, banks. In the middle eighties, quite a few were broke because of Third World debt or domestic oil and real estate loans. Cutting dividends would have signaled that the banks were in trouble, which would have led people to syphon out deposits in a hurry. That, in turn, would have made earnings even lower and the dividends decline even more—a spiral that some banks wanted to avoid at all costs.

However, to declare the same rate of dividends in the face of decreasing sales, revenues must be bolstered, so the organization raises prices or "adjusts prices upward so they are more consistent with the increase in our expenses."

Aristocracies, by and large, try to increase profits by raising revenues, not cutting costs. They do it, not by increasing unit sales, but by raising prices. Expenses sometimes may be cut by Aristocratic cultures, but only if they are forced to do so, and then it will only be on trivial items. As an executive in a moment of rage said, "They try to clean up a whorehouse by kicking out the piano player."

Raising prices in the face of a declining market share is like throwing gasoline on a fire. This action only accelerates the company's slide into the next stage of aging—Early Bureaucracy.

Mergers and Acquisitions

The Aristocratic organization is cash-heavy. If you compute the Dun and Bradstreet ratios of the Aristocratic and Prime organizations, the Aristocratic ratios are higher. The organization is conservative and liquid, because there are few demands for investments from internal sources. The organizational climate of accepting the present as desirable is stronger than the aggressive aspirations of any individual within the organization. Thus, few if any risk-taking endeavors are proposed. With its cash, the Aristocratic organization seeks new avenues for growth. Since there are no internal demands for this cash, it seeks growth opportunities outside.

Aristocrats often decide to promote growth by buying growth. This is done through acquisitions. And what do they buy? Not Infants. "They're too young and risky!" Not Adolescents. "They're too problematic!" Not Primes. "They're too expensive!"

Normal Aristocracies buy Go-Go companies. They get attracted to those companies because they want to get their hands on a new technology in a growing market. The Go-Go companies like to be bought out, because they are tired of trying to get organized and growing with their own internal resources. They figure the Aristocracy can do it more easily because it is bigger, richer and more organized.

But what might really happen? Every time the new acquisition wants to make a move, it has to complete a budget and a business plan for submission to the board. It takes the board three months to do anything, so by the time they've approved the action, it's too late—the opportunity has evaporated. After some time of this happening, the key managers of the Go-Go organization take a walk. The Aristocracy is left with a shell, because the biggest asset the Go-Go had was the entrepreneurs. If the Aristocracy appoints one of its own administrator types to run the Go-Go, even the entrepreneurial spirit might be lost.

The reverse situation can also happen. The Aristocratic organization, being cash heavy, is an attractive object for takeover. The most probable candidate to take over an Aristocracy, is a Go-Go organization which, in its eagerness to grow, has no limits to its appetite.

In both cases, the marriage is not easily consummated. When the Aristocratic organization buys a Go-Go, the latter is suffocated. What made the Go-Go exciting and vigorous was its flexibility— its speed in decision-making. Many decisions were made intuitively and the organization had little respect or place for ritual. With the Aristocratic organization, the climate is just the opposite. The ritual is rigorous: It requires budgets in a certain form, by a certain time, and with certain details, all of which the Go-Go organization finds stifling.

When the Go-Go acquires the Aristocratic organization, it is like a small fish that swallows a whale. Digestion takes a very long time. The Go-Go is in over its head with the problems of the Aristocratic organization. Milking cash out of the Aristocratic company will not transform it into a Prime organization, only a bankrupt Aristocracy. The vigorous Go-Go management introduces sudden and forceful waves of change. It sometimes paralyzes the Aristocrats with fear, making a workable merger even more difficult. The Go-Go might lose its growth momentum and orientation for several years while it is trying to digest its latest prey.

If the Aristocracy is very old and the Go-Go company cannot

easily solve the inherent problems of old age, the Aristocratic organization gradually consumes all of the Go-Go executive's time and both companies may go under. If an Aristocracy cannot acquire a Go-Go, it will merge with another Aristocracy. This further stymies the organization.

It is not strange then that recent studies on conglomerates show that the synergy that was supposed to happen as a result of mergers and acquisitions by and large did not occur. There is a clash of cultures that only a few managers know how to deal with.

At the advanced stages of Aristocracy, products are out of date. The clients know it, the sales people know it, and even the CEO knows it; but nobody does much about it. Complaints are filed. Meetings are held, but they are non-productive. In short, everyone is waiting for the first shoe to fall. In an effort to save their necks, many people leave the organization. Others, who cannot leave because they do not have attractive opportunities, accuse the deserters of disloyalty.

There is a sense of doom. The company tries to reverse the morale situation with gold medals for obscure achievements or with seminars in resort hotels where most of the time is spent vacationing, not working. The company may even build an expensive and unnecessary new building. Managers spend on form as if it affects the content. The same kind of behavior often occurs in failing marriages. The couple may try to cement the relationship by making new commitments, such as having a child or building a new house. They confuse cause and effect, input with output. First there must be commitment which is expressed in a new child or home, rather than having a child or a new house to create the commitment. The behavior is not to satisfy a functional need. It is to follow form, as if the form will force the function.

Why does this occur? Why the Finzi-Contini syndrome? Why are people hinting about problems and expecting someone else to do something about them? People know what is happening. Privately, they will be quite articulate in analyzing the problems. So why doesn't management provide leadership and act?

I have a theory which I call *the present value of a conflict*. We know that the value of a dollar received a year or ten years from now is not equal to a dollar received today. We have to calculate the present value of a stream of income over time. The same might hold true for the cost of a declining market share or a future problem.

A problem in the future is not as costly as the same problem facing us today. The anticipated, dreaded future might never occur.

There is a story that illustrates this point. Two thieves were thrown into jail and ordered to be executed. One of them sent a message to the Sultan saying that if he was given three years he could teach the Sultan's favorite horse to speak.

"How can you promise that?" asked the other thief. "You cannot teach a horse to speak!"

"Who knows," said the first. "In three years the Sultan might die, the horse might die or maybe the horse will speak!"

The same philosophy can be observed in an Aristocratic organization. Yes, they are losing market share, but right now, with their resources, it is a minor factor. In the future, who knows, they say, the government might change, government policies might change, the competition could go broke, customers might change their taste in goods, maybe they will survive or maybe even flourish. Note, they do not rely on their efforts to survive. They count on the environment turning in their favor. There is a joke I heard from a senior banker. It is about a certain country, let us call it Calico, but easily applies to any other country, corporation, or individual human being.

"As we all know," the banker said, "Calico has deep economic problems. There are two possible solutions to these problems. One is rational. The other is a miracle. The rational solution is that Saint So and So will come down from heaven and save Calico. The miracle solution will be if the Calician people get off their butts and start working real hard."

By the standards of the above joke, Aristocracies have *rational* solutions for solving their problems.

It is increasingly difficult to get cooperation across organizational lines to make changes happen. Compare this joke to another joke that applies to a Go-Go. A guy comes to a friend's store and says: "I am sorry I heard you had a fire in your store." "Sshh . . ." says the store owner, "it is tomorrow" . . .

The point is Go-Gos take charge of their life. Aristocracies want the environment to become favorable. The focus of control (on whom do they attribute the capability to make a difference) from Stable on gets increasingly externalized.

Why the reliance on external factors for taking action? Because future problems are not pressing in the present. The company is

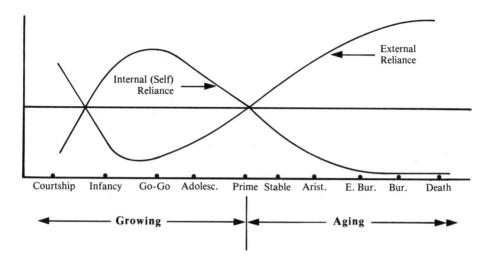

Figure 15: The Focus Of Control Over The Lifecycle

liquid and profitable. Taking action *now* means making waves and becoming embroiled in a political fight which has a price that must be paid by the individual making waves at that time, not three years in the future. The political costs of making waves *today* is higher than the present value of solving *tomorrow's* problems. Furthermore, there is a decreasing sense of control. The behavior that emerges is to allude to the problems without acting on them in the hope that someone else will do something.

That is what consultants are for. They are brought in to say what management would like to say without management having to explicitly admit anything. Management lets someone else "take the chestnuts out of the fire." Consulting reports are read but not acted on until Early Bureaucracy sets in. Why? Because by then the once-future problems are in the present and immediate action is called for. By that time however, the Sultan's horse is not talking, it is kicking and kicking hard. Market share is being lost, and there is negative cash flow and high turnover of good people. All the vital signs of an organization are screaming: "Emergency!"

Desperate over the continued loss of market share, with revenues and profits in a nosedive, the Aristocratic organization enters Early Bureaucracy. This does not happen slowly; it is quick and forceful. What happens is that the Aristocracy covers its losses through acquisitions and by adapting prices upward. As the prices go up, quantities start going down. At first, revenues go up because of the rising prices, but eventually the decreasing quantities have an effect and the revenues start declining rapidly. The organization finishes cashing in on the good will they so painstakingly built from Infancy. The artificial face lifts of price increases stop working because they are not the real thing. The real thing is to satisfy client needs; to provide real value.

The day of reckoning comes when they cannot raise prices, and acquisitions are no longer easily made. The truth surfaces rapidly. Then the niceties are gone. Knives are drawn and the fight for indivdual (not corporate) survival begins. Welcome to Early Bureaucracy.

EARLY BUREAUCRACY

In Early Bureaucracy, the following characteristics are typical of an organization's behavior:

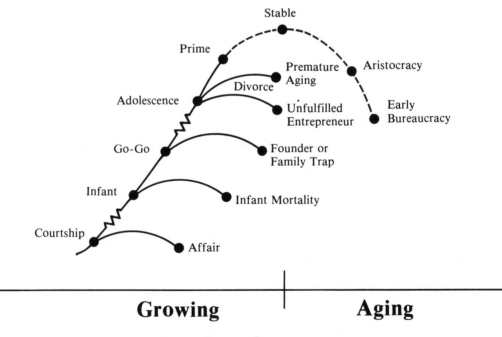

Figure 16: Early Bureaucracy

- Emphasis is on *who* caused the problem, rather than *what* to do about it (as if solving the *who* equals solving the *what*).
- There is much conflict, backstabbing and infighting.
- Paranoia freezes the organization; everyone is lying low.
- Focus is on internal turf wars; the external customer is a nuisance.

The Witch Hunt

During Aristocracy, if for a prolonged period of time there is neither a desire for change nor a results-orientation, the artificial face lifts of raising prices eventually have a negative effect. Finally, the day of reckoning arrives. The demand becomes inelastic and the increase in prices reduces total revenues; the revenues and market share steadily shrink. At that time, the mutual admiration society dissolves. The good old buddy days of the Aristocracy are gone, and the witch hunt begins. People try to find out who caused what to happen. With blades drawn, it's backstabbing time in the boardroom. The situation is not unlike what happens in a primitive tribe confronted with an extended drought or famine. It is time to appease the gods, which calls for a sacrifice. Whom does the tribe sacrifice? The fairest maiden or the finest warrior—the cream of the crop. Whom does the Early Bureaucracy sacrifice? The commodity they treasure most, and have the least of—the last vestiges of creativity. The head of marketing is fired because "We're in the wrong market with the wrong products." The corporate strategist or the engineering chief are the next to go: "Our strategy does not work; our products, technology, and advertising are obsolete." People are fired as if they were the cause of the problems.

People however, do not feel responsible for what is happening. The marketing head has claimed many times that the direction in which the corporation was following had to change. The strategist probably developed an ulcer worrying about the lack of organizational direction. The people complained in private, urged, begged and threatened; but, "it was like pushing wet spaghetti up the hill." They could not produce change from within. Those who seek to reform an Aristocratic organization from within often do so at the price of their careers. The organization eventually forces them out, even if it benefitted from their efforts. Thus, the creative employees the organization needs most for survival either leave or become useless and discouraged.

There is one main variable that distinguishes the Aristocratic organization from Early Bureaucracy—managerial paranoia. In the Aristocratic organization, there is a silence before the storm. People smile, are friendly and handle each other with kid gloves. In Early Bureaucracy, when the bad results are finally evident, instead of fighting competition as they should, managers start fighting each other. There are no gloves anymore, just bare knuckles. A ritual of human sacrifice starts. Someone has to take the blame; someone has to be the sacrificial lamb. So every year or every few quarters, someone is blamed for the adverse conditions of the company and gets fired. The paranoia stems from the fact that no one really knows who will be blamed next. So they watch each other with suspicion. CYA (Cover Your Ass) strategy dominates behavior.

It is not uncommon for people to circulate far-fetched explanations for what is happening. For instance, if the sales manager decides to give a discount, the other executives do not explain it in rational terms by referring to competitive conditions; rather they attribute it to a Machiavellian strategy on the part of the sales manager to discredit the marketing department and expose the incompetence of the marketing vice president.

This behavior accentuates the decline. Managers fight each other, spending most of their time turned inward, building cliques and coalitions which are constantly changing. Their creative abilities are not directed toward creating better products or developing a better marketing strategy, but toward ensuring personal survival by eliminating and discrediting each other. As organizational performance further declines, the people become even more paranoid. Since the better people are feared, they are either fired or leave. This cycle continues until the end result is bankruptcy, or a full Bureaucracy nationalized or subsidized by the government.

If the company is subsidized or nationalized, this is an extension of its life. It is reborn again. It should have died but it is being kept alive. It is an artificially living corpse. Thus, another Z appears on the life cycle curve.

What kind of people are left in such a protective environment? Administrators! Entrepreneurs come and go; administrators accumulate. Since the administrators have only to administer, the company converts itself into a full-blown Bureaucracy, with its sole

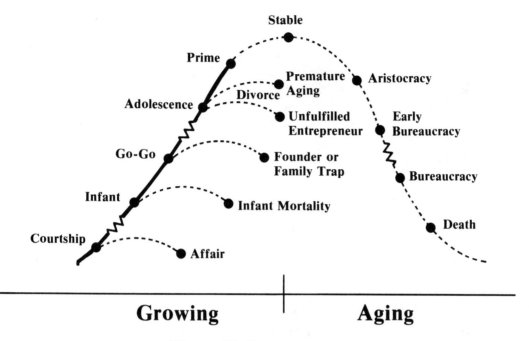

Figure 17: Bureaucracy

emphasis on rules and policies, and no obvious orientation toward results or satisfying customer needs.

BUREAUCRACY AND DEATH

In the Bureaucratic stage, the company does not generate sufficient resources of its own. It justifies its existence not by the fact that it is functioning well, but by the fact that it exists. It can hold off death only through artificial life support systems. What is the Bureaucratic organization like?

- It has many systems, with little functional orientation.
- It disassociates from its environment, and focuses mostly on itself.
- There is no sense of control.
- In order to work effectively with the organization, customers must develop elaborate approaches to bypass or break through the system.

Systems With Little Functional Results

A manager told me the following joke. A man went to Paris and wanted to know how to find the best jewelry store in town. He asked a friend who told him "go to Rue La Michele 25. I heard that is the best place." So he went there and was greeted at the door by a valet dressed in a red uniform with golden epaulets and shiny buttons. The valet tipped his hat and said, "What would you like sir?"

"To buy some jewelry."

"Left door," said the red-uniformed valet.

He entered and another valet, this time in blue, asked, "Are you looking for men's or ladies' jewelry?"

"Ladies'," he replied and was ushered down the right corridor where yet another valet, dressed in purple, asked if he preferred gold or silver.

"Gold."

"Corridor to your right please." Subsequently, he met three other valets who asked him his preference on several other things, and pointed him from one to the other in the proper direction. Finally, the last valet asked if he wanted diamonds or rubies.

"Rubies."

"Left door please." He opened the door and found himself in the street. Frustrated, he went back to the hotel.

"How was it," the friend asked.

"I didn't get to buy anything, but, boy, do they have a system!"

In the Bureaucratic organization, very little which is meaningful is accomplished. It acts like a broken record, repeating the same phrases over and over. The typical response to a question is "wait" or "someone will inform you soon," but there is no real answer. Once you get to know them, the managers are among the nicest people to meet. They agree a lot in public (not privately) and little if anything ever happens. There is no results-orientation, no inclination to change, and no teamwork; there are mostly systems, forms, procedures and rules.

One of the most distinctive characteristics of a Bureaucracy is the worship of the written word. When a client or another executive asks for or suggests anything, the typical answer is "write to me about it." Writing a letter to a Bureaucratic organization is often a waste of time, paper and stamps. It usually get filed. In the files of one such organization was a letter threatening to sue unless the writer's complaint was handled soon. The letter had been stamped "received on" and then filed. Since the letter contained a threat of legal action, the file clerk was asked why it had not been answered. The answer was that some needed information was missing.

A Bureaucratic organization is disorganized. Clients' efforts to get a decision on something are met with a request for another document. The organization does not ask in advance for everything that is needed, so the uninitiated client cannot possibly be prepared. Instead of showing its entire hand, the Bureaucratic organization shows one card at a time. This behavior occurs because no one in the Bureaucracy knows everything that should be done. Everyone has a small piece of the necessary information, and the client is expected to put it all together. New employees do not know salary policies, salespeople do not know marketing strategy; marketing people are not informed of company plans; finance does not know what sales are expected; production is not informed of how well the product is being received; and the customer does not know where to get effective attention. The customer service department often consists of a switchboard operator whose job it is to listen, record complaints, and answer them with a standard, routine letter—"We will do our best to . . ."

Disassociation

An older person can remember 1936 as if it was yesterday, but he often cannot remember what he had for breakfast that morning. Bureaucratic organizations are similar. They know all the rules, but they can't remember why they are in existence. If you ask why certain things are done in a Bureaucracy, the typical respone is "I don't know why" or more typically, you will get the answer— "Because it's a corporate policy." Bureaucracy runs on ritual, not reason.

Like an older person who does not want too much interruption in his life and cannot entertain the grandchildren for more than a few hours, these organizations do not like outside interruptions and actively create obstructions to outside interferences (customers). The Bureaucracy attempts to isolate itself from the environment, connecting to the external world through a very narrow channel. There are many examples of these narrow channels—such as having only one telephone line. A client must spend endless hours or days trying to get through to the company. If he goes to the organization, he is first sent to the dispatching window, which is only open a few hours a day. It's possible he'll spend the day waiting in line to find out where to go next. If he writes to the organization, it may take months to get an answer, and then it will be a form letter which frequently does not address his particular issue. Often, even this does not happen; the correspondence or file is simply lost.

Lack of Sense of Control

Why the disassociation? Why lack of action? Executives feel they cannot do or accomplish much although they know that they have to go through the rituals as if they are doing something. In other words, in order to make things happen, one needs the cooperation of others which in a bureaucracy is difficult to get because the changes necessary are complicated and a single executive cannot mobilize all the people needed across organizational lines to make those necessary changes. Thus rituals of going through the motions substitute action.

Bypass System

To get results from such an organization, a client must do the legwork himself. It seems as if the nervous system of the organization has broken down. The left hand does not know what the right hand is doing. One department rejects what another one requests. The client is puzzled, frustrated and lost.

How does an older person function when some organs are not operational? Usually, he is put in a protective environment (hospital) and connected to different machines that bypass the non-working organs. The same analogy applies to Bureaucratic organizations.

Business organizations that must work with a Bureaucracy usually have a special department with the full-time task of providing a bypass system. There are different names for these departments. In some organizations, they are forthrightly called government relations offices. In others, they are disguised as public relations. These departments become experts on the inner workings of the government agency and then divide their responsibilities. Mr. A will work with undersecretary Y; Ms. B will work with bureau director Z. Since Y and Z might not agree, or know what to do together, A and B decide what they want, and help Y and Z to make a decision desirable to them.

Business organizations spend millions of dollars annually just to find out what government agencies want or should want, and when and how they should be convinced of it.

At one of my lectures in India, an Indian CEO told me, "You Americans talk about market share and marketing strategies. That is irrelevant to us. What is crucial to our success is understanding the government's inner workings. Government policies on licensing, pricing, import quotas and labor relations can make or break us. It is more important than whatever the most successful marketing strategy can do. If a company figures out how to make the government machinery work in its favor, it gains the critical competitive edge. Those who have to develop know-how about the government and its working relationships, have to develop connections. This is difficult to do, so they are competitively disadvantaged. Government bureaucracy is my best ally. It is my best barrier against competition—better than any market positioning that you are talking about."

Bureaucracies are kept alive by the monopoly they have on certain activities—a captive audience which is forced by law to buy their services—and the external bypass systems that clients create. Pulling the governmental plug would put many of these Bureaucratic organizations out of business. In the United States, the taxpayers' revolt of 1978 was one way of doing that. I am not predicting that cutting taxes will enhance the administrative health of governmental agencies, but it would speed the death of some of them.

The health of a full-fledged Bureaucracy is very delicate. What appears to be a dangerous monster may actually be relatively easy to destroy. Bureaucracies that seem to be hard-to-change monstrosities may be rotten at the center and on the brink of bankruptcy. Any sudden change will ruin them. Bureaucracies which are forced to reorganize quickly often do not survive the effort. A new computer may throw a Bureaucratic system into a spin. The old system keeps running as if nothing has changed and, people ignore the new computer system, sitting next to it.

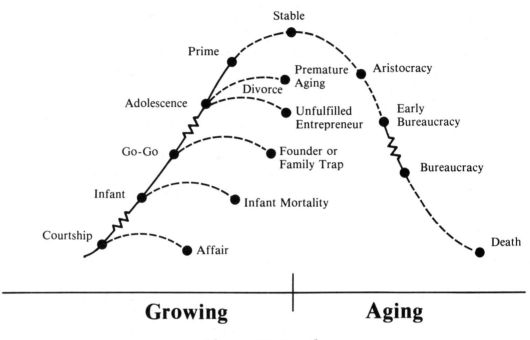

Figure 18: Death

Bureaucratic organizations may survive a protracted coma. This happens when they are able to operate in isolation from the external environment. Examples of such organizations include monopolies and government agencies. Unions or political pressures may keep them alive because no one dares eliminate an agency that provides employment. This results in a very expensive artificial prolonging of life.

Real death may take years.

Death occurs when no one is committed to the organization anymore. It can happen before bureaucratization occurs if there is no viable political commitment to support an industry or a company. In a Bureaucracy, death is prolonged because the commitment is not to the organization's clients, but to political interests that keep the organization alive for political reasons. If the organization depended on clients, it would have already died, because the clients deserted it.

In Brazil, Mexico and Israel, I encountered an interesting phenomenon. Some people come to work for government organizations in the morning, drape their coats on their chairs or otherwise make their desks look busy. Then they leave for their moonlighting jobs. In the evening, they come back and gather up their things as though they had just finished working. At the end of the month they come by and pick up their checks.

How can this happen? Where is management? Management might be doing the same thing. It can happen when the purpose of government is not to function for the marketplace, but to provide employment and a payroll. This political bribe is financed by the government printing money to feed the bureaucracies to keep them alive, or increased taxes that siphon savings away from investment. The result is either hidden or explicit inflation.

This summarizes the descriptive parts of the Lifecycle. Now let us compare growing to aging and analyze some general patterns of all the phases.

4

Comparisons: Behavior, Leadership, Goals, Form Versus Function and Determining the Location on the Lifecycle

There are distinct differences between organizations on the growing and aging sides of the Lifecycle curve. These differences were latent in the advanced stages of Prime. They begin to manifest in the first stage of aging—called **Stable**—and increasingly grow to dominate the organizational culture. The following table compares these subtle changes.

Growing Companies		Aging Companies
1. Personal success stems from *taking* risk	VS.	1. Personal success stems from *avoiding* risk
2. Expectations exceed results	VS.	2. Results exceed expectations
3. Cash poor	VS.	3. Cash rich
4. Emphasis is on function over form	VS.	4. Emphasis is on form over function
5. From *why* and *what* to do	VS.	5. To *how* to do and *who* did it
6. People are kept for their contributions to the organization in spite of their personalities	VS.	6. People are kept for their personalities in spite of their contributions to the organization
7. Everything is permitted, unless expressly forbidden	VS.	7. Everything is forbidden, unless expressly permitted
8. Problems are seen as opportunities	VS.	8. Opportunities are seen as problems

Growing Companies		**Aging Companies**
9. Political power is with the marketing and sales departments	vs.	9. Political power is with the accounting, finance and legal departments
10. Line calls the shots	vs.	10. Corporate staff calls the shots
11. Responsibility is not matched with authority	vs.	11. Authority is not matched with responsibility
12. Management controls the organization	vs.	12. The organization controls management
13. Management drives the momentum	vs.	13. Management is driven by the inertia
14. Change in leadership can lead to change in the organization's behavior	vs.	14. Change in the system is necessary to cause a change in the organization's behavior
15. Consultants are needed	vs.	15. "Insultants" are needed
16. From sales orientation	vs.	16. To profit preoccupation
17. From value added (profits) goals	vs.	17. To political gamesmanship

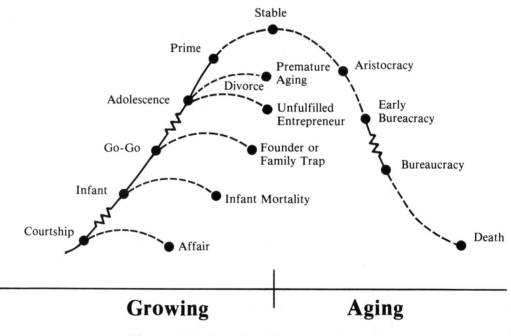

Figure 19: Growing Versus Aging

1. From Risk Taking to Risk Avoidance

During Infancy, the cost of risk taking was perceived as small because there was little to lose. During Go-Go, the risk was ignored; the company was growing quickly, and management became accustomed to intermittent feast and famine. People did not get especially upset if some adventures gave poor results, because other successes would compensate for them. Furthermore, in a Go-Go organization, there is a high level of permissiveness. People ask and receive forgiveness for decisions they have already made.

On the other hand, in a Prime organization there is a climate of repetitive success. Failure is unusual and it gets attention. It is analyzed, studied and punished. People are cautious. There is an organizational structure—a hierarchy and rituals to the decision-making process. Permission supersedes forgiveness. People ask before doing.

These subtle changes accumulate and produce an increased wariness of risk taking, which is what makes a Prime organization healthy. It is healthy because the Prime organization balances risk avoidance with risk taking. Before Prime, risk taking is stronger than risk avoidance. After Prime, risk avoidance dominates over risk taking. In Prime, it is balanced.

With success, people become increasingly content to enjoy, and rely upon the momentum that was created in the past. Their attitude becomes, "If it ain't broke, don't fix it," or "leave a good thing alone." Because they don't want to disturb what is going so smoothly, people start to perceive the cost of risk taking as being too high. *Now there is something to lose.*

As permission overtakes forgiveness, caution becomes a dominate pattern, and risk avoidance overtakes risk taking.

2. From Expectations Exceed Results to Results Exceed Expectations

An Infant organization can tell you how well it did in a year, only after that year has ended. Its people have difficulty predicting their future; the managerial behavior is *now*-oriented. They have a dream about the distant future, but it is vague at best. By definition, their expectations about that future exceed their present results. This phenomenon of expectations exceeding results continues into Go-Go.

In the Go-Go organization, there is experimentation. The organization will over stretch and eventually learn its limits. Management will attempt to budget and plan, but it won't really gain control over projected results. This is because the organization lacks an administrative system to provide a backbone, which would in time control the organization and bring about the desired results. In Go-Go, expectations can far exceed results. The deviations between budget and actuals can be staggering, with actuals as much as 200 to 300 percent above or below budget. Even when it is below budget, they do not correct the budget. They believe that the results will catch up. As a matter of fact, in Go-Go, they believe more than they think. They expect and aim for more and more. They are by and large unhappy with the results, no matter what the results are.

During Adolescence, the organization begins to learn how to regulate itself. By Prime, control is achieved. That is why a Prime organization can have the Go-Go's growth results, and at the same time, can predict and achieve those results. A Prime company can tell you what it is going to do, and do it with only minor deviations from its predictions.

In order to achieve repetitive predictability during Prime, budget systems are formalized, achievement is rewarded, and deviation is punished. Because of its past standards of more is better, deviations above and below budget are not treated equally. If actual sales are above the expected, people are rewarded, regardless of how large the deviation. If actuals are below the expected, people are punished, regardless of how small the deviation.

This system of reward and punishment determines how people behave more than the mission for which the budget was established. Over time, people increasingly focus on *how* to minimize undesirable deviations from the budget, and maximize deviations for which they will be rewarded, instead of focusing on *what* the budget and plans are attempting to achieve in the first place.

A way for people to minimize deviations and maximize rewards is to reduce expectations. During the budget process, people begin to aim at what they are *sure* they can exceed, or at least achieve. Each year, they aim increasingly lower to account for any uncertainties.

In the Infant and Go-Go organizations this can not happen.

People are rewarded by *what* they do, not by *how* they do it. There is hardly any budget. One is rewarded with a bonus based on actuals, like a commission. When budgets and reward systems are based on *how* people meet their goals, their behavior changes. The reward system increasingly rewards the *how*, rather than the *what*. The system soon reaches a point where the more people lie about how much they cannot do (the more successful they are in convincing that 'it cannot be done'), the more they are rewarded. The reward is for *how well* they beat the budget. So, the lower the target, the better the chances are of beating it—and reaping the payoff.

It is analogous to horse racing. The man who wants to be sure his horse always wins only enters the horse in mule races. The horse wins for awhile, but eventually it begins to behave like a mule.

There is no long-term winning unless you're willing to take the risk of short-term losing.

People try to ensure that they never end up below budget by aiming low. Management could stretch it from the top down by not accepting low budgets, but that has other negative long-term repercussions. It creates a climate of distrust. Subordinates (on any level) aim low because they know superiors (on any level) will bargain to raise the target. Superiors bargain to raise goals for the budget because they automatically assume subordinates have aimed low. This begins a group dynamic of mutual deception. The budget that is finally approved does not reflect the real capabilities of the organization or the real opportunities of the marketplace. It is merely a reflection of the trust or mistrust between the different levels in the organizational hierarchy. Since the organization rewards results that exceed expectations, the corporate climate changes, the company becomes averse to risk, and starts accumulating cash.

3. From Cash Poor to Cash Rich

A company with expectations which exceed results is always hungry for more cash. Cash fuels growth. Because the organization wants to grow, it always consumes more fuel. Growing companies are always short of cash.

In an organization where results exceed expectations, cash

starts to accumulate. In the Aristocratic stage, we find highly liquid companies that do not know what to do with their cash—behavior that befuddles an entrepreneur of the Go-Go stage.

4. From Emphasis on Function to Emphasis on Form

The transition from function to form starts in Adolescence. That is where the transition from "more is better" to "better is more" occurs. In Adolescence, the organization realizes it can make more money (profit) by doing things right, rather than by just doing the right things. As a matter of fact, through a lot of pain, the Adolescent organization realizes that doing the right things in a wrong way, is costing a bundle. They realize profits can be generated by cutting things, rather than adding things.

Entrepreneurial types (founders) make profits by increasing sales. Administrative types make profits by decreasing expenses. The entrepreneurial type asks, "What *else* can we do?" The administrative type asks, "What *less* can we do?"

The administrative type of behavior and orientation is functional during Adolescence. It is time to cool off from the hyperactivity of Go-Go. It is time to trim the extra leaves and branches so energy can be directed, rather than defused. Doing this sets the focus on form rather than function. Because form is almost non-existent in the Go-Go organization (it is perceived as unnecessary), the marginal utility of any system (form) developed during Adolescence is of great benefit, increasing the emphasis given to it. In Prime, form and function achieve balance. After that, the development of form has a decreasing utility, but it continues to grow.

As increasing emphasis is given to form at the expense of function, in the latter stages of the Lifecycle, all that is left is form. People go through the ritual of rain dancing, although they know it won't bring rain. People continue to go through the motions of budgeting, although they know the numbers are not at all realistic. They behave as if by worshipping the form, the function will somehow occur. If any function does exist, it takes place underground—in *spite* of form. This displacement of function by form happens because form, when first introduced, improved the function. That's when form became legitimized and desirable.

Why does form take over from function? Why does it keep growing in spite of decreasing marginal utility? Because it is easier emotionally and psychologically to implement the form than to perform the function. I use the words *implement* and *perform* on purpose. To implement means to repeat rituals. It does not require creative energy. It is not accompanied by anxiety, the by-product of uncertainty, which is always present when we do something new. To perform a function, one must adapt to changing realities. This means change, which creates uncertainty, which in turn creates anxiety and uses psychological energy.

Form is simple. We do not have to think, we only have to repeat what we are used to doing. Over time form wins over function because it is emotionally less taxing.

As long as function exists to some degree, even illegitimately, form can survive. When no functionality is provided, when form is barren, a breakdown will occur and a rebirth of function (new Courtship) will take place.

5. From *Why* and *What Now* to *How, Who,* and *When*

The switch from function to form can be noted in the organization's focus in group dynamics and decision making, as shown in Fig. 20.

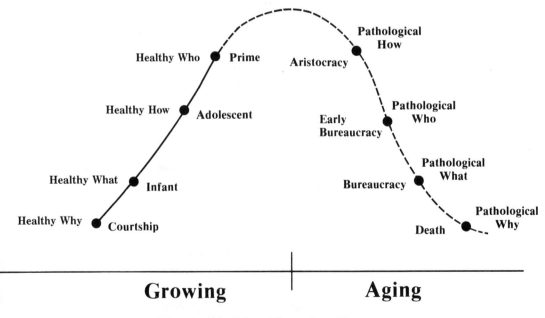

Figure 20: The Changing Focus

During Courtship, the people talk mostly about *why* something should be done. *What*, *how* and *who* are mentioned only in passing. In Infancy, after the organization is born, one only hears *what* to do, *why* is hardly mentioned; it is even bothersome to some people. *How* and *who* are irrelevant as long as the *what* is achieved.

Ignoring *how* and *who* eventually has a price. The organization becomes such a mess by outgrowing itself, that *how* and *who* can no longer be ignored. First *how* takes over in the group dynamics and decision making. That's what the Adolescent organization is spending time on. It is trying to establish *what* and *why* by focusing on *how*. The *who* is healthy and proactive. "Whom do we need to do the job?" This *who* orientation becomes pronounced in Prime. They pay attention to human resource factors, staffing decisions, and getting the best people money can buy.

In Aristocracy, the *how* is pathological. It is not *how* to do *what* and *why*. It is *how* period. It is how for the sake of *how*; it is a ritual.

In Early Bureaucracy, *who* is pathological. It is witch hunt time; people are looking for *who* did it (past tense), rather than who they will need to do it (future tense). Instead of looking at what a person can do for the organization, they look for what is wrong with what the person is doing.

In Early Bureaucracy, *what* becomes pathological; the organization is lost, asking itself desperately *what* should we do to survive. It is not the healthy, proactive, forward, energetic *what* of Infancy.

In Death, the *why* is pathological; why should it exist? It has no right to.

6. From Contribution to Personality

The increasing emphasis on form at the expense of function has manifestations in personnel administration. In the growing stages, what really counts is what people produce or contribute. Even if they are "skunks," it's OK, just as long as their contribution is valuable. As form takes over, the *how* becomes more important than the *what*. *How* the person behaves, talks, dresses and *whom* he knows become more important than *what* the person does for the organization. This behavior is facilitated by the fact that the organization may be so large, and the interdependencies so complex, that it is almost impossible to attribute any specific contribution to any individual, unless he is a salesman or production worker. The higher up the organizational echelon, the tougher it is to evaluate an individual's personal contribution. So the organization focuses on the *how*, as if it could predict the *what*. When the *how* becomes dysfunctional, because increasingly it is not functionally-oriented, all that is left is a *who* orientation. Thus, in growing organizations, one is hired and promoted because of his contribution, in spite of his personality. In aging organizations, one is hired and promoted because of his personality, in spite of his contribution.

7. Is It Permitted or Forbidden?

More than 20 years ago, I did my doctoral dissertation on the management system of Yugoslavia,[1] and I noted something very interesting. When the country was under the Russian Central Planning System, the climate that prevailed was, "If it is not explicitly permitted, assume it is forbidden—do not take risks." When Yugoslavia moved to free itself from the Russian Central Planning System, and tried to introduce market forces as the regulator of the economy, a change in climate occurred. People had to start taking risks if they wanted to operate in a market economy. That required a behavior that assumed "If it is not explicitly forbidden, it is permitted—so let's try."[2]

This change is not an easy one to make. It is easier to assume that something is forbidden, than to assume that it is permitted because nobody can hang you for what you *don't do*, or as the Sephardic saying states: "In a closed mouth, flies can't get in." Two stories can help illustrate the point. A Bureaucrat once said: "I do not know why they fired Smith. *He did not do anything!*" They expect inaction and reward it. Action creates troubles internally. Thus those who are team players, that is, make no waves, and accept the status quo, are usually rewarded and promoted.

Another story is about two salesmen from different shoe companies who were sent to sell shoes in Africa at the beginning of the century. One informed his company, "There is no market here.

---

[1] Adizes, I., *Industrial Democracy, Yugoslav Style*, First Printing—Free Press: New York. All subsequent printings: Adizes Institute, Santa Monica, CA. 290 pp., (1971).
[2] The same change sought by the economic reforms in Poland in 1987.

Everyone is barefoot." The other one reported, "An incredible market. Everyone is barefoot." The first response came from an aging company, the second from a growing company.

The Talmud says: "For a believer there are no questions. For the skeptic, there are no answers." The same goes for organizational climates. Growing companies are believers. Aging companies are skeptics. Growing companies create new needs, they have a vision. Unless proven wrong, they assume they are right. Aging companies exploit proven needs. They are risk-averse, skeptical and have an attitude of "until it's proven right, assume that it's wrong."

8. Are Those Problems or Opportunities?

For the entrepreneurial type, there are no problems, only opportunities. He sees in problems opportunities to do something else (or better). But, by following too many opportunities, he creates problems. That is why, in a Go-Go company, it is crisis by management, rather than management by crisis.

For the administrative type who thinks more about *how* the ideas will be implemented, opportunities are problems. "How in the world are we going to make it work?" is his preoccupation. The administrative types perceive opportunities as problems of implementation that are sometimes insurmountable.

As administrators take over from entrepreneurs from Adolescence on, opportunities are increasingly seen as problems, and those who point at opportunities are perceived as the problem makers. Eventually in Aristocracy, the innovators are identified by the arrows in their backs. The company is stymied and does not proact and eventually it does not react to change. The switch from opportunities to problems is accompanied by a change in the power centers of the organization.

9. From Marketing and Sales to Finance and Legal

The role of marketing and sales is to exploit opportunities. That is why in the growing stages of the Lifecycle, those departments carry the flag; they have the power to determine what product, system or idea will live or die. Line departments dominate and in growing stages, there is no corporate staff function to speak of. In Prime, staff departments are developed to plan and control and provide centripetal forces. The center of power moves to the executive committee, which includes staff and line representation. When the organization moves into the aging stages, the center of power moves further into the staff departments—the finance and legal departments—whose role is to prevent the company from making mistakes. Their role is to say "no!" And they do. Line departments increasingly lose power as the system becomes increasingly centralized.

10. From Line to Staff

This change in authority and power is more than just moving it from one department to another. The switch is from line to corporate staff. Those who do not have the responsibility for results, now carry the authority over those who do. Before, marketing and sales had the responsibility to produce results, and they had the authority to do so.

This removal of authority, away from the line to the corporate staff, causes centralization in decision-making and the aging of the company. The organization loses flexibility and capability to react (or proact) to a changing environment.

The switch in the power center has further repercussions.

11. Responsibility Versus Authority

In young companies, authority is clear; responsibility is not. In aging companies, responsibility is clear; authority is not. This is more than a game of words.

In a growing company, there is much to do, and everyone is expected to pitch in. The lines of responsibility are not yet well drawn. Everyone is expected to do what needs to be done. Authority, however, clearly rests with the founder. While responsibility is fuzzy; authority is clear.

The Adolescent organization started delineating responsibilities and depersonalizing authority. As a result, in Prime, responsibility and authority match. As the organization ages, it needs to realign its structure to reflect environmental change, but that is easier said than done. Structure changes the constellation of political powers, which is resisted. With responsibilities not functionally designed to act, one must seek the cooperation of others. That means that

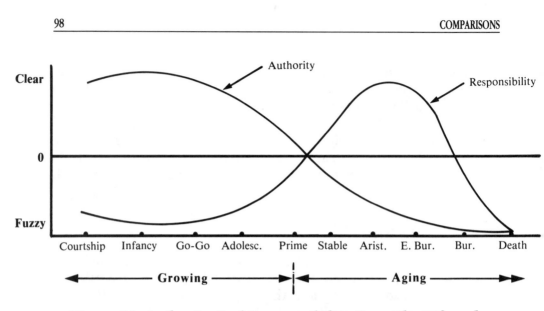

Figure 21: Authority And Responsibility Over The Lifecycle

others have power. Authority without power is weak. Those with authority feel powerless, which is managerially equivalent to the feeling of not having workable authority. The end result is that eventually, authority becomes unclear. When both responsibility and authority are ambiguous, the company is dying of old age. It is not clear who should or can act, and if they neither proact nor react, eventually they become obsolete and die.

The repercussions of this change impact the organization's sense of control.

12. Who Is Managing Whom?

One day I had to make an afternoon presentation to the top management group of a company. It was at a famous retreat that had horses for rent. I decided to use the morning to rent a horse and gallop up the hill and down the valley. After a few minutes of riding, I realized the horse had been rented out for many years. It knew the path by heart. It also knew how long an hour was without knowing how to read a watch. I kicked it to go up the hill. It moved two steps to the right and stopped, swishing its tail back and forth. "Perhaps it prefers the valley to the hill," I thought. So I kicked it to go left. It went two steps to the left and stopped. Its ears inclined forward, and I got the message. If I wanted to ride, I would have to behave myself and get back on the path. Now who was managing whom? I sat on the horse, looked left and right, and *acted* as if I was in control. But for the rest of the ride, I tried not to upset "the system" too much.

Many businessmen, looking for a challenge, take on a governmental bureaucracy. In their vision, they see themselves galloping up and down the landscape. Soon, if they are intelligent, they recognize the power structure of the organization and start muddling through—no more than two steps to the right and no more than two steps to the left. On the surface, they act as if they are in control; underneath they carefully watch each step, because the system is stronger than they are; if they disturb too many power centers simultaneously, they can be thrown off. The same thing happens to political parties in power. When they were the opposition party, seeking power, they made many promises. But once they gain power, they find those promises very difficult to keep because the governmental bureaucracy has its own inertia and has its own vested interests established, reinforced, and sanctified over the years.

By the time a company has aged, its administrative systems, policies, precedents, rules and guidelines dominate behavior. The decisions and reward systems of the past are what determines the company's behavior, no matter how much the management attempts to appear in control. In a sense, the company itself, rather than any particular person, is "managing" management. This sounds bizarre. Many people cannot understand how a system could manage itself. So when there are problems, they look for a culprit—*someone* who is causing the trouble. That is why organizations, when they experience difficulties in later stages of their Lifecycle, go through witch hunts and ritualistically fire people who are singled out and blamed for the company's troubles, although they personally caused few, if any, of the problems. Someone was in control of what is happening and thus this attribution is not rootless, but that was many life stages ago prior to Adolescence. Since then, the system took over and no single individual is fully in control.

13. Momentum or Inertia

In growing companies, one must direct the momentum. It is like a race horse. To keep it running, one feeds it, exercises it and keeps it healthy. All one needs to do is direct the horse, and it will do its job. However, directing an old mule will not make it a race horse. One needs to retrain a mule to race before one can guide it in the right direction. With a mule, one has to utilize the inertia. In the aging stages of the Lifecycle, a manager will try to capitalize on the inertia. Instead of attempting to change direction, he will try to find something good out of going "wherever the hell that mule is willing to be going." The older the organization, the more management will try to utilize efficiency at the expense of effectiveness in order to shine.

14. What To Do—Change Leadership or Change the System?

In the aging organization, a typical mistake is to believe that a change in leadership will rejuvenate the company. Changing the rider won't make a mule into a race horse. Changing the rider will change the results only in the growing stages of the Lifecycle, and only if there is a race horse in the first place. New leadership will help in the aging phases only if it changes the system, and spends its time, not racing the mule, but converting it into a race horse. (We will look at how to change organizational cultures in the analytical and prescriptive part of this book.)

This was a point of contention I had with journalists who wrote about my work with Bank of America. They felt the leadership of Sam Armacost, the president and chief executive, had to be changed because he did not produce immediate results. I urged further analysis. If you see an old truck standing on the road, what is your first instinct? Would you change drivers? What if the driver is busy under the hood? If the driver is doing nothing and the truck is not moving, then change the driver. But, if the driver is busy fixing the truck, even if it is not moving, why would you fire him? Maybe he does not know how to fix the truck. Then first check to see how well he is fixing it. Let us look at the *process*, not at premature results. Management theory is preoccupied with management *by* results, *by* objectives. My focus is on management *for* results, *for* objectives, and *by* process. The focus is, and should be on the *process*.

In growing organizations, it is the founder who sets the character of the organization. In the aging part of the Lifecycle, it is the organization's climate that determines the style of the organization's leadership. The driving and driven forces exchange place.

In the growing stages, it is the leader who attracts the people with his message. In the aging phases, the people choose the leader who reflects what they want. The saying "people deserve the leadership they get," applies to the organization in the aging stages of the Lifecycle.

In the growing stages, leadership leads the people. As the organization ages, leadership follows the people. In the growing stages, changing leadership changes organizational behavior; in aging we must change the behavior of the organization in order to change the leadership. Changing the leadership in an aging corporation without changing the system, is like taking a *hand out of water*. It doesn't make much of a difference to the ocean.

The leader in aging cultures is the result, not the cause of organizational behavior. In an aging corporation we must look not just at the results leadership is producing, but at what change in culture it is initiating so that *eventually* the desired results will be produced. These changes must be in the system—the structure, rewards and information systems. The changes must be in the mechanism of the truck, not just in the direction the truck is traveling. Changes in product line, pricing and advertising are superficial. They may create some temporary results; but one has to address the *cause* of the problem: Why were there wrong products, wrong prices and wrong promotions in the first place? One has to treat causes, not symptoms. Who should do that?

15. Internal and External Consultants Versus Insultants

To deal effectively with the causes, and not just the symptoms of problems (which means to deal with authority and responsibility structures, information and reward systems), is to deal with the guts of the organization. Expect pain when meddling with the organization's power centers. This means getting neck-deep in company politics. Consultants typically give advice on what to do. They pride themselves on the length of a relationship with a client; they cannot afford to be fired. As a result, they cannot disturb corporate politics. If they want to keep an account, they have to avoid causing pain.

A consultant, who cannot afford to lose a client is the wrong remedy for aging organizations. At best all he does is relieve symptoms. What an aging organization needs is someone who can change the power structure. I call these people *insultants*—consultants who can afford to give pain and risk losing the client.

It is very difficult for an internal agent of change to be an insultant because he cannot be knee-deep in organizational politics and have any kind of career life expectancy. He is too low on the totem pole and will be rejected, that is, fired. Internal consultants, such as organizational development staff specialists, can be effective in instituting organizational change in a growing organization. In these companies, there is a perception of a growing pie. The turf wars are not very violent and the dangers of crossing political boundaries are not so severe. Furthermore, there is excitement and the company's successes tend to compensate for the pain. In aging organizations, outside insultants are best suited to the job. (As pointed out in the Introduction to this book, I have created a training and certification program for it.)

16. The Transition

a) From Sales to Profit Orientation

At each stage of the Lifecycle, organizational goals change. The goal of an Infant organization is obvious. Cash! The organization needs to grow, thus it needs working capital—"milk"—and the faster it grows, the more cash it needs. It might even sell its services at a loss in order to generate cash. However, once it reaches Go-Go it has survived the cash crunch. What is the next thing it looks for? Growth, measured in sales and market penetration. Go-Go managers, when asked how they are doing, typically say: "We sold 35 percent more." The word *more* in a Go-Go organization usually refers to more sales. In Adolescence, the goal becomes profits. Now the *how* begins to take on importance. The goal is not only more *sales*, but more *profits*.

The transition from a sales to a profit orientation is extremely difficult, because both the bonus system and the hiring practice are geared to sales. During Infancy and Go-Go, the organization becomes addicted to a sales orientation. A person's performance is based on how well he can produce sales; that's what counts. Now that the organization is looking for profits—seeking to work smarter, not harder—that behavior has to change. To change behavior, the organization's goals and reward system must also change. The type of people who are hired and how the organization trains

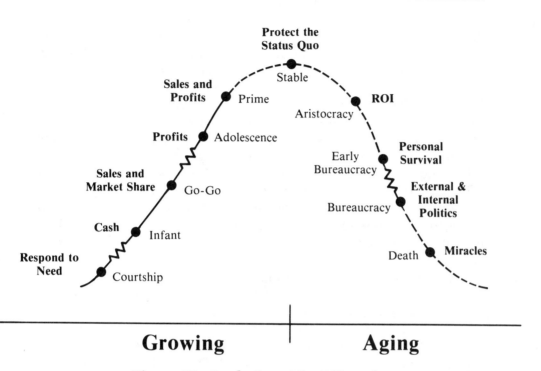

Growing | Aging

Figure 22: Goals Over The Lifecycle

them must be considered. There must be a transformation in the consciousness of the organization, a change that is relatively difficult for some organizations to make. It is a shift from being quantity- to quality-oriented in making decisions. Form begins to rival function, and there is a struggle between the two orientations. That is what makes Adolescence so difficult a place in the Lifecycle.

In Prime, function and form, quantity and quality have the same weight. Thus, in Prime, the organization's goals are both sales and profits. It can actually have more sales *and* more profits; something Go-Go organizations strive for, but cannot achieve.

Go-Go organizations ask: "How can we have more sales *and* more profits?"

My response is: "You must take the time to get organized and systematized first, or as Bikram Choudury, a famous yoga teacher says, "The road to heaven is through hell."

To realize its dream, the Go-Go organization must first go through the pain of Adolescence.

Leaving Prime means the organization has begun to lose its

flexibility. The finance and accounting people now take over the levers of power. The *how* becomes more important than the *what*. In the process, the organization switches clients.

b) From Customers to Capital

In Courtship, all the interests of the groups that will comprise an organization or impact it are considered and evaluated how they are going to benefit from the establishment of the organization. When the organization is born, one by one those interests are expressed, satisfied and balanced and integrated with the other interests until they are fully integrated and balanced in Prime. With aging, one by one the interest groups lose their power until in Bureaucracy only the "shadows" of these interests are left—called politics.

For the Infant organization, the customer reigns supreme. In Go-Go, the organization becomes the personal sandbox of management—they are the dictating clients. In Adolescence, the organization itself with its own needs outside management becomes the client and starts protecting its own interests. In the Prime company, capitalization is professionally analyzed. That's where capital interests come into play in addition to the human factor as interest groups that emerge and coalesce with all the above interests. Customers, management (top and middle), capital, labor and present and future customers get balanced. As adaptation to change declines in the Stable stage and in Aristocracy, customers become less and less important. The personal goals of management also become less important because they are not the driving but the driven forces as the rules of the game dictate the show. Later, in Early Bureaucracy, the goal is personal survival, people are jumping the ship. In Bureaucracy it's political survival, which means outside interest groups dominate rather than the interests of the parties that comprise the organization. This whole process results in goal displacement; deterministic and constraint goals exchange places.

c) From Cash to Politics

Deterministic goals are those goals we want to maximize; constraint goals are those conditions we do not want to violate. Serving the market was a deterministic goal in Infancy and the Go-Go stages. Profit was a constraint goal. Dividends were viewed more as payment on a bond—it was the minimum that had to be paid to the

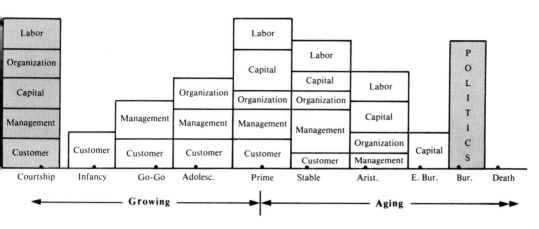

Figure 23: Interests Over The Lifecycle

owners (if at all) to keep them financing the company. Dividends were not the goal—owners were looking for the appreciation of their stock, not for fast yields. The goal was to maximize sales while keeping profits at the minimum acceptable level.

In Adolescent organizations, profits become a measure of significance and more sales do not necessarily produce more profits. Sales now become the constraint goal, and profits the deterministic goal. This goal displacement does not come easily. In Adolescence, although profits are to be primary goals, the sales orientation still dominates the culture since the organization became addicted to this sales orientation in Infancy and Go-Go—and more is still better. Thus in Adolescence, it is hard to know if profit goals are deterministic or constraint goals. Managers oscillate between seeking more profits and more sales, wanting them both. When they cannot achieve these incompatible goals for their location on the Lifecycle, they get annoyed and frustrated with each other, and internal marketing flourishes.

In Prime, the organization seeks and achieves growth in sales and profits. Both goals are deterministic. The constraint goals of what not to do are derived from the organization's strategy of expansion.

From Stable on, profits increasingly become the deterministic goals and sales, the constraint goal. Management learns to make more money through interpretation of accounting books than from managing its market. Because profits—measured in earnings per share—are the goal; the place of the customer as the client is taken over by the investment community, who buy and sell stock. If it is not a publicly traded company, the owners become the demanding, rather than the giving factor. It is now the organization's turn to feed, rather than be fed.

As the organization enters Stable and as it continues into Aristocracy, it believes that it exists in the marketplace to produce profits. It begins cutting back services (advertising, and research and development) in order to maximize those profits. In doing so, it may also cut out the factors that stimulate flexibility and entrepreneurship. Since the organizational climate encourages short-term profitability, those who seek this goal gain greater standing in the political power bank of the organization. There are fewer people in the organization who fight for resources to be allocated to change. What those people promise will be realized in the long-run, and the cultural climate does not encourage long-term yields. It supports the short-run. People who activate change step on too many toes and are labeled insensitive and non-team players. For their efforts they are politically isolated and functionally insulated. Eventually, they stop trying, quit or get fired. This to be a general phenomena. I noticed that with my parents, the older they got, the more impatient they became. With aging, the system shortens its horizon; it becomes short-term oriented.

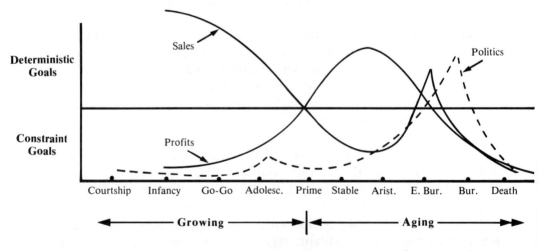

Figure 24: Deterministic Versus Constraint Goals Over The Lifecycle

When the organization is in Aristocracy, it is milking time. Owners are trying to get *beyond* their return on investment in a hurry, the shortest payback they can get. As a result, they are consuming not just the fat, but the flesh as well.

At the next stage, Early Bureaucracy, when the fighting starts, the goals change once again. It now becomes *individual survival—* not organizational survival. The goal is not dividends, not return on investment, not sales. It is who is going to survive and who is going to be fired. Politics take most of the managerial energy.

In Bureaucracy, there is blissful silence. Since the organization is under a protectorship, there is nothing to fight for. What one does in order to survive or be promoted is go through the motions. As long as you behave by the book, there is nothing to worry about. If you lie low enough, make no waves, do not offend or threaten, and as long as you avoid confrontations—you may become the president. The important goals are to be an asset, not a liability, from a political rather than economic point of view.

Goal Displacement	Deterministic	Constraint
Infancy	Cash	Founder's quality of personal life
Go-Go	Sales measured in market share profits	None if the founder can get away with it—he is testing the limits
Adolescence	Profits	Sales in dollars
Prime	Profits and sales	Strategic decisions
Stable	Protect status quo	Do not make waves
Aristocracy	Return on investment	Sales in unit terms
Early Bureaucracy	Personal survival (cash flow)	Political goals
Bureaucracy	Political goals	Political constraints

How to Decide Where a Company Is on the Lifecycle Curve

Years ago a friend of mine asked me if I wanted to measure the age of my heart. That sounded strange to me. Since my body and my heart were born at the same time, I thought they were the same age. I learned something new. This friend had a highly sophisticated, computerized exercise bicycle. You could attach a device which measures the heartbeat to your finger tip, and then punch your chronological age into the computer. After some strenuous bicycling, the computer would inform you how old your heart was.

That made me think. All parts of our bodies do not age at the same rate. While chronologically, I could be 40 years old, my heart could be older or younger compared to other 40-year-old people. Organizations have the same characteristics. Some units age faster than others. Some remain in almost perpetual youth. An accounting department can go from Infancy to Aristocracy in 24 hours. Healthy marketing departments, on the other hand, seem to remain in a perpetual Go-Go stage.

In reading the preceding descriptions and comparing them to your own organization, do not try to place organizations you know into just *one* place in the Lifecycle. Different units in the organization can be in different places. Where the organization is overall, is analogous to where a person is behaviorally in respect to his or her age. We have to generalize. Analogous to having to ask how a person behaves psychologically and physically *most* of the time; we have to analyze how the organization, as a total, behaves *most* of the time.

You will find there is a distribution within a distribution. For instance, if an organization is in Adolescence, it will sometimes exhibit the characteristics of a Go-Go and sometimes those of a Prime, but, most of the time, *most* of the behavior is of an Adolescent. This is normal. In times of stress, the organizational culture will retreat to the previous stage in the Lifecycle. When it is strong, it will evidence signs of the next phase. (This fact helps me analyze whether the organization is advancing or retreating therapeutically.) In the pathological stages, there are no signs of desired forward movement on the Lifecycle. Companies act as if they are stuck. When they try to get unstuck, they regress to the previous stage. It is as if they confuse forward with reverse and retreat into a behavior they recognize and with which they feel comfortable. This is usually a behavior that was successful in the past and got them to where they are now. For reasons we will explain in the next section, they are not able to take on the problems of the next stage. They are chronically preoccupied with problems of the present, or worse, of the previous stage.

A healthy organization has a normal distribution within the bell-shaped curve of the Lifecycle. This means that some of the time, it behaves as if it were in its previous position in the Lifecycle and some behavior is derived from the next position on the Lifecycle. Most behavior, however, stems from its main position on the curve. If it is healthy, the standard deviation in its behavior is small.

There is another point that is very important to understand in diagnosing organizations. The pathological stages of growing organizations resemble the pathological stages of aging. For example, there is Aristocracy in the Founder's or Family Trap, and there is Bureaucratic behavior in premature aging. One can find Aristocracy in pathological Go-Go. The diagnosis and therapy of such organizations is more complicated and requires a more advanced text.

This completes the descriptive part of the Lifecycle of corporations. Now let us proceed to learn why this behavior occurs and what can be done about it.

Part II

THE ADIZES THEORY OF MANAGEMENT: TOOLS FOR PREDICTING, ANALYZING AND TREATING CORPORATE CULTURES

Introduction to Part II
Tools for Analysis

What is the role of management in the Lifecycle presented thus far? It is to provide leadership and keep the organization in the healthy part of the Lifecycle, preventing or treating pathological problems along the way. The leadership should bring the organization to its Prime and keep it there. That is leadership—the function of management. Our next focus will be on how management can effectively do this. This section will present a theory of management that explains the organization's behavior on the Lifecycle and provide the tools for changing the organizations location, i.e., for changing its culture to the desired one.

The Role of Management as Leadership

In order to manage an organization, one's self or a society, or to solve old problems and move on to bigger, new ones, we must make good decisions and then efficiently implement them.

From experience, we know that some excellent decisions, even though they stand the test of time, never get implemented. In personal life, we call them New Year's resolutions. They're usually good decisions—to stop smoking or lose weight—but they aren't always implemented. At the same time, some decisions that we know are bad decisions, do get implemented. We decide to smoke another cigarette or we decide to have another piece of chocolate cake.

The quality of a decision does not predict the probability of its implementation. Moreover, I found that quality decisions and efficient implementation are generally incompatible. What causes an organization to produce outstanding decisions will undermine the efficient implementation of those decisions; and what causes efficient implementation will undermine the quality of the decisions.

Let me explain this further by looking at political systems. Which system is designed to produce high-quality decisions by having freedom of the press and political parties that argue and differ on what to do? A democracy. However, it's difficult to implement decisions in a democracy. The freedom of dissension that occurs

112

during the decision-making stage can cause a lack of discipline during implementation.

Which political system maximizes efficient implementation by forging ahead without debate? A totalitarian regime—whether communist, fascist or a theocracy. In such a system, disastrous decisions can be made because there is no open flow of information or free exchange of ideas and judgments. An unchallenged personal bias of the leader can be enforced with tragic results.

Good management requires democracy during the decision-making stage and dictatorship during implementation. I call this *democratship*.

Why decision-making and implementation? Are they both necessary and sufficient for good management? We need to make decisions because we are constantly facing change. If there was no change in our environment, we wouldn't have to make any decisions. We would simply re-implement decisions that we made yesterday. The higher the rate of change, the more decisions we have to make and the more complex they are going to be. To make decisions and not implement them is an academic exercise in futility. Thus, in order to analyze the quality of management and leadership, we must analyze the quality of decisions made, and how effectively and efficiently these decisions can be implemented.

This has importance for the Lifecycle theory presented earlier. In the introduction to this book, I explained that where an organization is on the Lifecycle depends on two factors: predictability, which is affected by self-control, and flexibility.

Flexibility and self-control depend on 1) how we are organized to make the decisions we make and 2) how we are organized to implement them.

To understand Lifecycles—why organizations have a predictable pattern of change, what causes the movement or lack of movement along the Lifecycle, and how to propel a developmental

MANAGEMENT/LEADERSHIP

Decide   **Implement**

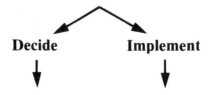

movement along the Lifecycle—one has to understand the factors that determine how decisions are made (discussed next in Chapter 5) and the factors that determine the effectiveness and efficiency of implementation (Chapter 6). The two factors generate inter- and intra-organizational conflict. Conflict is energy. If it is directed correctly, it is constructive; if not, it is destructive. We must understand the causes and the nature of conflict in organizations, and what to do about it (Chapter 7).

5

Predicting the Quality of Decisions ═══════

How can the quality of a decision be predicted before it is implemented? Evaluating a decision after the fact is *relatively* easy. I emphasize the word relatively, because even that is not totally simple; there are uncontrollable external factors that impact results and it is difficult to determine which results are due to the decision made, and which results are due to external factors. It is relatively easy, however, to evaluate a past decision than a present decision, because for a decision made in the past, we have all the information after the fact. So we can analyze what happened and when it happened. I developed a theory and techniques that help predict decisions rather than post factum evaluate them.

Professional managers in comparison to management researchers prefer to *predict* the quality of a decision rather than to analyze its quality after it has been implemented. The value of such a tool is in predicting the decisions of subordinates and in diagnosing a company, whether to purchase it, or in order to treat it. The better we know the future behavior of an organization, the better we will be able to proactively take the necessary corrective actions.

How can we predict the quality of a decision made by an organization? Let's start with a scenario. Let's take four people whom we have never met before and give them a case study of a problem that occurred in a certain organization. The case write-up should include all the information that's necessary to diagnose the problem and to recommend the solution. Let's assume that these four people know nothing about this case, the company, the industry or the country where the problem occurred; they bring no additional information whatsoever to the case at hand. Let's send the four into seclusion to study the case, identify the problems and arrive at a solution. They should write down the problem and the solution, put it in an envelope, seal it, and deliver it to you. Now let's give the same case to four other people whom we also have never met before and who also have no additional information beyond that included in the case study.

When we are faced with the two sealed envelopes, what would you predict? Are we going to have two different problems with two different solutions, or the same problem and the same solution?

Any experienced manager will respond that the problems will be different and the solutions will be different. If we mix the two groups, create two new groups composed of people from the previous two groups, we get two new sets of problems and solutions. We will get as many different problems and solutions as there are permutations of group composition.[1]

Why are the problems and the solutions different?

Because the people are different.

Aha!

In order to manage, do not look at the envelope; look at the people who wrote what is in the envelope. To manage means to deal with the people who solve problems, not just to solve the problems by yourself. Too many people say: "I love to manage. It's people I can't stand." Those managers (or mismanagers) miss the point.

How can one decide what is the right problem and the right solution though?

There are two questions that need to be answered before opening the envelope and if the answer to either of the questions is negative, you probably have the wrong problem and the wrong

---

[1] If the problems and solutions are different, then what is the *real* problem and the *real* solution? As a manager you might make the typical mistake of opening the first envelope and saying "This is the wrong problem and the wrong solution," then opening the other envelope and saying the same thing. Then, with a winning smile, you might say, "The *real* problem and the *real* solution are . . .". How do you know *you* have the *real* problem and the *real* solution? Maybe what you have is another envelope, which really means that you have another opinion.

solution. If the answer is a positive one to both questions, open the envelope because you probably have or are approaching the right problem and the right solution. The two questions are: 1) Were all the roles (functions) of decision-making performed? and 2) How were these roles performed together?

THE FOUR ROLES OF DECISION-MAKING (PAEI)

What do we mean by *quality of decisions* in problem-diagnosing or problem-solving, and how can we predict this quality?

There are four roles that need to be performed any time we make a decision, if it is to be of a high-quality. By *quality*, I mean a decision which makes the organization effective and efficient in both the short and the long run. If the decision does not meet those criteria, it is defective—of low quality.

There are four roles which need to be fulfilled if the decision is going to make an organization effective and efficient in the short and long run. We'll discuss those four necessary factors in detail, because they explain the development of organizational cultures and the *why*, *when* and *how* an organizational culture changes in its Lifecycle. Furthermore, these four factors explain *why* an organization's decisions may be defective and predict *what* kinds of decisions will be made and *how*.

Anytime one of the roles is missing, there will be a predictable pattern of defective decision-making, which I have called *a mismanagement style*.[2]

The first function in decision-making is the (P) role, which makes the organization effective in the short-run. The (P) stands

ROLE	ORGANIZATIONAL IMPACT	TIME RANGE
• (P)	effectiveness	short-run
•		
•		
•		

---

[2] Adizes, Ichak. *How to Solve the Mismanagement Crisis*: First Printing, Dow Jones Irwin (1979). All subsequent printings Santa Monica, California, The Adizes Institute (1979).

for **(P)**erform the **(P)**urpose of the organization. What is the **(P)**urpose that must be **(P)**erformed? Is it profit? A story from Greek mythology can illustrate the point.

Five people are walking down a narrow path on the top of a mountain. The path is so narrow they must walk single file. There is a deep canyon on the right and a very steep incline on their left. They have been walking for hours, singing, joking, laughing, whistling and talking. For an organizational behaviorist, anthropologist, psychologist or social psychologist, there is an organization to the group, and these professionals could write books about the behavior of the five people interacting with each other.

For us practicing managers, there is no organization until this group arrives at a point on the path where there is a rock so large that it blocks their passage. None of them can move it *alone*. At that moment, an organization from a managerial point of view is born; the managerial process has begun. The group needs to plan, organize, motivate and control how to move the rock.

The managerial process exists when there is a task to be performed, a task that requires task *interdependence* between people. If the rock could have been lifted by a single individual, there would be no need for an organization and there would be no management (except management of one's self). The moment the task requires more than one individual, management of the organization is required.[3]

The first role of management in decision-making, is to define the purpose of the organization. What is the function for which the organization exists? Every organization must have a reason to exist—a rock to move—a focus for the interdependency among people.

Whenever I work with an organization I ask the group of top managers, "Why are you together? What does accounting have to do with marketing, or personnel with R and D? What's the purpose of your organization's existence? I always get the same answer—profits. That is the wrong answer. I gave this same answer in interpreting the **(P)** role in my previous book.[4] Economic theory has

---

[3] If the five people were walking down the path, and that walk had a purpose which required interdependence among themselves, like exercising or mountain climbing, there would have been a management process from a managerial point of view.

[4] Adizes, *How to Solve the Management Crisis*, op. cit.

taught us that the purpose of economic entities (business) is profit. However, many organizations are so preoccupied with profits that they are going bankrupt. Why? If you focus on profits, shouldn't you generate profits? No. You are confusing input with output.

Profit is like love, health and happiness. If you focus on happiness and say "I must be happy today," you may become quite miserable. If you say "I must be healthy," you may become a hypochondriac. And to say "I must be in love" can create a great deal of hate. What you must ask yourself is what *makes* you happy, healthy or fall in love, and then focus on that.

Profit is analogous to playing tennis. Profit is the score board. You cannot play successfully if you are watching the scoreboard all the time. As a matter of fact, you should ignore the board and just play the best you can. Follow the ball and hit it across the net. Organizations that focus on earnings per share and profit margins, rather than the input and throughput that produce the profit, might be going bankrupt, not in spite of, but *because* they are overfocusing on profit. They are focusing on the score board and not keeping their eyes on the ball.

If you hit the ball effectively, which means if you satisfy client needs and do so repeatedly and efficiently (for which the other three roles are also necessary), you will win the tennis game. Winning means you will be profitable.

What then is the reason to be of a business organization? What is the "rock," the "ball" a manager must focus on? What should be the (P)urpose that the organization should (P)erform?

Let us go back to the stage where the founder was dreaming about starting an organization. What did he see in front of him? Profits? No. He saw an *opportunity* to make profits. Note the choice of words—opportunity to make profits, which means profit is an output; opportunity is the input. We have to focus on the input if we want the output to occur. We have to hit the ball, exploit the opportunity, and treat every volley as a first volley. The game is not over until it is over. What is the opportunity that the founder noticed? It was an unsatisfied need in the market place. A need he believed he could satisfy better.

From a managerial point of view, the distinction between profit and not-for-profit organizations is not valid in my opinion. Both organizations have clients and both organizations, to be effective, they must satisfy clients' needs. The end result is different for businesses that want economic profit and for not-for-profit organizations, which might want political survival. What the input management must focus on is the same: *To (P)erform a service, and to satisfy the needs of the clients for which the organization exists*, i.e., to add value.

Every organization—whether it's a unit within a larger organization or the large organization itself—has clients for which it exists. There is no organization and no management without clients. The clients of some departments—like the sales organization—are called customers; the accounting department and the personnel department only have clients, not customers. Their clients are within the organization.

Each organization by definition has a reason to be. It is to satisfy clients' needs which cannot be satisfied by an individual.

The behavior of an organization that does not focus on its clients' needs is analogous to cancer; it exists and consumes resources, but doesn't serve any client's function. It only serves itself.

When a manager makes a decision, he must first ask himself what the (P) role is. Who are his organization's clients? What are their needs? Which needs can, and will the organization satisfy? This is the (P)urpose of the organization that he is managing. This applies not just to top management, but to any manager including the lowest supervisory level.

If the (P) function is performed, the organization will be effective because it will satisfy the needs for which it exists. This can be measured by repetitive demands for the services of the organization, which in business is called brand loyalty. Are the clients coming back for more? If the people are not coming back for more of the same service or product, it means their needs are not being satisfied and the organization is not effective.

Profit, then, is the resulting indicator of how the four roles are performed, and thus how effective and efficient the organization is in the short- and the long-run.

• (P)erform (P)urpose	• effectiveness ⎫	short-run
•	• efficiency ⎭	
•	• effectiveness ⎫	long-run
•	• efficiency ⎭	

Profits

What are the other three roles?

ROLE	ORGANIZATIONAL IMPACT	TIME RANGE
• (P)	effectiveness	short-run
• **(A)**	**efficiency**	**short-run**
•		
•		

It takes more than just being effective to make an organization well-managed and profitable; the organization must also be efficient. That efficiency is provided by the **(A)** role. To **(A)**dminister means to systematize, routinize, and program the activities of the organization so the right things are done at the right time and with the right intensity. Proper **(A)**dministration prevents an organization from reinventing the wheel every time a wheel is needed. If this function is properly performed, the organization will be efficient.

(P)erform a service	-effectiveness (short-run)
(A)dminister	-efficiency (short-run)

Profitable in the short-run

However the **(P)** and **(A)** roles can create effectiveness and efficiency in the short-run only. The organization will be profitable, but not for long.

Again, let's take the example of playing tennis. Hitting the ball over the net into the opponent's field is the **(P)** role—the volley was effective. We **(P)**erformed the **(P)**urpose for which we hit the ball. In training to play tennis and repeatedly routinizing movements to utilize minimum energy for maximum impact, we provide for the **(A)** role—and made our game efficient.

Winning a volley does not mean winning the game; to win a game more needs to be done than winning one volley.

Two additional functions must be performed in order for the organization to be effective and efficient in the long run. The first one is the **(E)** role.

To win a tennis game, you need to do more than just efficiently

ROLE	ORGANIZATIONAL IMPACT	TIME RANGE
• (P)	effectiveness	short-run
• (A)	efficiency	short-run
• **(E)**	**effectiveness**	**long-run**

hit the ball over the net once. In order to hit the *next* ball, you must be ready to hit it, which means anticipating where the next ball is going to come from and being in position. That requires strategic thinking. So as a good player, as you hit the ball, you must be thinking what you should do next. Should you run to the net? Should you go back to the center of the court? You must be ready for the next volley. I call this the **(E)** role—**(E)**ntrepreneuring, providing proactively—not reactively—for change.

In this role two factors are necessary, creativity and risk-taking.

You must be creative to proact for the expected environment. You must imagine what the future is going to look like so you can prepare for it. **(E)**ntrepreneuring is analogous to planning—deciding what to do today in light of what you expect tomorrow to be. In order to plan, to perform the **(E)** role—you must be creative enough to imagine the future.

Being creative is analogous to having the ability to see through the fog. When you look through the fog, you have limited information and the validity of the information is constantly changing. You see bits of scenery and as the fog moves, the scenery disappears and the information changes. A creative person can take those bits of information, put them together like a jigsaw puzzle, fill in the jigsaw holes in the mind and imagine what the total picture could be.

Creativity is necessary for building scenarios of the future in order to predict the changes that will occur; but it's not sufficient for taking present action in light of that future. In order to act, you must be willing to take risk.

Going back to the tennis analogy, what makes a player unable to proactively move to where the next ball is going to hit? One obvious reason could be that the ball is moving fast, and the player is out of shape and slow. Another reason could be that perhaps he cannot predict the behavior of his opponent and imagine where the next ball will land. A third reason might be that he doesn't want to take the risk of moving on the court until he knows *exactly* where the ball is going to land. He waits for the ball to land, and once he knows where the ball is—once there is certainty—he advances toward the ball. Obviously that is too late.

Many managers behave that way too. They will say, "The event has not occurred yet. We don't know how the market is going to behave. Let's wait and find out what the reality is going to be, and then we'll do something about it."

In a rapidly changing environment, the time of reaction can be so slow in comparison to the speed in which changes occur, that the organization is continuously in a reactive mode. That is the reason I do not use the word *adapt* to a changing environment. The role of (ε)ntrepreneuring is not to adapt to the changing environment. Adapting means being reactive, not proactive. We must proact, project what the future is going to be, and then do something about it. We don't have the luxury of waiting for the future so we decide then what to do.

The (ε) role makes the organization effective in the long run by making it proactive. We will be able to hit, (P) the next ball, and have a successful next volley too, if we predict the future and take the risk in getting ready for it.

Decision Role	Impact
(P)erform service	-effective (short-run)
(A)dminister	-effective (short-run)
	Profit, short-run
(ε)ntrepreneur	-proactive, effectiveness (long-run)

These three roles are necessary but not sufficient if the organization is going to be effective *and* efficient in the long-run. The fourth role, which provides for efficiency in the long-run, is the most difficult to explain, especially in Western society.

Let's look in detail at this role, because it might explain the success of the Japanese management style over the Western management style. It will also explain why the Japanese might eventually lose their competitive advantage.

An observant, practicing manager could show examples of organizations that have been managed by a person who excels in

ROLE	ORGANIZATIONAL IMPACT	TIME RANGE
• (P)	effectiveness	short-run
• (A)	efficiency	short-run
• (E)	effectiveness	long-run
• **(I)**	**efficiency**	**long-run**

the (**p**)erforming service role, the (**a**)dministration role, and the (**e**)ntrepreneurial role. That (**pae**) manager has made decisions that focused on the needs of customers and the organization has become highly effective—(**p**). He has been extremely efficient and runs a tight ship. No resources were wasted (a function of (**a**)), and the manager has been highly (**e**)ntrepreneurial, projecting new needs in the marketplace and proactively taking action to satisfy those needs. However, what happens when such a manager, who is a rare bird, dies or leaves the organization? By and large the experience is that the organization suffers a serious difficulty and in some cases it dies.

In order for an organization to survive in the long-run, the organization must be independent of any individuals that comprise it. An example is the Catholic church. It has existed for 2,000 years and it might exist for another 200,000 years—independent of who is the Pope. That has happened because it is an organized *religion*.

If we took religion out of the Catholic church, it would probably be subject to the same difficulties of survival as any other organization. This suggests that an organization, in order to survive in the long-run, needs a "religion" that unites the organization in a transcendental way, far beyond what any single individual can do. These are the values, philosophies, rituals, patterns of behavior and beliefs which unite the people beyond the immediacy of the function they are to perform.

The (**i**)ntegrating role is to develop this culture of interdependency and affinity, so as to nurture the unique corporate "religion." This is done by *changing an organization's consciousness from mechanistic to organic*.

To change means to do something today, so tomorrow will be different from yesterday. (**i**)ntegration does not happen by itself. We have to do something in order for it to occur. In performing the (**i**) role, a manager must be actively engaged.

Organization is more difficult to explain. Frequently in my lectures when I ask someone how large his organization is, and how many people work for it, the person responds by looking at the organization chart or the salary list; and that's the wrong place to look.

In order for a manager to know how many members of the organization he is supposed to integrate, he should look at the rock from our previous example—the need that he must satisfy with the organization he is managing. There is a task-interdependency that must be managed. The question is who are the people whose interdependency must be managed? Some of the people are paid with salaries, others are paid with commissions, or perhaps he pays them by taking them to dinner and massaging their egos. How he pays is irrelevant, as long as it is ethical. What is relevant is that he provides the reward that moves the rock.

A typical mistake of an inexperienced manager is to claim that he cannot do a job because the people he requires to do it, do not report to him exclusively. There is no manager—in my experience with hundreds of organizations and thousands of managers—who has *all* the people he needs in order to do a job reporting to him. The president of Bank of America, Sam Armacost, supported this point when he said "You don't need to own a highway in order to drive on it. You just need to have a token to get on it."

A good manager first identifies his "rock"—his responsibility or task—by identifying the clients' he is supposed to satisfy. The next question is, "Whom do I need to complete this task?" The third question is, "What rewards do I give these people in order for them to help carry out the task?" Some will be paid in salary. Some will be paid in another way.

A manager is as good as his ability to analyze the (P)urpose of his organization and the needs and wants of the people needed to accomplish that purpose. A deficient manager is one who moves only pebbles, not rocks. He focuses only on those tasks that only the people who work for him can do.

As a matter of fact, I believe that a manager can be rated by the degree of IOUs he possesses. In the bank of favors, the more people he has who owe him favors, the more he will be able to cash in on them when the day comes and he needs to move his own rock. Support your colleagues. See how and where you can be helpful. Help them move their rock, and build your bank account, because the day will come when you will need them to help accomplish your own task.

A good manager is one who recognizes interdependency across organizational lines and does his best to support and cooperate with others, a person who is also supported in return. In short, a good manager is a team player.

Who the members of the organization are depends on the task that needs to be accomplished. This usually includes more than just the people who directly report to the manager or that are in a salary dependency.

The next word we need to explain is *consciousness*. Every organization has a personality and a pattern of behavior or style. Once we know the organization, this behavior is predictable. Thus, in a Bureaucratic organization, we can predict that files will be lost, response time will be long, delays and responses may be inadequate. When we integrate, the (I) role should change an organization's consciousness, behavior, culture and system of beliefs from mechanistic to organic.

What is *mechanistic*? Look at a chair that has four legs. You identify it as a chair because you can sit on it. If you could not sit on it, it would not be a chair. It is defined by what it does.

Look at a hammer. It is a hammer, if it is used to pound nails. If it was used to harm someone, it is not a hammer, it is a weapon. If it was hung on the wall as folk art, then it is not a hammer; it's an object of art and decoration. It is defined by what it does.

What will happen to the chair if one of the legs breaks? It will stop functioning as a chair; you will not be able to sit on it. In order for the chair to perform, someone from the *outside* must repair the chair.

Why doesn't one of the other legs move to the center of the chair and create a stool so the function of the chair can be continued? The obvious answer is that in a machine or object, there is no internal interdependency between the parts. It is dependent on external intervention to fix any breakdown if the machine is to function. A multi-billion dollar spaceship fails to function because of a few dollars worth of deficient O-rings. That is the nature of the mechanistic consciousness where there is no internal interdependency of parts to perform the function of the total unit. In organizations, it can be called parochialism or tunnel vision. Each person is thinking only for himself. Each department functions as an independent; acting by itself and not as part of the total system. If the total system is to perform, someone must manage the interdependence because the parts cannot do it on their own.

Now take an *organic* consciousness and juxtapose it onto a mechanistic consciousness. Look at your hand. What will happen if one of the fingers breaks? The hand will still continue to perform. Why? What makes a hand is not five independent fingers, but five fingers that each "think" like a hand. The other four fingers will cover up for the broken finger so the hand can function. If you lose three fingers, you still did not lose the hand, because the two remaining fingers will try to perform like a hand. If you lose the whole hand and use a mechanistic claw, you must have physiotherapy to teach you how one part of the claw works with the other. You must teach the parts of the claw to behave like a hand. You will be performing the **(I)** role, creating a sense of interdependency and identification with a higher cause for which a part exists.

Here is an analogy. Three people are laying bricks. The first is asked what he is doing.

"I am laying bricks."

The second one is asked the same question.

"I am building a wall."

The third is asked.

"*We* are building a place to worship God."

The third man understood the interdependence and the purpose of that interdependence. When that happens, no one is indispensable. It makes the organization efficient in the long run.

	Role	**Functionality**
(input)[5]	**(P)**erform service	Effectiveness (short run)
	(A)dminister	Efficiency (short-run)
	(E)ntrepreneur	Proact (effectiveness in long-run)
	(I)ntegrate	Organic (efficiency in long-run)
(output)	Long term and short term	Profitability

An Exercise

It is essential that we understand the four functions of decision making. The following story and exercise illustrates the concepts of the **(PAEI)** roles.

When my two sons were very young, they came to me fighting about a xylophone. In my family, the children share all their toys. One claimed that it was his xylophone and the other one said, "No, I touched it first." They wanted me to resolve the problem; and the problem was obvious—one xylophone, two fighting toddlers.

---

[5] The throughput is how to "manage" those four roles.

Let's see what the **(p)**, **(a)**, **(e)** and **(i)** solutions might be to this problem. Let's stop and think: It is important that the reader fully understand and integrate the **(paei)** analytical tools.

What do you think is the **(p)** solution?

In many of my lectures, when I ask this question, some of the participants will say that the **(p)** solution is to make the kids shut up. "Take their xylophone away so they stop crying." It's not the **(p)** solution. The confusion here is obvious. In order to find the **(p)** solution, you have to start by asking: What is the rock and for that you need to ask, who are the clients and what are their needs? If you identify the wrong clients, you will have the wrong solution. If you take the xylophone away and force the kids to quiet down, who was the client and whose needs did you satisfy? Obviously your own, and that's a mistake many managers make. They try to satisfy their own needs rather than those of the clients for whom the organization exists.

So lets start again. Who are the clients? The kids. What are they fighting about? What are the needs the xylophone will satisfy? There could be several needs. One is to make noise. Another is to draw the parent's attention. A third is a sibling rivalry—a competition between them to discover who is superior.

Please notice that you will not solve the problem until you satisfy their need. If their need is to make noise, a solution could be to bring some pots and pans from the kitchen so one can make noise with the pots, and the other with the xylophone. However, if the clients' (children's) need is to draw attention or to win a confrontation, bringing the pots and pans will not provide the solution. You have to continue seeking a potential solution that will be realized only when the needs have been satisfied.

What would be the **(a)** solution? Stop and think.

Here, you must look for routine, repetition, law and order. You have to do it by the book and apply the family's standards. It could be based on whoever touched the toy first, whoever had it first, or whoever had it longest. Perhaps the younger child must give in to the older one, or the older child must give in to the younger. Or maybe they just flip a coin. In the **(a)** solution, satisfying the children's immediate needs is ignored. The focus of an **(a)** solution is on the needs of the family unit as an organization for consistency: *the same rule must be applied when the same conditions* exist. You apply some order, some rule, and then you enforce it. The client now is not the children, but the family unit. To maintain efficiency in your parental (managerial) energy, future situations must be solved in the same way as the present one. Thus the routine, law & order.

The (E) solution to the problem will be to proact—project another, more powerful need that might detour the children from their immediate fight over the xylophone. An (E) solution is not just any creative solution. It is thinking about more powerful needs to serve as a diversion from the xylophone (look for the next ball to hit). The potential solution might be to suggest watching television, playing soccer, or going to the movies, which I found to be a consistent winner. You have to do what satisfies a more powerful need, rather than the immediate need.

The (I) solution is the most difficult to identify. In an (I) solution, you want to move away from dependency on external intervention. You want to avoid having your children come to you to resolve their differences. The moment you hear "Daddy" or "Mommy" and you are asked to resolve a problem, it should be clear there is no organic consciousness between your children. It is mechanistic. They are asking somebody from the *outside* to come in and resolve the problems they have among themselves, rather than solving the problems between themselves.

The (I) solution should create an environment in which the children will be motivated to find their own solutions. An example would be to take away the xylophone, send them to their room and tell them not to come out until *they* solve *their* problem of who should have the xylophone.

Notice that the children are going to cry even louder for a while, because they wanted somebody from outside to give them a solution. Outside refereeing is easier for them than having them solve the problem by themselves, but an (A) solution of providing the solution and enforcing it, will only be good in the short-run. Finding their own solution is more difficult and forces them to deal not only with the xylophone, but also with their relationship. Chances are, in the long-run when the parents die, as adults, they will not substitute the parents with lawyers and courts to resolve their differences. What we want to do in the (I) role is to make the children *interdependent* rather than *dependent* on external intervention.

If you went with them to their room and moderated the discussion to help them find a solution; or if you asked them to agree on rules for sharing toys and then you enforced the rules, how would that be defined in (PAEI) terms? What if you made them make their own rules and also made them enforce those rules themselves? Would it work? Why or why not?

THE (PAEI) INTERDEPENDENCY

If (P)erformance, (A)dministration, (E)ntrepreneurship and (I)ntegration functions are performed, the organization will be effective, efficient, proactive, and organic, and that means it can be effective and efficient in the short- and the long-run; but those rules are interdependent and undermine each other.

Let's look at the interdependency between these four functions.

(P) focuses on *what* is to be done. (E) focuses on *why* it is to be done. Another way to ask why is to ask what for, which means that (E) is the long-term (P); and (P) is the short-term (E). The significance of this distinction is that it explains how (P) and (E) interact.

Have you ever experienced a situation where someone said, "I've been working so hard I haven't had time to think." "People who work too hard have no time to make serious money."? What that means is that they are so focused on *what* they are doing, (P), that they have no time to think about *why* they are doing it, (E).

In our personal lives, if we have a disastrous marriage, we usually don't want to think about the *why*. We tend to get overly involved in *what* we are doing, avoiding the need to sit down and analyze why we are doing what we are doing.

As we have seen, (P)erformance impacts (E)ntrepreneurship, and the reverse can be true as well. (E)ntrepreneurship impacts (P)erformance. People in production might complain to the corporate planners and to the people in engineering in the following manner: "If you guys don't stop changing your minds, we will never get anything done."

In order to get action, we must freeze the planning process when it is understood as a process of producing change. We have to decide when to stop changing, so the action can start. If there is too much change, very little can be done. Take countries where there is too much change. It produces paralysis. To help stop inflation in Brazil during the 1980s, new laws and new government economic policies were constantly being introduced. This produced so much uncertainty that action was undermined. **(E)** threatened **(P)**, meaning that the more erratically they fought inflation, the more they fueled it. The higher the inflation, the more crisis-oriented the politicians became, and they changed laws and policies frequently to demonstrate action. During high inflation, Argentina changed its Minister of Treasury almost annually, inciting inflation, rather than restraining it.

(A) and **(I)** are also interdependent; **(A)** focuses on the *how*, while **(I)** focuses on the *who* and with *whom*. Both are *how*-oriented, except that **(A)** is a mechanistic *how* and **(I)** is an organic *how*. Here's an example of their incompatibility. Where is there more crime: in a large, highly-industrialized city, or in a small village where most people know each other? The obvious answer is more crime will occur in the larger city. Crime can be attributed to the sense of alienation that people feel, to not having a sense of belonging or an interdependency. There is an **(I)** deficiency.

A typical answer to crime, however, is to have more law and order, which is an **(A)** solution to an **(I)** problem. It should be noted that the more **(A)** solutions we attempt, the greater the **(I)** problem will be. The legal environment will become more intensive, people will be more likely to sue each other to resolve their disputes and they will begin to rely less on the social values to govern interdependencies. Crime can be arrested by **(A)** means, but to be solved it needs an **(I)** solution, in socio-economic terms.

It is the usual tendency to provide **(A)** solutions to **(I)** problems because **(A)** solutions require enforcing rules rather than thinking about the spirit of the solution and what makes sense. **(A)** is the more efficient *how* in the short-run, while **(I)** requires more time, but has a longer-lasting effect. **(I)** is the long-term *how*. The more we rely on the short-term *how*, the greater will be the long-term *how* problems that emerge over time.

Another example: Which country is strong on **(I)**, and has a competitive advantage because of it? Japan. Its culture has a strong sense of interdependency, affinity, and inter-loyalty between corporations and their employees. **(A)** is low. They have the lowest number of lawyers per capita in the free world.

Which country is growing in (a) and declining in (i)? The United States. How can the United States beat Japan's advantage?

Export (a). That will undermine (i). How can (a) be exported? Send business professors to teach the Japanese traditional management theory: span of control, unity of command, the exclusive rights of management versus labor, elitist managerial decision making, and a management theory based on adversary relations. All the above concepts increase (a) and then threaten (i). Mechanic *how* will substitute organic *how*. (a) will substitute (i) because it is more potent in the short run, it has a faster impact; (i) takes a long time to develop.

Let us look at (p) and (a) interdependency in a tennis example. Hitting the ball into the opponent's court any way you can is to provide the (p) role. It makes your game effective. By training to use your hands and body correctly, you learn how to be efficient, to have maximum hitting power with minimum energy. That is the (a) role. Imagine a player who trained and became so programmed and efficient in hitting the ball a certain way, that he might complain if the ball is not sent to his racket in the way that he is most efficient, rather than have his racket follow the ball and try to be effective.

Bureaucracies behave that way. They systematize themselves to be efficient to such a point that they stop being effective. These are the managers who might say, "This would be a wonderful business to run if it was not for the customers." The customers, by changing their needs and demands, mess up the organization's efficiency. The bureaucratic managers would rather be efficient and ineffective than effective and inefficient. They would rather be precisely wrong than approximately right.

If a large bureaucratic organization wants to be more effective, it has to be less efficient, especially if you compare short- with long-run. Short-term efficiency can be detrimental to long term effectiveness.[6] Achieving both effectiveness and efficiency simultaneously both in the short- and the long-run takes a managerial skill we will have to talk about in another book.

The (e) and the (i) roles are also incompatible. The (e) role

---

[6] For mathematical proof, see economic price theory on how short- and long-term variable and fixed cost curves behave. See: Stigler, George Joseph. *The Theory of Price*: (New York: MacMillian Company, 1966), p. 155.

of creativity and risk-taking, usually attributed to an individual, can be hampered by the sense of affinity, belonging and group pressure that is characteristic of the (I) role; (E) individuals who are creative sometimes find the (I) process stifling. On the other hand, individual creativity which is a deviant behavior from the norm, can threaten the sense of affinity and unity that is a product of the (I) role.

(PAEI) AND THE LIFECYCLE

If the four roles are incompatible and threaten each other, it is impossible for a simultaneous, balanced performance of the four roles to emerge instantly when an organization is born. The subsystems which facilitate the functionality of these roles have to be developed and in doing so, they threaten other subsystems that provide for the other roles.

The Lifecycle sequence occurs because there is a predetermined sequence of how each of the roles emerges and later submerges as another role emerges, and how the two eventually balance and allow a third to emerge, diminishing their own importance. Eventually—in Prime—three of the four roles come into balance. If all four roles come into balance, it is apparently a very special case; neither I nor any of my Associates have ever seen such a case.

Problems exist in an organization because all four roles with their subsystems are not fully developed from the start. The problems emerge because as the subsystems develop there is a struggle between the subsystems that functionalize the roles. A normal Lifecycle curve is one in which the sequence of role development occurs, and a new emerging role is solidified and institutionalized with a normal, predictable struggle. Once those problems (struggles) are removed, the organization is ready to move into the next stage, for a new role to emerge and to deal with the new problems that stem from such a development.

Pathological behavior occurs when the organization gets stuck and cannot proceed to develop the next function or role. In fact, when an organization encounters such difficulty, it usually regresses back to a former role; unable to proceed forward, it retreats to the familiar.

Understanding what is normal and what is pathological is essential if the change process is going to be assisted in any way.

The sequence by which the roles develop is predetermined, and thus the problems created by the incompatibility of the roles are predictable. With the power to predict problems in advance and the knowledge of which role deficiency is creating them, we can facilitate the development of that role and remove the problems. We have a diagnostic and therapeutic theory.

But there is more to it. Not only organizations have a culture which is dependent on where they are on the Lifecycle. Individuals have a personality too that expresses itself in a style of behavior—how they make decisions and the characteristics of those decisions.[7]

Management Styles

Since the (PAEI) roles are incompatible, it is rare that an individual can fulfill all the four roles simultaneously and excel in doing so. We are all mismanagers to different degrees, by virtue of being human. Some of us are more mismanagers than others though.

When one or more roles are totally not being performed, I call that a mismanagement style. If the roles are performed to the threshold performance needed, I call that a managerial style. It has its normal, to-be-expected human deficiencies.

In the extreme case of (P---), in which the person has the (P) quality to the exclusion of any of the other roles, we get a Lone Ranger. He focuses on the task at hand, but can't administer, has no vision or willingness to consciously take risk. He is not entrepreneurial and he is not sensitive to people, their values and group dynamics. This person is a doer and that is the end of it. He was promoted to be a manager because he is diligent, dedicated, hard-working and loyal. He's productive in spite of not having (A)dministrative, (E)ntrepreneurial and (I)ntegrative capabilities.

The result is a person who works very hard. His timetable is FISH (first in, still here). His desk is a mess. He manages by crisis. There is no delegation, no training, no long-range or even short-range planning and his subordinates are gofers. He reacts, he doesn't

---

[7] For detailed description and analysis of management styles see Adizes, *How To Solve the Mismanagement Crisis*, op. cit.

proact. He focuses almost exclusively on *what* now not on *how*, *when* or even *why*.

How about the **(-A--)** style? I call him the Bureaucrat. He arrives and leaves on time, regardless of what needs to be done. His desk is clean and his papers are in neat piles. Subordinates learn that what they do is not important; the how they do it is. The Bureaucrat manages by the book. What the subordinates do is not as important as long as they come in and leave on time. While the Lone Ranger has no staff meetings (he has no time), the Bureaucrat has many. But in the meeting, they focus not on the war, but on "who stole the strawberries," as per the style of Captain Queeg in the "Caine Mutiny. The Bureaucrat runs a very well-controlled disaster; the company is going broke, but on time.

How about the **(-E--)** style? I label this individual the Arsonist. When does he come to work? Who knows? When does he leave? Who knows? But the subordinates must be there before him and wait to leave just after him. Since no one knows when he comes and goes, it means his people are on call 24 hours a day, 365 days a year.

Does he have staff meetings? Yes, but no one knows when. Is there an agenda? There is none that anyone knows about in advance or that he respects. Does he expect his people to be nevertheless prepared? You bet! So people come to a meeting with their whole office in a mental suitcase. They have no idea what will be discussed or for what they will be attacked. Who does all the talking? The Arsonist. What do the subordinates do? They roll their eyes ("here we go again . . .") and hope he will forget what he wants or change his mind. This type changes his mind so frequently that no one really knows what the final decision is. "It is too late for you to disagree with me. I already changed my mind," is a typical response. Subordinates are all waiting for the dust to settle so something can be done. The more the Arsonist tries to activate his staff, the less they do.

How about **(---I)?** I call him the Super Follower. This manager does not lead; he super follows. He senses ahead of everyone else what direction the power wind is shifting to, how the undercurrent is changing and then positions himself as the leader of that current. To test the changing political climate, the Super Follower sends up trial balloons, which take the form of hedging when he speaks.

"I have a suggestion to make, but I don't know if I agree with it. . . ." "I suggest we declare dividends . . . but I don't feel too strongly about it . . ." In Mexico, they call this his type *pez enjavonada"*—soaped fish—just can't catch him. His subordinates serve as informers—to tell him what is going on. This mismanager has many meetings, but who is talking? Everyone else. He is listening, keeping his cards very close to the vest. Subordinates have a hard time concluding what exact direction he wants them to take. While they are waiting for clear instructions from him, he is sniffing the air, attempting to discover what it is the subordinates will agree to.

Since all of these are mismanagement styles, what is needed is a **(PAEI)** style. A person who is task-oriented, dedicated, hardworking, **(P)**; organized, efficient, thorough, conservative, **(A)**; a creative risk-taker with a global view **(E)** and sensitive and people-oriented, **(I)**. This person exists in textbooks, which is what is wrong with the whole theory of management—it is based on the perception that such a person exists or can be trained.

We are all mismanagers to different degrees because none of us is perfect. What is needed for **(PAEI)** decisions, if the decision is going to be proactive and effective, efficient and organic, is a complementary team.

A frequently encountered complementary team is the **(PaEi)**, **(pAeI)** team—the Mom and Pop store, even when the store is a multi-billion dollar company.

Anytime we have a complementary team, there will be *conflict*, which stems from the differences in style. Different styles necessarily mean different ways of thinking. Thus, conflict is necessary and indispensable for good decision making. Or, as it says in Zen writings, "If all people think alike, no one is thinking too hard." People who do not like conflict should not be managers. As Harry Truman said, "If you can't stand the heat, get out of the kitchen."

Is all conflict desirable? No! Conflict can be a source of growth or a source of frustration that stymies a person or an organization. The first is constructive; the second is destructive.

What makes the difference between functional and dysfunctional conflict? We can look for an example in personal experience.

The reason people divorce is usually the same reason they married in the first place. They marry because their complementary styles attract. But, interrelating means differences, and if those differences cannot be worked out, it means destructive conflict and eventually divorce. Conflict can also mean growth. It can make a marriage better.

What makes the difference in whether or not conflict will be constructive, functional and growthful?

Conflict is constructive when it produces the desired change. There is no change without friction and the difference between revolution and evolution is the degree of friction and the form that the friction takes.

There is no movement in a vacuum. We must be disturbing something and the disturbance is what creates the friction. An example will be walking from point A to point B. It creates friction between our feet and the floor. Now let us look at another example. Rub one foot against the other, continuously. It produced heat and friction, but it did not take you anywhere (unless you have an itch). The friction was not functional. It did not produce the desired change.

Desired change occurs when the conflict produces learning. When two people disagree, and because of the disagreement, each one of them learns something new, the desired change has occurred in their mind, and thus the conflict was functional. The learning produced a better decision than existed before there was conflict.

But, when will learning occur?

When there is a learning environment.

What are the conditions for a learning environment to develop and exist?

Learning occurs when there is *mutual* respect, and that means accepting the legitimacy of the other party being different or thinking differently.

It's a lesson I learned after much personal pain. Without respect for the other party, conflict is destructive.

Now, let us go back to the beginning of this chapter.

The two questions we have to answer before opening the envelope and evaluating the quality of a decision are: 1) Was there a complementary team that could perform the four **(PAEI)** roles? and 2) Was there mutual respect between the parties?

If there was no complementary team, the decision was biased. If the team was composed of four **AS**, they probably diagnosed the problem as insufficient rules and regulations, and their solution was to make more rules and regulations. If the group was comprised

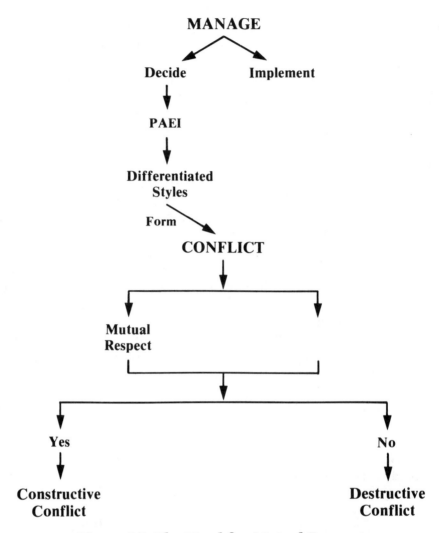

Figure 25: The Need for Mutual Respect

of four (**E**)s—*warning*—do not open the envelope. The side effects of their solution can be worse than the problem they tried to solve in the first place.

To produce a better, well-balanced decision than anyone could produce alone, we must have a complementary team and the interaction between the members of the team must be right. The team members must have mutual respect and learn from each other's differences of opinion. The components and the interaction between the components must be right.

For decision making, we need a complementary team whose members have respect for each other. Nice. But what about implementation?

6

Efficiency of Implementation ════════

INTRODUCTION

The quality of management depends on the quality of decisions made and on the quality of implementation. The quality of decisions depends on whether the four (PAEI) roles were performed, the subject of the previous chapter. Quality of implementation depends on the effectiveness and efficiency of that implementation, the subject of this chapter.

Effectiveness is measured by its functionality: Did implementation produce the desired results? Efficiency can be measured by how much blood, sweat and tears a manager must put into implementing a decision.

EFFECTIVENESS OF IMPLEMENTATION

Many outstanding decisions never get implemented. Personal decisions such as losing weight, giving up smoking and deciding to start exercising often remain nothing more than New Year's Resolutions. In the same way, many organizational decisions—to enter a new market or introduce a new product—never get carried out.

What determines if a decision will be implemented effectively?

There are several factors. First, a decision will be implemented in the spirit it was made if the decision is well-defined.

Defining a Decision

A decision has four dimensions. Any time one of the dimensions changes, the decision changes too; it becomes a different decision. The four dimensions are:

What to do	—	**(P)**
How to do it	—	**(A)**
When to do it	—	**(E)**
Who should do it	—	**(I)**

There is also a fifth, hidden dimension. The *why*. It is hidden because it is included in the *when*. The timing of a decision is derived from the reason for the decision. *Why* we do something has to be operationalized into *when* it needs to be done. One cannot decide *what* is the right timing, unless one knows *why* the decision was made. Thus, *why* is hidden inside the reasoning that leads to the *when*.

The sequence of making a good decision must reflect the **(PAEI)** components. First, we have to start with *why* we are making a decision. Once that is understood, we should proceed to the component of *when* a decision should be carried out, *when* it should have its impact. In light of the *why* and *when*, the *what* is determined. The *why*, *when* and *what* affects the *how*, which after being analyzed, might reverse some *what*, *when* and *why* components of the decision. Last, we decide *who* should do it, which might reverse the *how*, if, for example, the person is unavailable or unwilling. This can change the *what*, and affect the *when* and even the *why*; we might have to change the reason for what we are doing. In other words, the *why* might change in light of the *when*, *what*, *how*, and the whole process repeats itself as the decision is refined.

If all **(PAEI)** dimensions are not considered, the decision is not complete. Frequently, *what* to do is decided, but because the *how* is left open, the decision might be ineffective. We might regret the implementation; the *what* was done, but in such an undesired way that the joint result of *what* and *how* is undesirable.

A decision is not complete if the *when* and *who* are not decided too. Two decisions with the same *what* to accomplish, but with

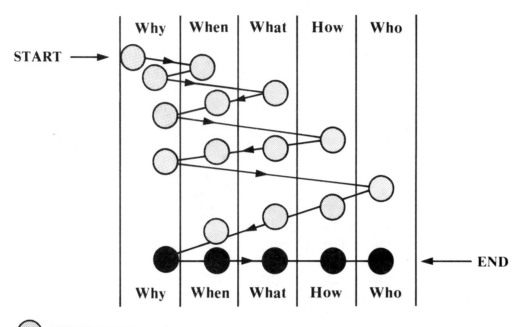

○ **TENTATIVE DECISION**

● **FINALIZED DECISION**

Figure 26: Decision-Making in the (PAEI) Sequence

different timings, become different decisions. By the same token, *who* should carry out a decision impacts the nature of the decision; it impacts *how* and *when*, and, eventually *what* gets done.

A decision is not finalized until all the four **(PAEI)** roles are expressed in their decision-making dimensions: *why, when, what, how,* and *who.*

The validity of this point can be seen with children who challenge their parents' position.

"Can I have candy?"

"No, it is not good for your teeth."

"Why?"

I explained to him. He did not give up though.

"But can I have it if I do my homework?"

"No."

"Can I have it after dinner?"

"No."

Then he went to his mother to see if she would agree. Note that my son was challenging each of the **(PAEI)** decision components. First, he challenged the *why*, then the *how*, then the *when* and at the end, he challenged the *who*. *What* he can do was not finalized until all the dimensions were finalized.

The four dimensions interact. *What* affects the *how* and vice versa. Thus, the proper sequence in which to make a decision is to discuss and finalize the *why* first. Once the *why* is decided, the **(PAEI)** dimensions can be finalized. A decision is finished when there is agreement on *why* something should be done, *when* it should be done, *what* is going to be done, *how* it is going to be done, and *who* is going to do it.

The *who* factor is not just the name of a person. Here, we must look at *why* that particular person should or will do it—what personal or cultural factors might project or impede him from efficiently implementing a decision.

The four functions, **(PAEI)** are imperatives; it is imperative that they are fulfilled, otherwise the decision will be faulty. (In *How to Solve the Mismanagement Crisis*,[1] I give descriptions of the predictable decision-making styles that will emerge whenever one or more of these four functions are not fulfilled.)

Figure 27: Imperatives of Decision Making.

---

[1] Adizes, *How To. . .* , op. cit.

Whichever sequence we follow, a decision is not made until the *why, when, what, how* and *who* is fully spelled out.

The *what, how, when,* and *who* (**PAEI**) dimensions of a decision can be depicted as a square.

These four functions have two dimensions to them:

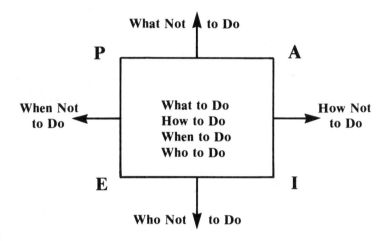

Figure 28: The Dimensions of Decision Making

A decision must be bound. We should know what to do and what not to do. If a person knows what *to do*, but doesn't know what *not to do*, he does not know what to do. He will have to find the missing information through experimentation.

Has your boss ever given you a new responsibility and told you what to do? You probably went down the hall to your colleague and asked him what he thought you should do. Why were you asking? The boss already told you what to do. What you were probably asking for was advice on *how* to do it. Behind the question of how to do it, you were trying to find out *what not to do*. You did not want to stick your neck out. You wanted to know where the organizational land mines were.

If you are the boss and you tell subordinates *what to do* and it does not get done in the spirit you intended, one of the reasons could be that someone else told them *what not to do*.

What a person does is a combination of what he thinks he should *and* what he thinks he should not do.

Take children, for example. If you only tell them *what to do*, but you do not tell them what they *should not do*, they do not know how to behave. It is an open-ended assignment. The children know what to do only when they also know what they should not do. The same thing applies to the *how*. We know *how* to do things only after we have also learned *how not* to do them.

Try the following exercise. Put a partition between two people— Joe and Frank. Have Frank tell Joe how to tie his shoes. Then tell Joe to do as he is told, so there is no question that he followed instructions, but to purposely give the worst possible interpretation to those directions. For instance, if Frank tells him to put one end of the shoe lace over the other, Joe should do it, but only after he put the lace over the other shoe also.

There is no way the shoe laces will be tied correctly. We do not know how to do anything new until we learn from experience *how not* to do it. The same applies to the *when to* and *when not to*, and to the *who to* and *who not to* components.

Good decision making requires continuous back and forth communication to correct mistakes in understanding. If a new decision does not get implemented correctly the first time, you should realize that the people you assigned to the job are not dumb or intentionally trying to subvert and sabotage your beautiful idea and decision. They do not know, *what, how, when* and *who*, until they know at different degrees of understanding *what not, how not, when not* and *who not*. You do not know the answer to these questions either, until you are confronted with the possibility of what, when, who and how not to.

There is a catch though. What not to do is endless, and you cannot imagine or predict all the endless possibilities.

Thus, what gets done in organizations is not what is expected but what is inspected, corrected and reinspected until no more corrections are necessary. By that time the decision is obsolete, the situation has changed and you have to start all over again. As soon as you relax and feel in control, smile and start all over again. That is called continuous experiential learning from life, and those who feel they have graduated, should not try to manage.

A decision will be effective if it is well spelled out, and that will happen when all four imperatives of decision making (**PAEI**) are spelled out and put in their two dimensions (yes and no).

However, even if the decision is well-defined for implementation, that is not enough. The (**PAEI**) dimensions will make it effective but not efficient. Somebody must be able to carry out the decision and see to it that it is implemented efficiently.

EFFICIENCY OF IMPLEMENTATION

Having a well-defined decision with the four imperatives is a necessary condition before implementation can occur. Having the four imperatives, however, is not sufficient to implement the decision. A manager needs certain energy in order to carry out the decision. The sources of that energy are authority, power and influence.

Authority

I define authority as the right to make a decision—to say yes *and* no. This is a formal right inherent in a person's job independent of his power, connections or education.

The above distinction of yes *and* no is not a mistake. Most people would say yes *or* no. If we would have defined authority as the right to say yes *or* no, it might mean that someone has the right to say yes, but not to say no (which is very rare); or that he has the right to say no, but cannot say yes (which is very common).

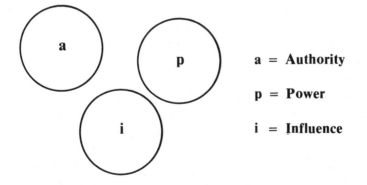

a = **Authority**

p = **Power**

i = **Influence**

Figure 29: Sources of Managerial Energy

When people can say no without being able to say yes, it bureau-cratizes an organization and causes it to lose its ability to relate to a changing environment. New needs which emerge in *what, how, when* and *who*, must be addressed by means of changing the way the organization does things. This cannot be done because only a few can say yes, and they are hierarchically distant. Those who can say no, are many, and they are usually omnipresent. The prob-lem and its potential solution are filtered by so many no-sayers that it never arrives to the yes-sayer. It is not strange that effective consultants request access to the top person. That is where a *yes* can be obtained.

Authority to say yes is necessary, but not sufficient. In many countries, authority and 25 cents won't even buy you a cup of coffee. "So what" is often the attitude of employees who fear little if any-thing.

Power

The second source of managerial energy to implement decisions is *power*.

I define power as the *capability* to punish or reward. Because carrying out some organizational tasks requires the cooperation of more than one individual—to lift the rock requires a working interdependency, whoever else is needed to cooperate in implement-ing a decision, if he can withhold that cooperation, has power. How much power a person has depends on how much we need his cooperation and how much of a monopoly he has over what we need.

Falling in love can be an overpowering experience. You might say, "I need you. I want you. I can't live without you, and you are the only one." When are we free from the continuous pain and ecstasy of being in love? When we do not need the other person for anything or when that person is not the only one to whom we can turn to get what we need. Wonderful. We removed the pain but the ecstasy went with it. Life is empty because we did not allow it to be full.

Nikos Kazantzakis, the author of *Zorba the Greek*, has written on his tomb in Crete: "No more hope, no more fear, finally free."

We are free of any power over us when we hope for nothing

and fear nothing. But that happens only when we are dead. To be alive means to hope and fear, to want and need, to depend and expect, to ask for and to give; in one word: interdependency.

On whom do we as managers depend the most to carry out a decision? Our subordinates! And that's where the power is. This comes as a real surprise to many managers. They believe that the higher one climbs on the organizational ladder, the more power there is. Wrong. There is more authority there, and maybe authorized power. But the real, naked power is found lower on the ladder; and the lower you go, the more of it there is.

Here is an example.

In the early 1970s when appointments for postmasters changed from being political to professional appointments, I was asked to train a new crop of top post office executives. To study the needs of my client, I spent one day at the San Francisco annex where mail is processed. I wanted to see how the mail could get misdirected. I wanted to follow a piece of mail from the time it was dropped into a mail box until it arrived at its destination.

In the process of handling mail there is a point where it is classified into zip numbers for sending it to the zip code post office. To do that, mail is put on a conveyor with fronts facing in the same direction. Now this is not just a few pieces of mail. San Francisco annex at that time processed six million pieces of mail a day.

So imagine a gigantic conveyor with people arranging all addresses so they point in the same direction. Then there are the Blind Belindas—machines consisting of a conveyor belt, a rubber hand and a typewriter keyboard. The rubber hand picks one piece of mail and puts it on a stand in front of the person who sits behind the keyboard. The person looks for the zip code number and types in a magnetic code that is stamped on the back of the envelope. Then the conveyor picks up and directs the piece of mail to a pigeon hole with the proper zip code.

I stood behind one of those processors. The speed at which the mail is put in front of the workers' eyes is fantastic. The problem is compounded because people have all kinds of handwriting and odd places to put the zip codes on envelopes. By the time I found the zip code, the automatic preprogrammed conveyor had already taken the envelope to some destination.

There were 16 Blind Belindas working simultaneously. The job of sorting the mail is mechanistic; the person uses only his eyes and fingertips. He uses his brain only as an information processor. People might go crazy if they had to do this task for four or eight hours straight. So the processors take a 10-minute break every 30 minutes.

I wondered who assures that these processors are not playing Bach or Chopin on the keyboard while looking for badly scrawled zip codes? They could be sending Washington mail to Hawaii and St. Louis mail to Denver.

"How do you check on their work?" I asked the supervisor.

"We sample what is in some of the zip code pigeon holes."

"Sample? How can it be a meaningful sample? There are six million pieces of mail a day. How many can you sample to make it meaningful? And if you find a misdirected piece of mail, what do you do? How do you know who did it? There are 16 Blind Belindas."

"Well, each piece of mail gets stamped on the back by the machine that processed it."

"Great," I said, "but who did it? People change seats every so often."

"Well, we don't know that," he admitted.

Whoa. If my mail arrives, it is because *someone there cared* about doing his job correctly. If he did not want to do it, my mail would still be wandering around the world. There is no way anyone can economically control this process. Even if the supervisor checked 100 percent of the mail who would check on the supervisor? His manager? And who would check on him? If we continue this analysis, we can easily see the president of the United States spending all his spare time sorting the country's mail.

It dawned on me that it is the people on the firing line who have power to make or break managerial decisions. Period. The people have the power whether managers want them to have it or not; whether they should have it or not. This is a reality.

I remember another incident. I was touring a shoe manufacturing company. At the shipping department, a worker told me with a grin and in confidence, "Do you know what we do? We put one shoe of one size and one of another size in the same package and send it out." I could see the president, CEO, chairman, executive committee, strategic planner and consultants laboring, sweating to make a sensible strategy on how to penetrate the market. And here is a $3.15-per-hour guy who can reduce that strategy to shambles.

"Yes, but if I caught the guy, he would be fired instantly," said an executive who heard this story in one of my lectures. But how many unproductive employees can you catch? One? Two? Three? You can't catch all of them, all of the time. They can make your life more miserable than you can make theirs. If employees do not want to cooperate with you, they can make you a loser faster than you can fire them. Besides, anytime a company fires an employee, it costs money. The person was probably not productive for months before he was fired. His replacement will not be fully productive for the first several months after he is hired. It all costs money. So you might be punishing someone for poor performance and at the same time committing hara kiri. You need your subordinates as much, if not more, than they need you.

Who suffers from high blood pressure, sleepless nights, ulcers and heart attacks? Is it called executive stress or worker's stress? What do workers suffer from? According to the literature published by behaviorists, they suffer from daydreaming, boredom, apathy and alienation. So they turn their energy against the manager, because it is more interesting to see him twist in the wind. Secretaries have more ways to lose files than the human mind can imagine. Workers can go to the bathroom or to the coffee dispenser more times than you can count and if you try to control it, you spend all your time running to the bathrooms or designing forms to report on who went where or drank what. That again costs money in lost productivity, in filing, analyzing and processing information.

The subordinates have the power. Period! The sophisticated manager realizes this. The higher you go, the more power the people under you have. You climbed the mountain hoping to find power up there. Surprise! At the top of the mountain there is a sign, "It is down there!" It is your job to enlist your subordinate's cooperation, or you are dead as a manager, because you can't fire everyone. Unless you enlist your subordinates' cooperation (legitimize power and make it coalesced—see the following discussion on *CAPI*) the day of reckoning will come. Don't just control! Motivate instead, and only those who cannot be motivated, fire.

Influence

The third source of energy to implement a decision or carry out the responsibility for a task is influence. That is the *capability* a person has to make somebody do something without using authority or power. Influence usually stems from the information that convinces the person we want to direct, to act as desired. When he is convinced on his own, of the validity of the decision to be implemented, he has been influenced. That happens only when he acts on his own volition—not because he was coerced or scared into acting.

When we overlap the circles of authority, power and influence, we get different combinations of these three sources of energy. We get authorized power (*ap*), which is the legal right to punish and reward. We get indirect power (*ip*) which happens when the directing person believes he is influencing, but the focal person perceives power. This happens when we try to convince someone of something, but he is not convinced at all. He acts not because he is convinced, but because he does not believe that he can exercise his own independent judgment. He acts because he is scared or worried about the repercussions if he does not comply.

The third combination is called influencing authority **(ia),** which in the professional management literature is also called au-

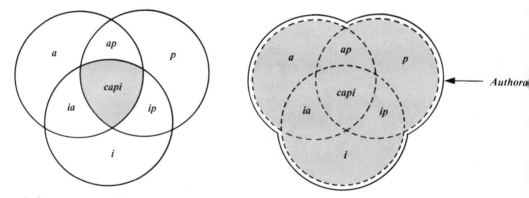

$$Authorance = a + p + i + ap + ip + ia + capi$$

Figure 30: *Capi* and *Authorance*

thority by acceptance or professional authority. This is a situation where we accept and co-opt the decision of our superiors.

The heart of these three circles is *CAPI*: Coalesced Authority, Power and Influence. All the possible combinations are called *authorance*, which is authority plus power, plus authorized power plus indirect power plus influence plus influencing authority plus *CAPI* (See Figure 30).

Let us see how this model works in reality.

Look at the situation of a mother trying to convince her child to eat spinach. She uses different components of *authorance*. In the beginning, she might say, "Eat it, it's good for you. Popeye eats spinach and look how strong he is. You will be like Popeye." She is using the influence component of her *authorance*. If the child still refuses to eat, she will allude to the father who will be home soon. This is indirect power, and it may cause the child to eat the spinach. If, however, he still refuses to eat, the mother might get angry and punish him. If the punishment is acceptable by the value standards of the family, that is authorized power. If not, it is power without authority. If the child still refuses to eat, the mother might make the classic mistake managers make, by pleading, "Why don't you listen to your mother? Am I not your mother? Why don't you ever do what your mother tells you to do?" This means she is using the last resort of her *authorance*, which is authority. It is a mistake, because after she uses her authority, there is nothing left for an encore.

What she could be using to affect her child's behavior, is influencing authority. She could eat the spinach herself in front of the child to serve as a behavioral model; and the child might emulate her.

CAPI is used when she says, "How about eating some spinach," and the child immediately eats it because he believes it is good for him, he worries about the repercussions if he does not eat it, and he respects his mother's suggestions. In that case she has control.

Let's superimpose *authorance* on a decision, on the responsibility to carry out a task. Here are three identical tasks, identical responsibilities with different compositions of *authorance*.

In the first case, *authorance* almost equals responsibility.[2] *CAPI*

---

[2] They do not have to be equal, because the lines are not lines, but areas.

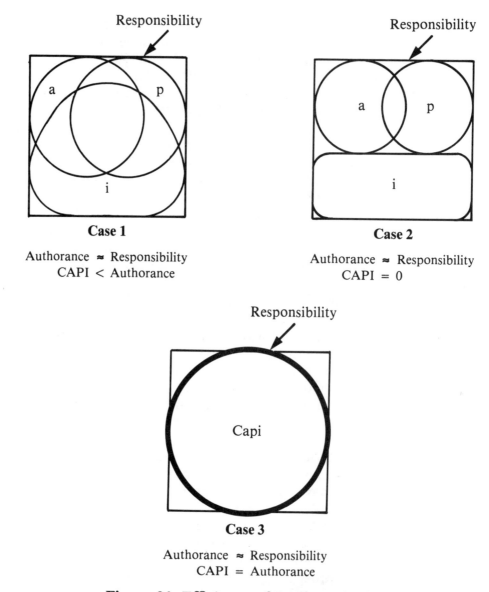

Figure 31: Efficiency of Implementation

is smaller than *authorance*. How does this manager carry out his responsibility? Part of the task the manager carries out with authority but without power, which means he can tell people what to do; however, if they don't do it, he cannot punish them effectively. He has limited power that is accepted and formalized. The manager carries out another part of his responsibility by using power. He somehow communicates that he will withhold his cooperation in providing something they need. Thus, they will complete his desired action out of fear or worry. A third part of his responsibility the manager will carry out by influencing, which means that he will try to convince people and hope for the best because he has no authority and no power.

He can carry out a very limited amount of his responsibility with *CAPI*, which means he has total control only in a limited area of his responsibility. In that area, all he has to do is decide, and the subordinates will carry out the task.

In the second situation, this manager has sufficient authorance but zero *CAPI*. The three circles are not overlapping. The manager still can carry out his responsibility, but obviously with less ease, because there is no area of responsibility in which he has unchallenged control.

In the third situation, *CAPI* equals authorance, which almost equals the task. This manager is in control over almost every part of his responsibility. He has authority, which he can back up with power and influence.

The three managers can carry out their tasks and responsibilities equally, but not with equal efficiency as measured by blood, sweat and tears expended. How much psychological energy is necessary for the task to be completed?

The least efficient manager, which means the one who sleeps the least at night, is manager No. 2. The most efficient one, who spends the least psychological energy, is manager No. 3.

I call this phenomenon managerial efficiency. It is distinct from organizational efficiency which measures labor efficiency, and capital efficiency. I am looking at managerial efficiency as the psychological energy a manager must expend to carry out his responsibility.

While manager No. 3 is the most efficient, he is also the rarest.

No manager can control anyone. You have to motivate people and no punishment per se will produce all the control a manager wants.

A manager must have humility, and that comes with experience. Beginning managers use power; they fire people or threaten to fire them. With time, they learn that the trick is not to control, but to create a controlled situation. How is that done?

While a single individual might not have total *CAPI* over his task, a group of people might jointly have the required *CAPI*. In order to put the *CAPI* together, a manager must create a win-win environment for the various interest groups that comprise *CAPI*.

In an organization where the *CAPI* is split between different people, the authority usually lies with management, which is authorized to make decisions by the board of directors. Usually power lies with the subordinates who can cooperate or not cooperate in carrying out the decisions. Influence usually lies with the technocrats, the professionals who have the know-how for making the best decisions in technical terms.

This can create a conflict of interests. The interests of those in authority could be growth, market share, sales, profits, return on investments or dividends. Those with power (the employees) might want more security at work, a higher-quality of work life and better salaries. The technocrats might want the biggest research budgets, the best equipment, and the most precise, accurate professional solution to a problem.

In the short-run, those interests are incompatible and the conflicts that ensue from it might paralyze the efficient implementation of decisions. For this conflict to be resolved, a win-win climate is necessary. A commonalty of interests is called for. That however, is utopia, because it is not operationally possible to have a win-win climate and a commonalty of interests at any point of time continuously and forever. Conflict over diverse interests is normal at any point in time. What to do, then?

To operationally obtain a win-win climate in the short-run, there must be a vision of win-win in the future, and mutual trust among the people who together comprise *CAPI* in an organization. They must trust that they will benefit from the long run win-win, even though there is a win-lose in the short run. If there is no trust between people, the short-run conflict of interest will dominate their behavior and thus impede the efficiency of implementation.

One can predict how effective the implementation of a decision will be by how much *CAPI* any individual has over the decision to be implemented. When one individual does not have all the necessary *CAPI* alone, we should analyze how much mutual trust and win-win vision there is among the people necessary for implementing the decision, the people who jointly have *CAPI*.

Fascism, communism and all totalitarian regimes are efficient in implementing decisions. *CAPI* is unified by force, and as a matter

of fact that is the predominant factor in their policy-making decisions. Democracies, on the other hand, are effective because of how
they make decisions, but they are not efficient because *CAPI, by
law*, is split into the branches of government. To be an efficient
democracy, there must be mutual trust among the differing parties
that comprise that society and govern it.

On a corporate level it can be predicted how well a decision
will be implemented by asking if an individual can control the
implementation, and if not, whose cooperation does he need for
implementation? Is there a win-win climate among those whose
interests are affected by the decision and how well do they trust
each other to share that win-win in the future.

7

The Nature of Conflict and
What To Do About It

To manage, we must first decide and then implement. For a quality judgement to be made during decision making, a complementary (PAEI) team is necessary.

For efficient implementation, the parties whose cooperation is needed for implementation should have common interests in implementing the decision *CAPI*.

Different (PAEI) styles generate conflict. Self-interests can conflict with common interests *CAPI*. Thus, conflict rising from form (styles) and content (self-interest) is common in organizations. It comes with the territory called managing. It is necessary and indispensable. There is no conflict only when no new decisions are made, or no implementation of new decisions is necessary, which means only when there is no change, and that happens only with death.

As it was discussed in Chapter 5, conflict is either destructive or constructive. It is never benign. It is constructive when it is functional; it is destructive when it is not channeled. Conflict is like energy or rushing water. Unless it is utilized for a purpose, it finds its own purpose. By definition, it does not stand still.

Conflict is constructive when a functional result or a desired change occurs. That happens when learning occurs, because learning is a change in the state of mind; there is growth. When does learning occur? When there is mutual respect. We do not learn from people we do not respect.

Respect is necessary for learning and thus for making better decisions, but it does not direct implementation. For that, trust is necessary. People will allow, and foster change that impacts them, if they believe that it will benefit their self-interest. Since it is impossible to assure such an outcome, trust is necessary if change is going to occur efficiently.

The task of management is to channel conflict which is potentially a destructive force to be constructive by developing and nurturing a climate of mutual respect and trust in an organization.

Mutual Respect

What does respect mean? Emmanuel Kant says that respect is accepting the sovereignty of the other person. In international relations, when a country is sovereign it means that it can make its own decisions without another country intervening. The same thing applies in interpersonal relations. We respect other people when we accept their sovereignty to make their own decisions. They don't have to make decisions the way we want them to make them. We don't have to agree with each other, but if we are going to learn from each other, we do have to understand each other. When we respect another person who disagrees with us, there is a chance we can learn from that person's disagreement; and the quality of our decision improves.

Let us look at the English language. The English word colleague comes from the Latin words to arrive together. Thus, colleagues are people who started from different points of view, but arrived at the same conclusion by learning from each other about their differences in opinion.

What turns conflict into a destructive force is the lack of respect. What destroys a marriage is not the existence of conflict. A marriage with no conflict is a marriage that is dead, dying, or about to die. People marry each other *because of*, not in spite of, their differences. Psychotherapists report that the reasons people marry are the same reasons they divorce. They are attracted by their differences. They fall in love with the differences, with the qualities that one lacks and the other person possesses. Jointly they are perfect, and subconsciously, I believe, they try to have such a perfection so their children will be perfect.

However, when they tie the knot, an organizational unit is

established with tasks to be accomplished. They try to put their differences to work and conflict emerges which, depending on *how* it is handled, can produce a growing relationship or a pitiful disaster. In order to stay married, mutual respect is essential. In that case, a disagreement is an opportunity for growth; the spouses learn something new about each other and about their marriage. When there is no respect, neither partner listens to what the other has to say, much less understands his mate's position. The marriage dissolves, or should dissolve.

What breaks up a marriage is not the existence of conflict, which is to be expected, but *how* the conflict is handled.

Some years ago, I read an article in the *New York Times* that summarized research on couples. Several hundred married couples were studied from their college years on. The researchers tried to find out whether there are personality traits that can predict which marriages will succeed or not. They could not find any significant variables as to which differences in personalities make for better couples. But they did find that what made the difference in whether or not a couple stayed together, was *how* the couples handled their disputes, regardless of what the personality differences were.

(PAEI) Conflict, and the Lifecycle

Looking at the Lifecycle of an organization, we see that the organization has problems at every stage; that's due to the fact that the four functions are never in total balance at any point in time— the four (PAEI) roles are never fully developed and equal at the same time. There is always a lack of balance, even in the normal stages of the Lifecycle. Why the lack of balance? Because it is the lack of balance that enables movement and growth. Balance is death. There is no energy for change.

Try the following exercise. Stand very steadily, on both legs with your hands clasped in front of you. You feel comfortable and in control, don't you? This looks like the normal state to be in. Right? Wrong! If you stay like this you die. You can't go to get food, go to the bathroom or go to sleep. Now try another posture. Stand on one leg, extend the other in the air as if in mid-walk, with one hand forward and one hand behind. You are out of balance, and will probably have difficulty standing on one foot for very long.

This does not look comfortable and normal, does it? No it does not, but that is the desirable posture because you are between points. You are coming from getting food, and going to do something else. What seems comfortable in the short run is very uncomfortable for the long run and what seems uncomfortable for the short run is comfortable for the long run.

The lack of balance between the systems—the processes, people's styles and structures—that comprise an organization and give birth to and nurture the **(PAEI)** roles, produces conflict. Lack of conflict will be very comfortable in the short run, but it will lead to death in the long run. Conflict is uncomfortable in the short run, but could be very constructive in the long run, depending on what we do with that conflict.

The difference between pathological and normal conflict is not whether there is conflict or not, but whether the conflict is propelling the organization to develop the strength it needs in order to function. Pathological conflict occurs when the conflict leads the organization, the individual, or the system to repeat itself rather than go forward. It does not locomote change. Since it has to be channeled, the energy can not stay in one place, it might change whatever is in its way—it becomes destructive.

It will not work for a marriage, a business, or a society.

During a normal Infancy, the dominance of **(P)** and weakness of **(A)** **(E)** and **(I)** creates normal problems of obsession with quantifiable results at the expense of the process. It is a reactive environment where the lack of patience is accepted as normal. But, it sows the seeds of destruction for later on.

The lack of control and a planning process causes the organization to go out of control during the Go-Go stage; the lack of patience from Infancy, with the typical arrogance of a Go-Go leads to a lack of tolerance, which in turn leads to a lack of mutual respect which, in turn can destroy an Adolescent organization.

In Go-Go, this imbalance creates the normal problems of overemphasis on the *what* and the *why* without sufficient attention to the *how* and the *who*. That's why there is a switch from management by crisis to crisis by management.

During Adolescence, the imbalance creates normal problems that stem from the conflict between **(A)** and **(E)**, which could be ameliorated if there is a conscious effort to reduce the attention paid to the (P) function, and instead pay attention to the **(I)** function.

What is the nature of mutual respect in the Lifecycle? Let's look at respect as a reward system. During the Courtship stage, the prospective founder does not get respect yet, he is a dreamer. During Infancy, the respect goes to the doers, to the producers.

There is admiration and infatuation with the founders during the Go-Go stage, because the results they achieve are so incredibly good. During Go-Go, the founders get a religious type of admiration they were not accorded during Courtship. The high rate of growth and the unexpected expansion build a certain sense of arrogance in the organization, and especially in the founder.

I have seen companies where the founder began developing delusions of grandeur. In one pathological, high-tech case, having a repetitive growth of more than 300 percent a year, the founder felt invincible and started relating to himself as a reincarnation of Jesus Christ. In another situation, the founder of such a company suggested that he could solve, not only the problems of his own company, but of the whole country. He thought of running for political office, because he believed that he had God-bestowed powers. This self-infatuation and self-admiration can be shattered almost overnight. It happens when the organization experiences a major crisis in the advanced stages of Go-Go, and causes the organization to move into Adolescence. Then, instead of mutual respect, there are mutual accusations, fights, cliquish behavior and total disrespect.

From Courtship to Adolescence there is usually no *mutual* respect. There is respect for a person. There is the disease of *personalitis*, or leader worship. The leader personifies all that the organization wishes to be. This *personalitis* can be one of the difficulties the Adolescent organization will have when respect for one person must be transformed into *mutual* respect in order for the organization to move into Prime.

If not completed, the transition from individual to mutual respect can lead an organization to the Founder's Trap. Monopolization of respect indicates that there will be difficulties for the organization to advance along the healthy path of the Lifecycle. If the organization was founded, or is led by several people who have different styles and who have conflicts, but who work with mutual respect, the organization will grow and prosper faster in the long run.

If the organization moves into Prime, the respect is no longer directed to any single individual, but rather to the organization as a whole; as a result the people of the organization have a sense of affinity for, and feel the pride of belonging to an entity. In the Go-Go stage, the identification is with an individual. "I work for Stewart" versus "I work for IBM." In Go-Go the repetitive word when the founder speaks is *I*; during Prime, the repetitive word is *we*. (During Adolescence the word used is *they* or *he*, due to the struggle and in-fighting that occurs.)

After Prime, the respect changes again, but it turns into a ritualistic respect of form; not of the function, person or system. This is even more emphasized during Aristocracy where those who do not show respect are rejected, even if their disrespect is necessary for the organization to remain functional. The disrespectful are the (E)s, the skunks that the organization considers as enfant terribles.

When the organization ceases to function well during Early Bureaucracy, disrespect reigns and mutual accusations run rampant. If the organization survives and is given external support in spite of its lack of functionality, there will be respect for people in public, but not for the organization, and not for each other when they speak about people who are not present. Bureaucrats are the least tense people I have ever worked with. There is no pressure to perform, no pressure to offend anyone, and no pressure to make waves. Because individuals will survive regardless of how they perform, respect is disassociated from performance and it exists regardless of what happens in the organization. Form is everything. If you play by the rules, don't make waves, and don't offend the other players, they will not offend you. But that, of course, is superficial. On the surface, Bureaucrats appear very respectful of each other, but behind each others backs they are very disrespectful.

In Death, as in Early Bureaucracy and Adolescence disrespect is exhibited, it is not covert. There is the bitterness of defeat, and all feelings are out in the open.

In comparing the growing and aging stages, there is respect throughout the Lifecycle, except during Courtship, Adolescence, Early Bureaucracy, and Death. Prior to Adolescence the respect is directed toward an individual. In Prime it is to individuals and the team as a system. From that point through Aristocracy, respect is directed to the system only. In Bureaucracy there is the appearance of respect while disrespect is the true attitude of the people.

Why is there disrespect and why is it exhibited during Courtship, Adolescence, Early Bureaucracy, and Death? The common denominator seems to be that there is a major turning point, a major disturbance in the development of the organization. The common denominator for Courtship and Adolescence is birth pains. In Courtship the idea is born. In Adolescence the organization is born as a separate entity from the idea or the founder that gave it the initial impetus for birth. Birth comes through pain, and where there is pain, disrespect can be manifested unless the pain is directed and produces functional results.

The common denominator for Early Bureaucracy and Death is the dying. Early Bureaucracy is the announcement that the end is here, which could be followed by the actual death of the organization—bankruptcy. If the organization is hospitalized—gets external help—death can be postponed. Then the disrespect is postponed until the organization does finally go bankrupt.

There is an interesting conclusion from this. There is no growth without pain. But pain can cause growth or it can stymie the system, depending on how it is handled. It is energy that unless it gets directed, since it cannot be contained it becomes destructive.

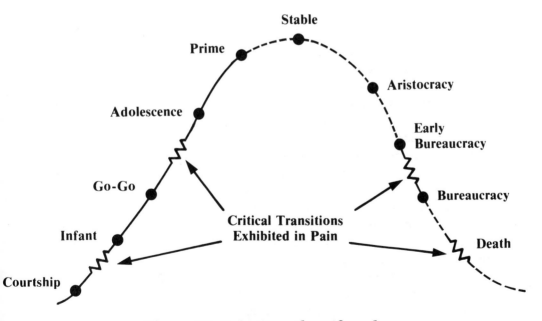

Figure 32: Pain Over the Lifecycle

Winners are identifiable by how they lose, how they handle pain. It is easy to win, and experience the joy of success. How one overcomes defeat indicates the strength the person has—that strength is what can make the person a winner if the opportunity arises.

Organizations should experience childhood diseases. It would be healthy for them as it is for a child. Childhood illnesses strengthen the system so it can handle problems later on. Management learns to handle conflict as the organization grows and this experience enables management to grow as the organization grows.

I agree with Red Scott, Chairman of Intermark. To discover whether or not hirees are potential winners, one of the questions he asks is if they had a personal tragedy or difficulty they had to overcome. That shows if these people had or developed strength. People who have only won are like spoiled brats; there is no way to predict how they will handle a loss, which is to be expected in life. There is no such thing as continuous winning, unless one cheats or is an underachiever, and those are not the people one would want to hire, anyway.

Mutual Trust

To implement a decision efficiently, *CAPI* is necessary. If an individual does not possess *CAPI*, then it must be coalesced. To coalesce people with authority, power and influence, we must coalesce the different self-interests. Management usually wants more, or better; it wants to build something. In all cases, management wants to do something to somebody through the organization. Those somebodies are the subordinates, who usually have interests different from management. It is logical that those who sell their brains or muscles, and who have no vested interest in building things, will not be interested in the long-run benefits, because they might not be there to enjoy them. They will want the maximum reward for the minimum effort in the short run. They will want to do less work for more money, while management wants more work for less money. There is a conflict of interests right there.

The technocrats—professional staff—have professional biases. If they are in marketing, they want the best marketing campaign. If they're in finance, they want the best ratios. The computer people want the latest in technology. Each special interest group has a professional frame of reference that it consults in making professional decisions. There is going to be conflict again. This time it is not due to style differentiation. It is a conflict of interests.

The reason that some decisions, which are good for the total system, are not implemented, is that it is not in the self-interest of a component of that system to forward implementation of the decision. On a personal level, while it might be a good idea for me to lose weight, it is not of interest to my taste buds to stop tasting fantastic food. This is sub-optimalization; the interests of a subsystem undermine the interests of the totality.

Conflict of interests can destroy any organization. It is not that we do not understand each other, which is the source of conflict in (PAEI). We do understand each other. We simply do not agree because the decision does not serve our individual self-interests.

A joke can bring this point home.

A pig and a hen were very good friends for a long time. So the hen thought it a good idea to start a partnership. "We are such good friends. We get along so well. Why don't we start a business together?" asked the hen. "That's a good idea, but what do you have in mind?" asked the pig. "Well, I thought we should open a restaurant chain which, to capitalize on our joint competitive advantages should serve ham and eggs." "Great idea, with sound strategy," said the pig. "But there is one problem. What is a mere contribution for you is a total commitment for me."

To implement decisions, there must be a commonalty of interests—a win-win climate. Such a climate cannot exist in the short-and-long-run forever. It is normal that at any point in time people can believe that there is a win-lose situation for that point in time.

To overcome this win-lose hurdle, there must be a vision of win-win in the long run. If people are going to remain committed to the organization in the long run, they must sense the organization's long-term commitment to them. People must have a vision of the organization where the short-term win-lose aspects will be eventually compensated by a win-win situation. They must know that there will be a reward later on for the sacrifices they make now.

The long-run horizon is not just a long-run forecast of events. It means a long-run common goal and long-run common interests through a common vision. How is the long-run vision and common interest going to be translated into the short run so as to make common interests workable in the present, when it is needed? The transformation vehicle is called *mutual trust*. It occurs when we trust that a person who has different interests from ours in the short run, will pay us back in the long run.

In traditional societies there is an extensive exchange of presents. In Japan, it is a social ritual. It is true for animals too. Professor Amotz Zahavi, a world famous zoologist, pointed out the following finding to me. He did extensive research of a certain flock of birds in the Negev desert. These birds are unique because they are very cooperative. How they do it, he said, is by doing things for each other as if to say, "I give to you because I trust that you will eventually give to me later."

We stop inviting people to our house for dinner, if after many parties at our table, they never reciprocate with anything. They are the takers, and we shy away from them.

There is no giving without taking in return. For that to happen, there must be mutual trust, because there is a time lapse between the episodes, and the implicit value of what is being exchanged is difficult to assess. One has to trust that somehow in the long run, it all washes out.

People who have no trust in other people neither give nor take. They do not take because they are afraid that they will have to reciprocate. They do not want to owe anybody anything. So they are alone and stay alone. These people should not manage, and they probably make bad spouses and parents as well.

How and when does mutual trust occur? In the Greek language, the word *friend* and the word *love* are the same—filos.

That made me think. When you love someone, if that person hurts, you also hurt. If anything bad happens to my children, I am in terrible pain also. It is a Sephardic custom that if anything painful happens to the one you love—child, spouse, parents—you will say "yo para ti" which literally means: "I wish I was in your place." It is less painful to be hurt directly than to empathize with the pain caused to someone you love.

"Love is that when I am with you, I feel best about myself," said Larry Wilson. Why does that make sense? Because love means interdependency, physical, emotional, psychological. If you hurt, I hurt. The more I love you, the more I feel as if we are one. Since we are one, when I feel that you are great, I feel I am great too. Love is not feeling miserable. . . . To love someone means to be integrated to the point that whatever happens to that person feels as if it has happened to you.

In Hebrew, the word friend comes from the word to be connected, as in being one (HVR). Thus, it makes sense that friend and love will be the same word, because whatever happens to your friend is as if it happened to you. It is as if you are organically connected.

Mutual trust happens when people are friends. Then, when one hurts, the other will also. You can trust a true friend, because he can't afford to hurt you. Hurting you will hurt him, because you are connected, you love each other. You can trust a friend because it is in his self-interest not to hurt your interests. You will never consider a person to be your friend if you can't turn your back to that person.

A team of colleagues who are also friends, is necessary for good management of any system, whether it is a corporation, a family, or a society. They can disagree on everything, except on one subject—they must share the same self-interests or have a vision of win-win and trust each other to share it. A perfect spouse then, is someone who is a colleague and a friend. This person disagrees with you in a helpful way, and there is no thought in your mind that the disagreement stems from a hidden self-interest that your spouse is promoting at your expense. Japan is successful because their management system is based on a culture of mutual respect and trust. In their culture, they respectfully listen to each other's disagreements. To offend someone is a serious matter and to lose face can lead to suicide. A system of life long employment fosters a commonalty of interests and long-term commitment to each other, which is based on mutual trust.

This subject of mutual trust and respect can be analyzed through an analogy of body language. When we respect someone, we turn our face to them and listen and disagree respectfully. Once a decision is made and we proceed to implementation if we trust the other person we turn our back—we know the person will implement the decision in our interest because it is in their self interest too. The disagreement is during decision making, not during implementation.

In many situations, the noise and the silence are upside down. People who do *not* disagree in order not to show disrespect nod their heads supportively and *act* like friends, but behind the scenes they disagree by promoting their own self-interests against each other.

A friend is not necessarily one who agrees with you. A friend is someone who shares your self-interest.

The essence then, of a healthy organizational culture is one where learning is nurtured and people truly care for each other. Conflict, as exhibited in disagreements, is accepted as long as exclusive self-interest does not propel people to destructive behavior and sub-optimalization. The disagreement is in how the common interest is interpreted.

For mutual respect, we need a learning environment with colleagues who know how to disagree without being disagreeable. For mutual trust, we need a climate of common interests that stem from interdependent self-interests. That is called love (not passion), like the love of a mother for her child. Friends love each other, care for each other's interests or they are not friends—they are acquaintances.

To manage well, we need a climate of mutual trust and respect. We need to surround ourselves with friends who are colleagues, people we love and learn from.[3]

Let us look now at the Lifecycle of organizations and how commonalty of common interests, or the lack of it, impacts behavior.

In Courtship, the long-run commonalty of interests is being built in; the organization is building its vision. A trust me climate is being created. If the founder does not succeed in creating a climate of trust, the restaurant chain for ham and eggs will never be. As a matter of fact, founders do not command such respect because their ideas are not proven yet. The only thing that will enable the birth of an organization is trust, a trust that the founder will deliver something that in the future will benefit whoever joins the endeavor in the present.

For organizational birth to occur the trust must be tested by

---

[3] This is spooky though. Tom Monihan, CEO of Domino's Pizza, owner of the Detroit Tigers and a Certified Integrator of the Adizes Methodology, pointed this out to me. There were studies done by serious researchers of people who were revived from clinical death. As we know, people who go through serious trauma often experience some change in lifestyles and their outlook about life. People who have experienced such a clinical death were asked if they developed a new outlook, a message on how to look at life. Although they never met or discussed their outlooks, they all essentially said the same thing: love and learn.

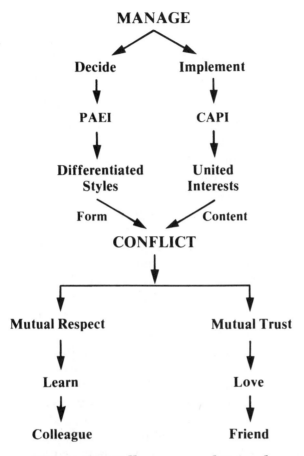

Figure 33: Colleagues and Friends

a commitment to undertake risk. Money is put on the table, people dedicate part of their lives to do the job and spend sleepless nights thinking about what to do with the organization.

In Infancy there is a commonalty of interests that is called survival, so there are no problems of implementation. Everyone does what needs to be done because of what Mary Parker Follet called "the law of the situation." The reasoning behind decisions is obvious and dictated by the situation; it is not an ego trip of a single individual.

In Go-Go, the ego, not the situation, drives the organization. Still there are no problems of implementation because there is no argument with success; there is infatuation with leadership and trust in a person and his genius. Trust in the leader is at its zenith here. Everyone who has a piece of the action is doing very well, so they let the founder do whatever he wishes; they trust him fully although the situation is pregnant and they feel it and are worried whether the boom can and will continue forever. They worry, but do not lift their heads or open their souls in public. Then the big bang occurs when the problems of advanced Go-Go creep in, and mutual trust goes to hell.

The disparity of interests that started at Infancy, which was bridged first by the dictation of the situation, and then by the success of Go-Go, begins to surface during Adolescence. The fact that the big bang is a major business misfortune, accentuates the disparity in interests which is located first in the authority structure, among the management whose task it is to overcome the problems. The (E) type wants to go back to what made the organization successful; he wants to do *more* of what he has done before, which to an (A) looks like throwing good money after bad money. The (A) type wants to put a lid on this runaway train—to control and conserve what was built. He wants to do less.

Another disparity of interests is between the organization and the founder. The founder who made more money than he ever dreamed possible, wants more free time, more of the amenities that go with success, and ego gratification through community involvement. But the organization wants a more stable, not a more remote leadership. The professionals want to stop the seat of the pants actions of the founder; it offends their sense of professional integrity or self-interest to preserve and sustain what they are trying to build. In Adolescence it is normal for a breakdown to occur between authority and influence. In pathological cases, the breakdown will ultimately cause the founding partners to split.

The organization's diminishing results make the long-term vision hollow. The vision created during Courtship has run its course by the time the company reaches Adolescence, and a new vision must be created. As the long-term interests lose their appeal, the short-term interests reign. It is a time of power games, and questions of who will buy out whom.

If this pathology occurs, the organization never reaches Prime. It will only proceed to Prime, if during Adolescence a new vision, a new long term win-win situation is created, and the trust is transferred from an individual into the system. This requires a coalescence of interests based on *self*-reliance. The vision cannot be the exclusive domain of a leader; the organization must share the vision of its future by planning for it. There must be mutual trust through self-trust.

Mutual trust and self-trust exist all the way into Aristocracy, where mutual trusts declines, which causes a decline in self-trust later, during Early Bureaucracy.

During Early Bureaucracy, the breakdown in interests is between power (labor) and an integrated authority influence (management and the professional staff). It is the top level that wants to cut out the bottom level. It is normal for the bottom level to fight for its survival. In extreme cases, the breakdown in interest goes even further. Management wants to fire the professional staff or they try to undermine management, and the witch hunt is on. There are different degrees of mistrust, and everyone is watching his back.

In Bureaucracy, there is a commonalty of interests again—survival. The organization is like a new infant, but one born with a whole set of silver spoons in his mouth. The prevailing rule is that as long as you do not publicly cry or soil your clothing; as long as you are not a *political* liability; you are secure. The level of trust or mistrust depends on political realities and not on what happens with the clients.

APPENDIX TO CHAPTER 7

Social Cultures and Economic Performance

For an organization to be well-managed and constructive, conflict must be harnessed. The sources of conflict are style differentiation (**PAEI**), and the disparity of interests *CAPI*. Mutual respect functionalizes conflict that stems from style differentiation, while mutual trust functionalizes conflict that stems from the disparity of interests.

Good management is necessary for economic performance, and a culture of mutual trust and respect is necessary for an organization to be well-managed. Thus, countries like Japan, Germany and Switzerland have excellent economic performance and excellent management without vast physical resources and without claiming leadership in business education. What they have is a *culture* of mutual respect and trust.

Shumpeter received world acclaim for his theories on economic growth. One of the cornerstones of his theory is the importance of entrepreneurial spirit for economic growth. A professional experience made me question Shumpeter's findings. During one week I lectured to CEOs of Israel, Greece and Germany. As I was lecturing the theory presented in this book, I had an illumination. If there are countries with an abundance of entrepreneurial spirit they would be Israel and Greece. The Jews and the Greeks have been wheeling and dealing for 2000 years. Germany, on the other hand, is known more for its (**A**) culture. How about Japan? They are not known for individual entrepreneurship, are they? They are known for their (**I**).

Which country has better economic performance? The entrepreneurial culture like Greece and Israel (discounting problems of security), or Germany and Japan? It occurred to me that Shumpeter discovered the importance of (**E**)ntrepreneurship because he was raised, educated and did his research in Austria, which is a German culture with an (**A**)dministration orientation, and where the complementarity of (**E**) is critically needed. What makes Germany, Japan and Switzerland successful is a culture of mutual trust and respect. In Switzerland if a person from a German canton travels to an Italian or French canton, he speaks Italian or French. They do not try to dominate, overpower or govern each other.

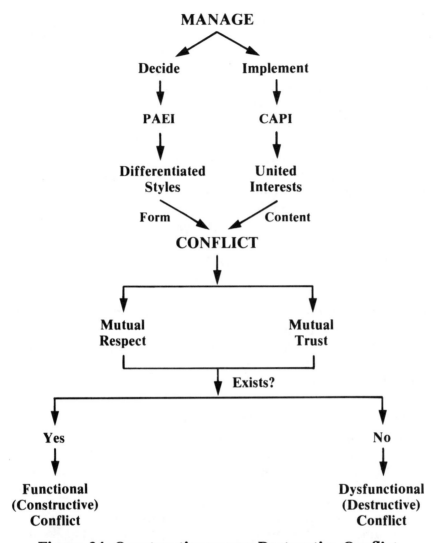

Figure 34: Constructive versus Destructive Conflict

What made the United States the biggest, richest, most successful nation in the world was not just size and economic resources.
Latin America has them also. Brazil alone is the size of the continen-
tal United States. The state of Sao Paulo is bigger than all of France.
In terms of physical resources Brazil, is not lacking. What made
the United States *AMERICA*, as a concept, as a brand name for
success, is a philosophy of mutual trust and respect. It is a melting

pot with predetermined rules of the game, which in essence are supposed to be mutual trust and respect required by law. Employment is supposed to be without bias of creed, color or race, and the sky is the limit. And, when the rules of democracy are broken, no one is exempt from the consequences. Look, for example at Watergate, a case in which the president was forced to resign.

The secret of success is not entrepreneurial spirit alone, but a culture of mutual trust and respect in which the entrepreneurial spirit can be planted and allowed to succeed. What makes for growth is not only the quailty of the seed, but also the quality of the soil in which the seeds can grow.

Israel and Greece could succeed more, if they would nurture a culture of mutual trust and respect. Look at Singapore. It is a small island, with no resources to speak of, multiple races, ethnic groups, religions, traditions, and languages. It has the potential of being an incredible trouble spot. Ruled with an iron hand, rules of respect and trust for each other have been established. The determined leadership of Prime Minister Lee Kuan Yew has developed a culture that made Singapore different from the rest of Asia, although the same problems were inherent in Singapore as in the rest of Asia. The following excerpt is from the *New Straits Times*, August 19, 1987.

KUAN YEW LAYS DOWN GROUND RULES

SINGAPORE, Tues.—Singapore's Prime Minister Lee Kuan Yew laid down the ground rules for the country's 2.6 million people—no communalism, communism, or religious extremism.

To Mr. Lee, who has ruled this country for the last 28 years, it is possible for the people to have a distinctive culture where all the races come into one mainstream but this may take a long time shaped by many generations of common historical experience.

Speaking about Singapore's special difficulties in nation building, the Prime Minister spoke for more than two hours on Sunday of the dangers of using race, language and religion to rally the people.

On Singapore's vulnerability as a nation, Mr. Lee who will be 64 next month quoted an American scholar who said "geography, history, language and culture have all conspired against the countries of Asia to make their task of nation building and economic development more difficult."

The scholar in his book also said the future was fraught with risks for every State in the region . . . outside forces might also set off internal chain-reactions within individual countries that could topple the Governments and wipe out the gains of past decades.

Mr. Lee said Singapore prefers to leave as little chance as possible to the dangers that might lead to the nation's breakdown and will continue to curb dangerous speakers exploiting race, language and religion.

Let us look at Sweden. One of the natural resources of that country has always been a culture of mutual trust and respect. The Swedish people go through endless pain to avoid confrontations, conflicts, and shows of mistrust and disrespect. It is one of the few countries where people trust and respect their government and the government trusts and respects the people. Sweden has not known labor unrest for hundreds of years. However, a welfare society has developed, which requires more revenues, and so more taxation. Some Swedes are joining the rest of the world and starting to learn how to avoid taxes. The seeds of mistrust and disrespect have been planted. In my lectures in Sweden I have told members of the Swedish government and parliament that any legislation that undermines their culture of mutual trust and respect is equivalent to a legislation that ruins their natural wealth and resources. A culture is an important factor for economic success, sometimes even more important than physical resources. That is what is making Japan the empire it is today. They have little resources to speak of. However, they have a culture of trust and respect that enables group creativity and long term interest projection that unite self interests of the short run.

Let us now look at Yugoslavia, a country whose management system I have studied in some depth.[4]

The self-management system has been repetitively criticized because it was evaluated in economic terms. I made the same mis-

---

[4] Adizes, I., *Industrial Democracy, Yugoslav Style*. First Printing New York Free Press, 290 pp., (1971) All subsequent printings, Adizes Institute, Santa Monica, CA.

Adizes, I., and Mann-Borgese, E. (ed.), *Self Management: New Dimensions to Democracy*, First Printing ABC/CLIO and The Center For The Study Of Democratic Institutions: Santa Barbara, California, 162 pp., 1975. All subsequent printings: The Adizes Institute, Santa Monica, CA.

take in my own books. Now I understand it differently. The Yugoslav self-management system should be evaluated in social terms; it succeeded in *debalkanizing* the Balkan.

Yugoslavia succeeded in creating a culture, which at least temporarily, overcame some of the disrespect and mistrust between the different nationalities there. I emphasize "some" in the above statement because it is far from being Japan or Switzerland in terms of acquiring mutual respect and trust. However, it has managed to move from a zero to, let us say a four on the trust and respect scale, which although an infinite improvement, is not enough for economic success. What is the alternative? Zero? A civil war! The system in Yugoslavia should be evaluated, not by what it has achieved, but by what it has prevented.

It appears that social cultures explain political movements and economic performance. For instance, I think that the reason developing countries are attracted to communism is that it *promises* mutual trust and respect. "Workers and peasants unite against exploitation and against injustice." Look at the flag—a hammer and sickle united. Listen to the slogans—"proletars of the world unite." They promise unity and equality. Communism *promises* law, order and rules of conduct that are simple to understand and apply. The promised results—trust and respect—look exciting. Totalitarianism promises efficiency.

What does democracy offer? Conflict and instability. In free markets, the qualified will make it, those who cannot, will be left behind. Does it *sound* like mutual respect and trust? It sounds more like disrespect and mistrust to me. It promises inefficiency in the short run, does it not? If there is effectiveness, it is promised in the long run through some hidden hand. It should not be strange then that short-term efficiency seems more attractive to developing countries than long-term effectiveness, relying on some inefficient hidden hand.

The problem, which should be clear by now, is that short-term efficiency produces long-term ineffectiveness, while short-term inefficiency produces long-term effectiveness. Bureaucratization of totalitarian regimes produces mistrust and disrespect (as is evidenced by Auschwitz and Siberia). What is promised is not delivered; it is just the opposite. By the time this becomes evident, the totalitarian system is a trap that even its leaders have difficulty escaping, see the case of Nikita Khrushchev. The inefficient democracy produces respect and trust because in the long run, the sky is the limit. Anyone can at least believe he has equal chance to make it. Without mutual trust and respect, a democracy could not operate. The democracy must protect trust and respect, if it is to survive.

From the previous tools of analysis provided, it should be clear that conflict is inevitable and desirable for good management. Management is a necessary and inevitable process, although the Yugoslavs in their self-management system tried to practically outlaw it, and the Israeli kibbutz movement tried to abolish its tenets through a rotation system. Management is there, and it must be there, because if there is a constant, it is change, which is accelerating. And someone must lead the process of proactive or reactive adaptation. That is called the managerial process. It necessarily means conflict, because in making a decision on what to do, styles clash; and in trying to implement change, interests clash. This conflict is inevitable, and it must be managed and functionalized.

Karl Marx tried to negate conflict as though it was a pathological development, an outcome of a bourgeois society where there is conflict of interests between the classes. His prescription was *the elimination* of conflict, through a system that unites the interests of a classless society. That could work for acquiring *CAPI*, but, even that is a maybe, because monopolization of *CAPI* negates conflict of interests on the books, while Milovan Djilas noted, new classes, other than those that Marx knew, develop in reality.[5]

But negation of conflict by creation of a unity of interests in a classless society is only *half* the equation. It deals only with *CAPI*. It deals only with the implementation of decisions. What about the making of decisions? To negate conflict, the communists also negate differentiation of opinion. Negation of political parties generates decisions that are not well-discussed and end up being disasters.

The end result of negating conflict is the negation of change. Communism is analogous to the example about standing still with your hands clasped in front of you. There is strength when there is no conflict and no friction. But, there is little movement to adapt or proact to change.

Mikhail Gorbachev is attempting to unfreeze the Soviet system

---

[5] Djilas, Milovan. *The New Class: An Analysis of the Communist System*, San Diego: Harcourt Brace Jovanovich, 1983.

by legitimatizing Glasnost, which means allowing openness in discussion. It means liberalizing and legitimizing different opinions. He cannot stop with just unfreezing (**paei**); if he wants a better-managed economy, he will have to unfreeze *CAPI* as well, and legitimize the differentiation of interests. That, I believe, he will not be able to do. The USSR is a powder keg of nationalistic interests. Freedom of speech will be followed by requests for freedom of action to reflect differentiated interests. At that point, Gorbachev will have to rescind Glasnot, or he will be rescinded himself by the bureaucrats that infest the Russian bureaucrat system. (Written Nov. 1, 1987.)

Democracy is the legitimate differentiation of political judgements (**paei**). Capitalism is the legitimate differentiation of self-interests (*CAPI*). Democracy and capitalism legitimize conflict and thus movement and change.

Communism, which seems so attractive because there is a promise of efficiency stymies change, which in the long-run means economic, social, and cultural atrophy. Capitalism seems unattractive—it promises conflict, differentiation of opinions, uncertainty and unequal distribution of wealth because the different interest groups are allowed to promote their self-interests. Nevertheless, the conflict also produces change. It produces growth and thus equal opportunity for all to have more. Communism promises equality which, through lack of change and thus growth, produces privileged classes who by definition have more at the expense of those who have to have less, i.e. an unequal opportunity to share. As Winston Churchill said: "Capitalism is an unequal distribution of wealth. Communism is the equal distribution of poverty."

The democratic system, however, has the seeds of self-destruction in it, as is evident when the system promotes freedom of those who negate respect and trust, and thus negate the democratic system in which they were born. It happened in Germany, when the Nazis ascended to power legally. Furthermore, for democracy to occur mutual trust and respect must be part of the political culture. That means (**paei**) = *CAPI*. What will endanger democracy is the growth of (**a**), big government, technocracy. As the society slips down from Prime it suffers economically, inflation or the trade deficit become troublesome, the time span for solutions will shorten and a big (**p**) will be asked to lead and solve the problems that can and will endanger democracy.

Communist countries are another threat to democracy.

Totalitarianism must expand geographically to import energy since it is an inefficient system in the long run. A political joke I heard in Eastern Europe makes this point.

Question: "What is the largest cow in the world?

Answer: "A Bulgarian cow! It feeds in Bulgaria and is milked in Russia!"

By disallowing freedom of speech, decisions that can produce disastrous change are made, and importing of energy is necessary to cover for it.

Can democracy work for developing countries? Democracy is *not* functional until after Adolescence. It works only after a system of mutual trust and respect is established. Prior to Adolescence there is no such culture. The culture is too dependent on a *leader*, on a person. For a democracy to succeed, a working constitution and a working educational system that imprints mutual trust and respect is necessary. That is why dictatorships abound in developing countries.

How can the United States help make those countries make the transition from dictatorship to democracy? Not by throwing aid at those countries or by sending military advisers there either.

It is 1) by not supporting any regime that is exploitative, unfair to its people, and that nourishes disrespect and mistrust. Aiding in the removal of Ferdinand Marcos from the Philippines was a step in the right direction. 2) By refusing to provide wheat, machinery, or any other commodity to a totalitarian regime. Those regimes will crumble from the sheer weight of being ineffective. We must contain and refuse to feed their ineffectiveness regardless of how profitable it is to us in the short run. 3) By instituting an educational program that correctly markets the effectiveness of democratic ideology, understanding that socio-political efficiency is an antidote to socio-economic effectiveness.

Part III

USING THE TOOLS TO PREDICT BEHAVIOR

Introduction to Part III

To manage effectively means to make the right decisions and implement them. Thus, quality of the managerial process is a function of the quality of decisions made and the efficiency of implementation.

In Prime, an organization makes good decisions and implements them well. It makes the right decisions to change and implements that change. The organization is both flexible and predictable.

But how does one become a Prime organization?

This Lifecycle phenomena occurs as the capabilities to make and implement decisions increase, as **paei** roles are learned and institutionalized and as interests that the organization serves become integrated and coalesced.

There is a deterministic sequence how the **(paei)** roles develop. There is a deterministic sequence how *CAPI* gets coalesced. There is also a deterministic sequence how and why an organization gets out of Prime and ages.

How **(paei)** develops is the topic for Chapter 8. How *CAPI* gets coalesced is discussed in Chapter 9 and why and how an organization ages in Chapter 10.

Once we understand how and why the organization behaves along its Lifecycle as discussed in Part III, we will cover what to do about it in Part IV of this book.

8

Predicting Corporate Cultures ════════

In Part I of this book, each stage of the Organizational Lifecycle was described. Are there reasons for the progression of an organization from one stage of the Lifecycle to another? Using the tools described in Part II, this chapter will discuss why corporate cultures develop as they do.

If we superimpose the (PAEI) roles on the Organizational Lifecycle, we can understand what happens at each stage.

COURTSHIP (paEi)

During Courtship, a commitment that will ultimately give birth to an operating organization is created; that is, a need is identified and commitment must be built to respond to that need. Thus, (E)ntrepreneuring is the most important role. It provides for the proactive behavior, it identifies the future needs in the present, and it generates the willingness to undertake the risk in satisfying the need. This is done by building a commitment which is manifested by excitement, or *falling in love* with an idea.

An organization is born when the commitment is tested. Organizations die when there is no commitment to its functionality—when we don't know *why* we are doing whatever we are doing. The vitality

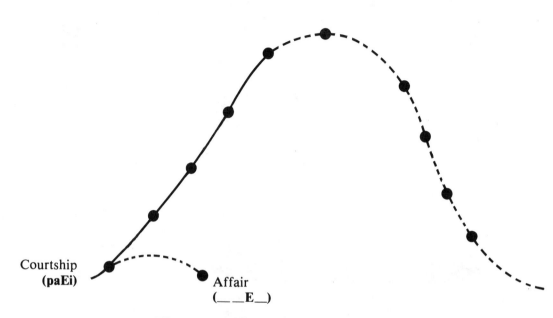

Courtship
(paEi)

Affair
(_ _E_)

Figure 35: The Culture of Courtship

of an organization can be measured by how many people are committed to the organization and its functionality.

Since all four **PAEI** roles are necessary for an organization to be in Prime, there must be ingredients of each at conception.

The **(P)**erforming **(A)**dministering and **(I)**ntegrating roles provide reality-testing for the **(E)**ntrepreneuring role during Courtship. The difference between normal and pathological Courtship is the presence or lack of the other three roles. A normal Courtship is **(paEi)**; a pathological Courtship is **(--E-)**, where the **(P)(A)** and **(I)** are missing. The organization does not experience any reality-testing of the commitment. Reality-testing considers *what* we are going to do—(P)—*how* we are going to do it—**(A)**—and *who* is going to do it *how and with whom*—**(I).**

When there is no reality-testing during Courtship, that is an affair; when the real test occurs, the Courtship will dissolve. The commitment will not pass the test. All four roles must exist, at least latently, in Courtship.

The reason **(P)**erforming **(A)**dministering and **(i)**ntegrating provide reality-testing of **(E)**ntrepreneuring, is that **(P)**erforming, **(A)**dministering, **(I)**ntegrating are incompatible with **(E)**ntrepreneuring. So **(E)**ntrepreneuring is challenged by *small* doses of **(P), (A)** and

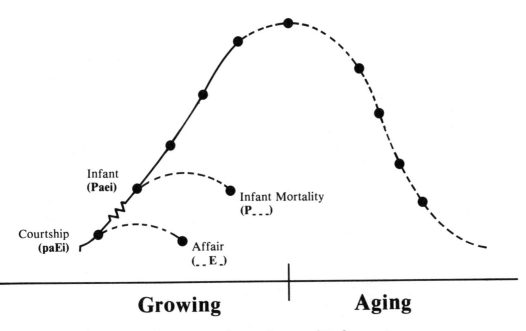

Figure 36: The Culture of Infancy

(I). If **(E)**ntrepreneuring was not challenged during Courtship, when the organization is eventually confronted with big **(P)**erformance demands in Infancy, it might dissolve. The needed commitment is not really there.

In simpler terms, the transition from romantic dreaming to actual doing is not an easy one. When an organization is conceived, we must *simulate* the reality which will confront the organization in the immediate future and throughout the Lifecycle. We must determine whether the organization will survive the simulation before the actual reality occurs. It is as if the seeds of future subsystems must exist at conception; as if the necessary ingredients of the future must be available from the start.

INFANCY (Paei)

The organization is born when the commitment is realistically tested and risk is undertaken. The most important role then becomes **(P)**erforming. **(A)**dministering and **(I)**ntegrating remain secondary as they were during Courtship. However, the increase in (P)erfoming decreases (E)ntrepreneuring. Why?

What propels the founder is his commitment to the organization: the crying need he believes he was destined to fulfill. So, when the organization is finally opened for business, the founder plunges in with gusto. It is a *do-do-do* time. That explains why the (P) role increases; but why must the (E) role decrease? Because there is interdependency between (E)ntrepreneuring and (P)erforming. If (P) is *what*, and (E) is *what for*, then (E) is the *long-run* objective of (P). When the short-run *what to do*—(P)—is released, the long-run *what for*—(E)—must take a back seat. (When short-run attention is incompatible with the long run, the short-run must win, because without it, "in the long-run, we are all dead," to quote M. Kaynes.)

The organization must perform the function for which it was established. If the organization does not deliver what it promises, it will quickly die. Furthermore, the risk the organization undertakes during Infancy must be covered by action and by hard work that delivers the commitment for which the risk was undertaken.

(P) is the functional orientation. This functional orientation exists with all infant systems, including humans. During the first months of life, a baby is totally focused on functional needs—eating, sleeping and being warm and dry. It is the same with an organization. The focus is on (P). It must have cash—liquidity—in order to survive. It is normal in Infant organizations that there is no time to think, no time to dream and no time to feel. It is all do-do-do. For example, it's normal that after a revolution the theoreticians of the pre-revolutionary era get locked up or executed; since the revolution has succeeded, it is a time to do and not a time to talk.

Those who dream and talk hinder those who take action. The Old Testament tells us that Moses died across the Jordan River as the dream of entering Canaan was going to be realized—a dream to which he had dedicated his life. He transferred the powers of ruling to Joshua, a doer, who could implement and act, rather than prophesy.

In an Infant organization, (A)dministering, (E)ntrepreneuring and (I)ntegration are low. The (P)erforming role is dominant, which is normal. It would be normal for an Infant organization to be managed by a person who behaves like a Lone Ranger, who does

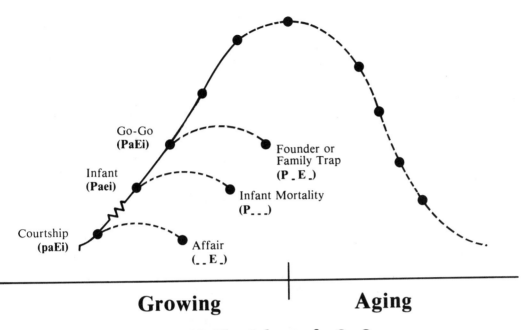

Growing | **Aging**

Figure 37: The Culture of a Go-Go

not delegate and works like a one-person orchestra. That's what the Infant organization requires. It's analogous to a mother who must feed, rock and change her baby all the time. It would be inappropriate for that mother to behave differently and try to teach the baby to play the piano, because what the baby really needs is to have its functional needs satisfied first. That is what the founder must do for the organization at this stage of the Lifecycle.

GO-GO (PaEi)

When the (**P**)erforming role arrives at the threshold of stabilization—suppliers are repetitive and stable and cash flow is secured because clients have started to repeat their orders—(**P**) is fully developed. This allows (**E**)ntrepreneuring to increase. Why? In Courtship, (**E**)ntrepreneuring was high and a vision was created. It decreased during Infancy because the vision was being tested. All energy went to deliver the first of that vision. (**P**)erforming had to be high. When the test is over, the energy is freed and is directed back to the vision, which propels the organization with full force again: (E)ntre-preneuring goes back up.

This sequence is important to note. During Courtship, (E) is up first. Then in Infancy, (P)erforming goes up and (E)ntrepreneuring goes down. During Go-Go, both must be stabilized together before the third role is allowed to grow. (P) and (E) means that both the *what* and the *what for* are being stabilized before the *how* role can be developed.

A pathological Infancy occurs if the (E)ntrepreneuring role cannot develop, if the organization remains in a perpetual (P)erforming orientation. The organization will be like an infant that never emerged from its functional orientation. It is preoccupied with food, sleep and wetness even though many years have passed. Obviously, this is a person who needs extra treatment because he is not growing normally.

It is the same for an organization with a negative cash flow, an unstable client base, that is continuously fighting for survival although many years have passed. Eventually it will die because the energy required for development is higher than the energy necessary for maintenance. Providing a continuous import of energy to maintain this organization might be prohibitive.

The Go-Go stage occurs when (P)erforming and (E)ntrepreneuring are at high levels. These high levels of (P) and (E) which are present during the Go-Go stage explain the behavior of the organization. A Go-Go is *what-* and *why-* oriented; it is results-oriented for the short- and long-run. There is a dream, as there is in Courtship, but the organization is trying to realize it instantly, as it did in Infancy. That's why the transition from Infancy to Go-Go is a transition from *management by crisis* to *crisis by management*.

A Go-Go company expands rapidly in many different directions, usually intuitively and in a highly flexible manner. It might over-commit itself in a very short time. It might run out of cash, not because the situation calls for it, but because the management over-commits the organization. The organization has little control. The difference between the budgets and actuals is high. Policies, if there are any, are violated, and the power is highly concentrated around the founder.

In Go-Go, the (A)dministrative role is low. It is still undeveloped, which explains the lack of systemization, the lack of order, the lack of an organization chart and the lack of clear definition of tasks and specialization. The organization is structured around *people* rather than around the *tasks* to be performed. In the Go-Go stage, the organization is adapted to the people rather than the people adapting to the organization's needs.

Pathological Go-Go occurs when the next role, the (A) cannot develop. (A) must develop next, since the short-range *how*, must be developed before the long-range *how*—the (I)ntegrating role—can develop. The need for (A) is less expressed if (I) is derived from the social culture in which the organization exists. That explains why Far East entrepreneurial families can build huge trading companies with little (A). They have abundant (I).

The development of (A)dministering is triggered by a crisis that management produced in its Go-Go behavior. The organization requires some stabilization, some order, some priority setting. This does not mean deciding what *else* to do. It means deciding what *not* to do which means focusing on *how* to do it. The organization turns its focus away from the *what* and *when* and onto the *how*. If this is not allowed to happen or if (I)ntegration does not exist because the family ties are not strong, the organization falls into the Found-

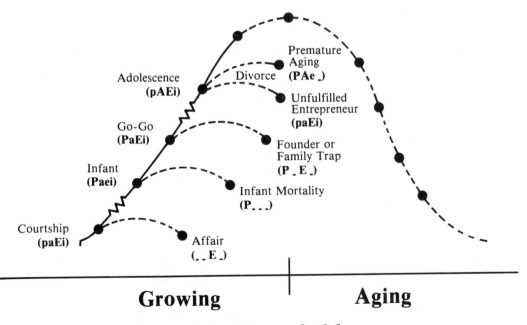

Figure 38: The Culture of Adolescence

er's or the Family Trap which is the pathological development of a Go-Go.

The trap stems from lack of institutionalization of the *what* and *why*—from the lack of (**A**)dministering or (**I**)ntegration of the (**P**)erforming and (**E**)ntrepreneuring functions. Without the (**A**) role, the organization does not function as a system. It is too personalized around someone who makes the decisions as he sees fit, rather than allowing a system to narrow down the choices. The organization is too dependent on the person leading it, causing the (**E**) role to become monopolized; the same principle holds for the (**I**) role. Strong social values serve as a substitute for the mechanistic rational (**A**) rules.

Institutionalization of (**P**)erforming and (**E**)ntrepreneuring allows decentralization of those functions without loss of control. This is a necessary factor for moving into Prime. There must be rules and policies, (**A**), or sound values, (**I**), that even the founder must be subject to. As the result of such a constitution, the organization as a system is born independently of the founder who established it.

ADOLESCENCE (pAEi)

What prompts movement from the Go-Go to the Adolescent stage is a crisis that requires paying attention to the (**A**)dministering role. The emergence of (**A**) comes with pain because it's a significant transition from *what* and *why*, which are quantity-oriented, to *how*, which is quality-oriented. It is a switch from "more is better" to "better is more" is a switch from an external to an internal focus. The organization reduces its attention on external client needs and begins giving priority to its own needs. This is what apparently happens with our adolescent children too.

The emergence of (**A**)dministering as a significant function has to come at the expense of either (**P**)erforming or (**E**)ntrepreneuring which are already developed. The new role requires "energy" for its development but has to be taken from somewhere. If it comes at the expense of (**E**)ntrepreneuring, it is pathological. If it comes at the expense of (**P**)erforming, it is a normal progression. Let us explain this in more detail. (See the summary about my doubts on this subject.)

First, we must realize that the development of (A)dministering cannot be without a sacrifice. It cannot develop without impacting (P)erforming and (E)ntrepreneuring. The reason this seems to be true is that the switch from function to form, when function is (P) and (E), and form is (A), is so distinct that there must be an impact. It seems as if an organization has fixed energy for its growth and if a new demand emerges, something must be shut off temporarily. Let's see it from the conception.

At the beginning, all energy goes to (E)ntrepreneuring. Once that role is accomplished, by successful (PAE) testing, only threshold energy is dedicated to (E) and the remaining energy goes to (P)erforming. Once (P) is stabilized, the next step is to dedicate the energy to stabilize the (P) and (E) roles together. With this accomplished, the energy can afford to maintain two roles. It is as if in the beginning, the system learns how to deal with one role at a time, then, when it learns how to deal with two developed roles, it takes on the higher challenge of it handling two roles, one of which is a new one. The new role is (A)dministering which is a form rather than a function, and function must give in to the rise of form. The question is which component of function—(P)erforming or (E)ntrepreneuring—will give in to the rise of (A).

(A)dministering is a short-term function, and thus its obvious substitute is (P)erforming which is also short-term. It is an easier transformation than developing a short-term role at the expense of a long-term role like (E)ntrepreneuring. But (E) could be a more attractive candidate. (E) could decrease when (A) increases, because the rise of (A)dministering was triggered by too much (E)ntrepreneuring to start with. It was a crisis that gave impetus to (A), and in crisis, it is normal that the organization will seek to protect (P). Furthermore, there is a tendency to sacrifice (E), because the long-term costs are not as high as the short-term costs of reducing (P). Thus, it is to be expected that the rise in (A) could decrease (E). The question is *should* it, not *would* it.

Sacrificing (E)ntrepreneuring makes the organization totally short-term oriented—(PA)—and will prohibit it from moving into Prime. It is therefore an undesired development.

It seems as if Adolescence is a testing time. Adolescence is where the screening is done; it separates those organizations which will advance and flourish from those which will flounder. It separates those organizations that have self-discipline and those that don't. Prior to Adolescence, the progression is normal; (E) must come first, then (P) is up and (E) is down. Then both (PE) are up. The sequence is smooth, as if dictated by the dynamics of organizational growth. The founder just follows the cues; but, during Adolescence, he is given a choice. The organization is even tempted: Will management take over or be taken over by the organization? Does management lead or does it follow?

I have noted over the years that what makes a champion in any endeavor, whether it is the arts, sports, business or even crime, for that matter, is not just talent. One needs talent to do anything well, but talent alone can be wasted. It will not produce a lasting impact. To achieve excellence, one needs self-discipline to control urges and short-term temptations. The greater the talent, the greater is the need for self-discipline. And in the Jewish tradition, the saying is: "Who is a hero? The one who can conquer his urges."

Self-discipline without talent is barren; talent without self-discipline is a torrent of sparks that don't catch fire. For a controlled burning, one needs a controlled spark. In Adolescence, the need for organizational self-discipline emerges. Without self-discipline the urge will be to lose (E)ntrepreneuring. With self-discipline and control, the organization will sacrifice (P)erforming.

Up until Adolescence, only talent is needed to manage an Infant and Go-Go; talent to sense what the market wants. In Adolescence, discipline emerges. Will it match talent? If it does not, the organization will wander around. If the rise in discipline kills the talent, the switch has been too sudden and the organization will become stymied. The desire should be not to lose talent, but to consciously use self-discipline and sacrifice short-term results instead.

To lose (P) requires self-discipline. The organization must consciously decide to do less of one thing so that it can spend more time doing something else, although it might show less immediate results. It must spend less time out there selling, and more time in meetings, getting organized.

Self-discipline is required to allocate resources to do *fewer* things *better*, even though past behavior of investing in *more* rather than in *better* produced the desired results. This is a significant change in behavior that does *not* occur naturally as it did when the organization moved from Infancy to Go-Go. On the contrary, during Infancy and Go-Go, organizations become addicted to (P). Weaning them away from (P) is often difficult.

My experience is that the switch will occur more easily if (i)nte-grating is present. The higher the (i)ntegration, the easier it is for (a)dministering to emerge at the expense of (p)erforming rather than (e)ntrepreneuring. This is explained by the fact that (i) is the long-run *how* that aids the long-run (e). These roles support each other. Thus, the emergence of the short-run *how*, (a) can be more easily achieved at the expense of the short-run *what*, (p).

Where did the (i)ntegration function come from? It was latent, small, in Infancy and Go-Go, right? Yes and no. (i) comes from the macro-social culture within which the organizational culture develops. It is derived from the values of the people who comprise and lead the organization. Thus, the Japanese culture provides (i) to its organizations. The organization does not have to develop it. It means that for a Japanese company, it is easier to get to Prime than it will be for an Israeli or Greek company that must develop it in an intense (e)ntrepreneurial environment with little (i)ntegra-tion. The role of Adizes[sm] in providing cultural change is to move an organization from Go-Go to Adolescence (from entrepreneurial management to professional management); it is to develop the (a)d-ministrative system through (i)ntegration.

Why is decreasing (p) a normal development while at the same time losing (e) pathological? Losing (e) means losing (p) in the long-run. By losing the long-term orientation, the organization will eventually pay the price of losing short-term orientation too. When an organization consciously sacrifices short-term orientation with-out losing long-term orientation, it is a temporary sacrifice. Rather than sacrificing the long-term effect for expediency, which in the process, dries up future growth, management should slow growth down temporarily and dedicate its energy to becoming more effi-cient. Normal Adolescence is **(pAEi);** pathological is **(PAei).**

If the organization is allowed to progress on its own dynamics, if management does not manage—showing judgment through self-discipline—the loss of (e) will be the normal development. The reason is that the growth in (a)dministration will threaten (e)ntre-preneurship. (a) and (e) are opposite roles, and thus are in conflict. This conflict can take the following form: the founder might hire a chief financial officer or vice president of administration to put his company in order. The new person performs the administrative role. He may develop some hostility toward the founder who per-forms the entrepreneurial role, because it is (e) which continues to change direction, bringing new opportunities into the company. For an entrepreneur, every problem is an opportunity. But, for an administrator, every opportunity is a problem, since this person is focusing on *how* to do it, and on the repercussions of doing it. Thus, what appears to be an opportunity for (E) is usually a problem for (A).

Eventually, the administrative type starts to see the founder as the company's problem, because the founder does not allow the system to stabilize. At that point, an alliance might develop between the chief administrative officer and the board of directors, which also seeks (A)dministrative stability. This alliance is at the expense of the founder who is perceived as being uncontrollable. If the power structure enables this alliance to be fruitful, the founder might be squeezed out of his own company. If he is not fired, he might find the atmosphere so unpalatable with support and enthusiasm for his leadership gone, that he might decide to start all over again with a new company. That's basically what I believe happened to Apple Computer's founder Steve Jobs. It could have been predicted I believe because his partner Steve Wozniak, who was the creative engineer, had previously left the company. That was the early sign of an exodus of (E)s from the organization.

The struggle between (E)ntrepreneurship and (A)dministration roles becomes more acute if the organization is a partnership. The company is started by a complementary team, usually a (PE) and an (AI) type. The (PE), who took the risk and brought opportunities to the company, usually is the leading force at the advanced stages of Go-Go. However, in Adolescence, new opportunities being sought by (PE) become too expensive as (A) perceives them. So, (A) begins to resist the plans of the (PE) person in the partnership. It might take the form of (A) saying, "One more idea, and I'm going to break out in a rash," and (E) thinking, "Why did I get involved with an inactive, placid, non-risk taking partner? I built this company *in spite* of him, and now he is becoming a barrier for future growth."

By and large, the (A)dministrative type wins the struggle. This happens for several reasons. First, an entrepreneur believes that he can successfully put down roots elsewhere. Furthermore, (E) does not like the realities of running a highly-complex organization. He enjoys building an organization more than he enjoys running it. He hates details and the complexity accompanying details. (E)ntrepreneuring is incompatible with (A)dministrating. (E)ntrepreneurs prefer the wide-brush approach to solving problems but wide-brush solutions are not functional since the side effects of the solution can be more dangerous to the organization than the problem to which the solution was applied.

The founder starts dreaming of the good old days when the company was small, flexible, and responsive. Now it seems too big for him to handle, and he becomes positively predisposed to leaving the company, starting over, and having something small and exciting again. The (A)dministrative type has no place to go, and besides, he likes to manage a system. Thus, his tendency is to try and buy out the entrepreneur. The board of directors, or those in power, side with the (A)dministrative type. They realize the need for consistency and order, which is something an unpredictable (E)ntrepreneurship does not provide. So this alliance of (A) with the board dominates. The end result is that (E) gets squeezed out of the company.

This phenomenon does not happen with only the founder. As systems and controls are introduced, as "no" is heard more frequently than "yes," other entrepreneurial types in the company, besides the founder, start leaving. There is an exodus of (E)s and an influx of (A)s. I call this phenomenon premature aging. The company aged before it arrived at Prime.

The way to avoid this pathological phenomenon is to consciously reduce the (P)erformance role so that (E)ntrepreneurship will not be diminished. This means management has to decide to cool off for a period of time and devote its attention to (A)dministration. For example, management can spend a year defining the organization chart, determining its corporate mission (not only deciding what *else* it's going to do, but also deciding what it's *not* going to do), developing training programs, salary administration systems, and incentive systems. If this is done proactively, the reorganization can avoid the emergence of future problems such as lack of salary administration, lack of clarity in the organizational structure and hiring tomorrow, people who were needed yesterday. By making a conscious decision to reduce (P), a company does not have to lose (E).

Choosing the right timing for reduction of (P)erformance is crucial. The difficulty stems from the fact that in the Infancy and Go-Go stages, the organization becomes addicted to (P). In Infancy, if someone does not produce, he is fired. The company needs functional orientation if it is going to survive; so, whoever produces is promoted. In the Go-Go stage, the orientation is for growth, as measured in terms of sales and market share. Again, the orientation is for quantity, and those who produce are rewarded emotionally and financially.

In the Adolescent stage, when the organization turns inward and needs more systems and order, there must be a significant change in who is recognized and appreciated under the reward system. The switch from a sales orientation, to a numbers orientation is not an easy one. There is a struggle between those who are internally-oriented and those who are externally-oriented. This can become offensive, with people calling each other *bureaucrats* or *Lone Rangers.*

A timely move to Adolescence can be achieved if management consciously determines when the organization is doing well and chooses that period to turn inward and get organized, then the pressure on (P)erformance is not as great. This kind of conscious self-discipline is rare. Those who have it are the real winners. To pick the right timing is difficult because, when the times are good, few people think about proaction. Usually the administrative orientation emerges when the company is in trouble, when it loses a lot of money in the advanced stages of Go-Go. This is a crisis which prompts the movement to the Adolescent stage, and the pressure is to increase rather than decrease (P).

Let's look at the family as an analogy for an organization. The way to avoid the trouble of adolescence is not by introducing strict rules when the child becomes a teenager. That will only cause him to rebel. There will be a serious problem when a teenager moves from permissiveness in childhood to strict rules in adolescence which were introduced as a reaction to the child's show of independence. A climate should have been established in infancy and in childhood while the child was still small and growing having a strong family identity. The stronger the family identity, affinity, rituals, and sense of belonging, (I), the less the need will be to establish mechanistic rules, (A), when the child starts showing independence in the adolescent stage of growth.

Jim Miscole, executive vice president at Bank of America, told me that in his family, when his teenage sons went on a date, his wife would say, "Just remember who you are and whom you represent." More rules and controls are necessary for those who do not

have that kind of value system to support them. The higher the
(I)ntegration, the less (A)dministration will be needed. On the contrary, the more (A)dministration we use, the less (I)ntegration we
will have. Note that (I) will *not* emerge unless threshold (A) exists,
and (A) mushrooms if there is no (I).

A higher (I)ntegration element makes the child's transition
from dependency on family to independence as an individual, less
acute and painful.

Adolescence is a difficult stage because the curves of *better*
and *more* are crossing each other and the struggle between form
and function is significant. A story from my own adolescence can
bring this point home.

When I finished high school, I was sent with an Israeli high
school delegation to France. We took an overnight trip on a train
from Biaritz to Paris. We all tried to sleep in one compartment
which could accommodate at best eight people and there were 20
of us. It took almost two hours for each one of us to find a place
for our feet, arms and head, and it took some accommodation to
find the right sleeping position. Some of us were on the floor. Some
were sitting on others' laps. One head was behind somebody else's
shoulder. The sleeping arrangement was structured around people.

Just as we fell asleep, somebody announced he needed to go
to the bathroom. Incredible commotion. The only way he could
go was by upsetting the entire group. One had to move a leg, the
other had to move a hand, this one had to move his body, another
screamed, "Don't step on my toes."

When an organization is structured around people and not
around a task, frequently it's easier to wet your pants than to make
a commotion throughout the whole organization. Thus, in organizations structured around people, change can become very difficult.
There is a saying that you can recognize innovators in such an
organization by the arrows in their backs. To make a change requires
so many buy-ins, so many approvals and arrangements that the
innovator simply gives up before even starting. Eventually, not
only one person is wet but a lot of people are wet and the place
begins to smell bad.

The general culture of the company is not a problem of an
individual, but it's a problem of the system. In such a system, the
allocation of tasks and administration of the organization is made
on an ad hoc basis, built on expediency rather than on the task

and the needs of the organization. Function is all. Form is ignored until dysfunction reigns and it becomes dysfunctional like in the previous analogy because there is no supportive form.

Prior to Adolescence, function is everything. Form is not as important. (ɪ)ntegration and (ᴀ)dministration are at low levels, (ᴘ)erformance and (ᴇ)ntrepreneurship are high. The organization is structured around people; the organization chart looks like a piece of paper a child has drawn lines all over. Eventually, the organization becomes too big and too complicated to manage. The interdependency starts looking like a Gordian knot that the more you pull, the tighter and more complicated the knot becomes. What makes the company succeed is change, but increasingly, change becomes a problem rather than an opportunity.

In a structure built around people, accountability for function becomes more and more confused. It becomes increasingly difficult to make a *controllable* change. Form must evolve to structure the function. The driving and driven forces exchange places. Until Adolescence, the organization is structured around people, people being the driving force. In Adolescence, the organization is the *driving* force and people become the *driven* force; they must adapt now to the organization's needs.

Controlled decrease in (ᴘ)erformance during Adolescence means paying less relative attention to results like sales. The organization turns its attention inward. The deterministic and constraint goals change places. Deterministic goals are those that we are intent upon achieving. Constraint goals are conditions we want to maintain. To not violate those conditions is a goal.

The deterministic goal of Go-Go is sales growth. The constraint goal is profit, which is a result of the efficiency of implementation.

In Adolescence, there is a goal displacement. Profit, the outcome of efficiency, becomes the deterministic goal, while sales growth becomes the constraint goal. It is now "we want maximum profits, and *no less* than x percent of sales growth a year," instead of, "we want *at least* x percent of sales growth a year, with no less than y percent profit margin on sales."

Profits during the Go-Go stage are happenstance rather than a predetermined occurrence. A Go-Go can explain why it *was* profitable rather than why it *will be* profitable. Even if it can explain why it was profitable, it cannot provide assurance that it can repeat its profitability, since there is not enough control over the system to make the desired actually happen.

If the organization survives Adolescence, which means that it does not fall into pathological behavior, it will move into Prime. In Prime, the role which will re-emerge is the one that was consciously put under control—(P)erformance.

PRIME (PAEi)

When the systems are in place, a function of (A)dministration, the organization can return to serving the clients, a function of (P)erformance. The organization then can have both profits *and* growth in sales (PAE). It can control its behavior to provide the profits as planned.

A Prime organization can be both oriented toward sales growth *and* profits. It is high-growth and high-profit in orientation, and it can afford to be. Let's see this transition again.

In Infancy, the goal is cash because the Infant organization is function-oriented, and what it needs to function is cash—liquidity. The Infant's typical complaint is, "We are undercapitalized," because its growth is faster than its ability to obtain the liquidity it needs for its future growth.

In the Go-Go stage, the goal is sales and market share; the basic assumption is that more sales mean more cash and profits. The assumption is that the profit margin is stable, and it takes a crisis for the organization to recognize that the profit margins have been declining. To achieve more sales, the organization has been sacrificing more and more profits by increasing the costs of obtaining those additional sales. At a certain point, more is not better. More is worse.

I have had the experience of proving through cost accounting, that by the time the company paid sales commissions and customer discounts on increased sales, as well as the cost of capital necessary to finance those increased sales, there were no profits left for the company. On the contrary, the company was losing money. That's why in some advanced Go-Gos, there is a phenomenon whereby individuals get bonuses for performance (measured in sales) while the company is losing money and going broke. This happens because the orientation of individuals and what they get rewarded for is not functional to the needs of the total system. What is occurring is called *suboptimalization*. Sales are not necessarily producing more profits, and if all rewards are oriented towards sales, the profits might actually suffer. (It also happens in developing countries. The phenomenon is called "rich people, poor country." It is *not* true that the richer the people become, the better the country becomes. That could happen in Prime countries like the United States and we *should not* assume that what is good for this country is necessarily good for young, third world countries.)

Why are individuals rewarded while the company is going broke? In a Go-Go organization, it happens because the systems necessary to evaluate the cost of what the organization is doing have not yet been established. Typically, a Go-Go will not have a good cost accounting system and it will not have adequate information systems. It is a patchwork of organizational structures, reward systems and information flows.

A Go-Go organization is opportunity-driven rather than an organization that drives its opportunities. This stems from the fact that during the Infancy stage, the organization was so hungry that any opportunity which enabled it to survive longer, was snatched up. When these opportunities came as a torrent in the Go-Go stage, remembering the Infant stage, the organization was afraid to pass on any opportunity. That's why the opportunities are driving the organization. It takes maturity and a sense of security and self-confidence to pass up opportunities. To do so, we need information, budgeting systems and control systems. These are developed during the Adolescent stage, and once these are developed, a Prime organization becomes an opportunity-driving organization rather than an opportunity-driven organization. Without such control systems, the organization becomes addicted to results. It rewards those who exploit particular opportunities, even though they might be undermining the totality.

In Prime, the organization knows what to do and what not to do. They know when to pass up an opportunity and why to pass on it. The organization has both talent and discipline. It has vision and self control. It is oriented toward quantity and quality. Both the form and the function are balanced, and they are functional. The organization can grow profitably.

Getting into Prime, however, is difficult. Staying in Prime is

even more difficult. When a Prime organization starts losing its
(E)ntrepreneurship, the organization begins to move out of Prime.
Why is the loss of (E) a cause for aging?[1] (E) provides flexibility;
it is the proactive force which changes the organization. An organization is dead when it cannot react to its environment. First, it stops
being proactive when it loses (E)ntrepreneurship. Later, because
of it, it will not be able to react either, thus losing (P)erformance
when it stops satisfying client needs, and unless there is a subsidy,
the organization becomes dysfunctional and dies.[2]

The change in behavior described in the previous chapter—
how the organization behaves after Prime and how it behaves after
Stable—is attributed to a decline in (E). The difference between
administrators and entrepreneurs is that for an entrepreneur, everything is permitted unless specifically forbidden. For an administrator, everything is forbidden unless specifically permitted.

I learned this from my research about Yugoslavia.[3] I researched
what happened to Yugoslavia as it tried to free itself from the
Russian model of running the economic and political systems. As
the Yugoslavs introduced market forces into their economy and
stepped away from central planning, they experienced extreme difficulties. In a centrally-planned model, where the (E) function is
centralized in the government and businesspeople are not businesspeople—but bureaucrats who carry out government orders and
plans—the behavior of management is bureaucratic. Everything
is forbidden unless specifically permitted.

When market forces are introduced and businesspeople have
to emerge as businesspeople, they must start behaving entrepre-
neurially. They must compete. Businessperson must be innovative,
creative, and willing to take risks. This behavior means they must
assume that everything is permitted unless specifically forbidden.

My previous research shows the difficulty of this transition
in style and behavior. It's easier to be an administrator than an

---

[1] See the Summary.

[2] Note: Solow, won the 1987 Nobel Prize in Economics, for a 1956 study
that claims that success of a nation stems from its technological developments,
and not from its labor force size or accumulation of physical resources. Technological developments are a function of (E).

[3] Adizes, Ichak: *Industrial Democracy—Yugoslav Style* (Santa Monica, CA:
Adizes Institute 1971). Adizes, Ichak and Mann Borgese, Elizabeth: *Self Management, New Dimensions to Democracy* (Santa Monica, CA: Adizes Institute 1975).

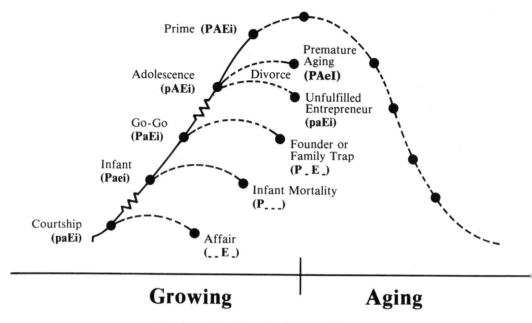

Figure 39: The Culture of Prime

entrepreneur, because it's less risky and less demanding. If people are asked only to follow rules and not to try to change them, when they eventually are asked to be creative and take risks, their past experience with the reward system works against this change. New reward systems must be introduced, and a change in style and culture is required.

I found that bureaucratic behavior is like a trap. It's very easy going in; very difficult getting out. Centralizing decisions is easy. Decentralizing is very difficult.

If you look at the Lifecycle curve, you will realize that Prime is not at the top of the bell curve. Prime is *on the way* to the top. The reason is that in Prime, there is still (**E**)ntrepreneurship, thus, there is still a source of flexibility which provides for organizational vitality as expressed in (**PAEI**) terms. Why does the organization continue rising to the pinnacle of the bell curve?

The bell curve expresses the *vitality* of the organization; vitality is defined as the organization's ability to be effective and efficient in the short- and the long-run. The vitality of the organization keeps rising, but at a decreasing rate, because the organization is losing its (**E**). When it is green, it is growing. When it is ripe, it is rotten.

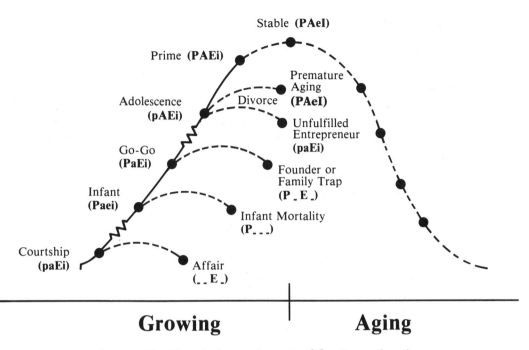

Stable **(PAeI)**

Prime **(PAEi)**

Premature
Aging

Adolescence
(pAEi)   Divorce **(PAeI)**

Unfulfilled
Entrepreneur
(paEi)

Go-Go
(PaEi)

Founder or
Family Trap
(P.E.)

Infant
(Paei)

Infant Mortality
(P...)

Courtship
(paEi)

Affair
(..E.)

Growing | Aging

Figure 40: The Culture in a Stable Organization

Thus, being in Prime is not a point in time; it is a *process*. When you are moving toward a certain point, it is better than being at a point. An analogy to personal life is that it's not important what a person is; what's important is who the person *was* and what he is *going to be*. What a person is, is transitory. We should focus on the process and not on the result. The process predicts the results.

STABLE (PAeI)

During the Stable stage, **(E)**ntrepreneurship decreases. Since **(E)** decreases, **(I)**ntegration increases.

As it was previously discussed, **(I)**ntegration could be high in the growing stages of the Lifecycle, but that's not a frequently encountered behavior and it is derived from the social culture. During Stable, we are describing an indigenous, organizational culture that is created within the organization. **(I)** goes up as **(E)** goes down. The long-term *what* goes down, which allows the long-term *how* to go up.

Why (E) Declines First

Why is (E)ntrepreneurship the first factor that decreases after Prime, when the code for Prime is **(PAEi)**. Why not (A)dministration or (P)erformance?

For (P)erformance to decrease, (E)ntrepreneurship must have decreased first. (E) predicts the behavior of (P). (E) is the long-term (P). (P) equals *what*; (E) equals *what for*. Thus, (E) has to precede (P).

Why (E) and not (A)dministration then? The reason is that (A)dministration has the highest survival rate. It is very difficult for (A) to enter an organization, but once it is in, it is very difficult to get it out. (A)dministration will not decrease on its own. It tumbles down when (P) is not functional anymore. (A) is destroyed by an uprising, by a new (E) or through professional change. Thus, in the sequence of organizational decline, (E)ntrepreneurship goes down first, then (P)erformance declines, then (I)ntegration, and eventually (A)dministration when a new Courtship occurs or organizational cultural change is completed.

Why (I) Increases

Now, let's understand how this transition from Prime **(PAEi)** to Stable **(PAeI)** occurs. It's not the increasing (I)ntegration which drives the decline in (E)ntrepreneurship. On the contrary, it is the decline in (E) that allows (I) to grow. But why is the decline in (E) expressed in the increase in (I)? Why will it not be expressed in the increase in (P) or (A)?

The role that has not yet come to the surface is (I)ntegration. In utility terms, the marginal increase in (A) has a smaller marginal utility than the first increment in (I), so (I) has to increase. The decline in (E)ntrepreneurship which is a long-term function, is exchanged for another long-term function, an increase in (I).

This increase in (I) as (E) declines can be explained by the fact that since the organization is successful and in its full vitality, its fight for survival is not acute. It can afford the luxuries of turning inward and paying attention to interdependencies between people and to the various values that dominate behavior. That can occur at the early stages of the Lifecycle as we discussed previously, but that will not be an indigenous cultural development. It will be a

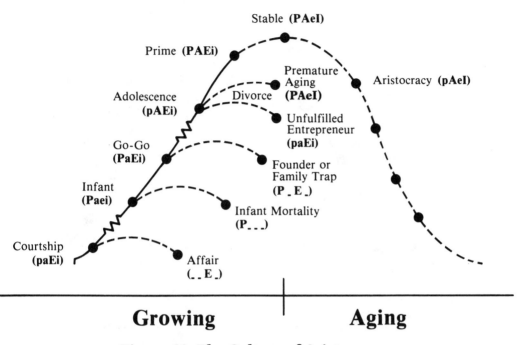

Figure 41: The Culture of Aristocracy

piggyback development—piggybacking on the existent social culture where the organization operates, or it will be nourished by a very people-oriented founder, which is rare because in this case, he must be excellent in three roles, **(PAI)**. None of the **(P)** or **(E)** roles can be sacrificed if a founder is going to be successful in building a company.

ARISTOCRACY (pAeI)

From the previous discussion of the interdependency between **(P)**erformance and **(E)**ntrepreneurship, if **(E)** is low long enough, it should be obvious that an eventual decline in **(P)** will have to occur. That's how we move into Aristocracy. The code for Aristocracy is **(pAeI)**, which tells us that the main orientation is on the short- and long-term *how*, rather than on the short- and long-term *what* and *why*.

The decline in **(P)**erformance means a decline in attention to function and increased attention to form. That's why in Aristocratic

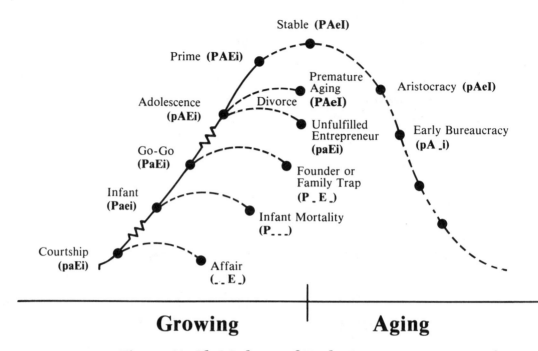

Figure 42: The Culture of Early Bureaucracy

organizations, rituals are of extreme importance. How you do something is more important than what you do. How people dress, how
they speak, how they relate to each other, how they obey the organizational rituals and unspoken values, is more important than
the results they produce. This can happen because an Aristocratic
organization can afford not to be functionally-oriented. It is basically
capitalizing on its past successes or resting on its laurels. If we
look at a balance sheet of an Aristocratic organization and compare
it even to a balance sheet of a Prime organization, we will see
that the financial ratios are higher in Aristocracy than in Prime.
Aristocratic organizations will be more liquid than those in Prime;
and this stems from the fact that an Aristocratic organization is
taking less risk, it's more numbers-oriented, and more security-
oriented than a Prime organization will be.

I have worked with many Aristocratic organizations that were
highly liquid. In one of them, during the executive committee's
meeting the financial officer said, "We have $300 million in cash.
Does anybody have any suggestions what to do?"

For the company to have $300 million in cash is not unusual.

What was unusual is that nobody came up with recommendations on what to do. This has occurred more than once, and from interviews I have conducted, this is not an unusual phenomenon for organizations in this stage of their Lifecycle. Top management is waiting to be told what to do rather than suggesting what to do, especially if doing something entails taking risk.

In an Aristocratic organization, there is the calm before the storm. People do not offend or cross each other. The climate is that if you lie low long enough, you might become the president. The tendency is to encourage somebody else to pick the chestnuts out of the fire.

EARLY BUREAUCRACY (pA-i) and BUREAUCRACY (-A--)

Organizational inaction while the world is changing eventually must have its repercussions. Clients do not come back. Their needs are satisfied better somewhere else. Furthermore, the Aristocracy prices were constantly raised so that the product not only is competitively obsolete, but is also overpriced. The desertion of clients impacts sales volume which impacts market share which impacts cash flow.

When liquidity is drying out, all organizational alarm signals are on: it's an emergency! The organization tries to revive (P) urgently. It cuts prices to encourage sales, but without cutting overhead, the company is selling at a loss. Cutting overhead in a hurry might be slicing not only fat but also flesh; so by firing people and discontinuing activities to reduce cost, the organization might be cutting its capability to deliver (P). The company is damned no matter what it does *in a hurry*.

When people in the organization cannot get results outside they turn inward, attacking each other. As the (P)erformance level goes down and cannot be easily resuscitated, (I)ntegration goes down. What stands dominant and looming like a monstrous shadow is (A)dministration.

The situation is bad and people need an explanation why. They must have a solution; they must have hope. The explanation people give to the situation is that new, energetic leadership is necessary. They look for *a person* to lead the organization out of the trap.

The tendency to believe that changing leadership will change behavior is developed and established as a successful cure, and rightfully so, during the growing stages. The argument becomes since it worked then, why not try the same cure now? Changing leadership is easy and expedient. Firing the president and hiring a new one is more easily done than changing the organizational responsibility, structure, information systems and reward systems. So the organization does what is easy and expedient rather than what is difficult and long-drawn. The result is a witch hunt. The first ones fired are those to whom the organization attributes the difficulties. And since the difficulties have been due to lack of adaptation to change (the products are obsolete), the ones to be sacrificed on the altar of organizational ignorance are those who had the responsibility to provide the organizational entrepreneurship. Those are the people in marketing, strategic planning, R and D, and engineering. Erroneously attributing blame to people, rather than to the need to change the system can hasten the death of the organization.

I believe this phenomenon stems from the fact that we continuously confuse causes and effects. In the growing stages, changing leadership would change the behavior of the organization, but this medicine will not work in the aging stages of the Lifecycle. A change in the system is necessary. It is the administrative system, functional in Adolescence, which is stymieing the organization now. Form is now stronger than function. On the margin, form reaches the point where it suffocates the function. If function is to be liberated from form, it has to change. This means the organizational system reflected in the structure of accountability, information flows and rewards has to change.

Aging is caused by a decreased (E)ntrepreneurship. In Early Bureaucracy, (E) does not just decline, it is ejected. That's why in Early Bureaucracy, the (A)s kill, expel and imprison the (E)s. This speeds up the destruction of the organization.

Throughout history, when a country was on the rise economically, they invited the Jews in. When the country was in trouble economically, the Jews got accused for it and were either murdered in pogroms in Russia or expelled from the country like in Spain.

This is not only the fate of the Jews. It happens also to other entrepreneurial races like the Chinese and the Armenians. In this case, it is not just anti-semitism. It is anti (E)ism.

Death is close when (E) disappears. (E) is what gives the organi-

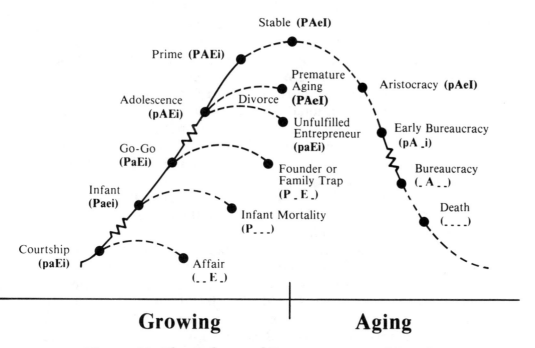

Growing | Aging

Figure 43: The Culture of Bureaucracy and Death

zation life and its disappearance is the organization's death. An organization is born when commitment is tested. An organization is dead when no one is committed to its existence.

With exclusive (**A**)dministration, all that is left is form for the sake of form as if form is the function itself (thus, the insistence on organizational rituals without understanding of their purpose or functionality). There is rain dancing although everyone including the Shaman knows it won't bring the rain. People remain for security, since they cannot be measured for performance, so there is no pressure to perform, compete or undertake risk.

This can work only if there is external support to pay for it because the clients will not pay for services they do not get unless they are forced to by law.

DEATH

With limited or no functionality, the organization virtually dies by not being effective in the short-and-long run. If it is a business organization, it will go bankrupt unless emergency measures are taken. These emergency measures are necessary in order to revive the functionality of the organization.

Sometimes the organization is kept alive artificially; this happens when the organization is important enough politically that external powers take on the responsibility of its survival. I refer to governments which nationalize or continually subsidize organizations although they do not satisfy the client needs for which they exist. The goals of the organization change from satisfying the external client needs for which it was established, to satisfying political needs, such as providing employment at any cost.

The organization then becomes a cancer. It usurps energy. Resources which could go for the support of Infant and Go-Go organizations are channeled to maintain the survival of non-functional organizations like Bureaucracies. Death occurs when these external subsidies for survival are removed. Not being functional and not having external support finally kills this organization. What appears to be an all-powerful, difficult to deal with Bureaucracy, is nothing more than an empty, dead shell which—once external financial support is removed—crumbles down having no internal support and no reason to exist.

Death will occur when this external support is discontinued, when the organization has to justify its existence by its functionality. Then it is evident that (A) is pure form that does not yield any functionality and a new (E)—a new courtship—is born.

As one organization dies, another cause is born on its ashes, if it is encouraged to happen. Otherwise the larger system is impacted and the whole society slowly declines economically.

To see whether any system, micro or macro, will die we should always analyze the environment of that system and how it encourages (E).

9

Predicting Who Has Control ═══════════

In Chapter 8, we analyzed how (**PAEI**) changes over the Lifecycle. In this chapter, we focus on the implementation, or how *authorance* changes.

As discussed in Chapter 5, *authorance* is all the energy management uses to cause behavior to occur. It is the combination of three basic ingredients: *authority* (the legal right to make decisions), *power* (the capability to punish and/or reward,) and *influence* (the capability to cause self-directed behavior through convincing of the directed party. Components of these elements include *authorized power*, which is the legal right to make decisions that can be accompanied by punishment and/or reward; *indirect power*, which is directed influence but perceived power; *influencing authority* which is the legal right to make a decision based on acceptance of the decision through cooperation. *CAPI*, which is coalesced *authority*, *power* and *influence*, produces control over the situation.

This chapter will help us analyze how the different components of *Authorance* change during the Lifecycle.

AUTHORITY OVER LIFECYCLE

In Courtship, the question of authority is not discussed. It is practically irrelevant. During this *falling in love* period before a marriage, no authority issues arise because there is no real task yet. It is a

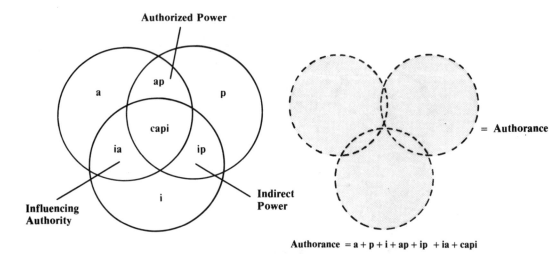

Authorance $= a + p + i + ap + ip + ia + capi$

Figure 44: The Components of Authorance

make-believe world where each person is careful not to scare the other one away. It is a period of sharing. Decisions are made together, with each person taking the time to convince the other.

When the organization is born and there are tasks to be carried out *NOW!* Time evaporates. We need to act: *NOW!* Decisions must be made, *NOW!*

This *now* requirement means one person must have the authority to make a decision because of the time pressure. Authority naturally is concentrated in the founder—the person who is the most committed, and who has made the biggest sacrifice for the company. If it is an equal partnership, the partners will have to spend a great deal of time together, deciding how to split responsibilities. This usually results in one of the partners emerging as more dominant than the other one.

In Go-Go, authority becomes even more monopolized. All the titles—chief operating officer, chief financial officer, chief executive officer, founder, president, chairman of the board—usually belong to one person. The organization becomes a one-person show, even if it is partnership or a public company. "I've created a monster here," said one of the partners about the equal partner that emerged as the leader. The founder communicates less and less with his followers, and, because the company is growing rapidly, there is the arrogance that goes along with that success. No one challenges this monopolized authority—yet. They do not dare. There is no argument with success.

In his arrogance, the founder feels the growth and success of the company is his own doing. He thinks it is *his* leadership (talent), good judgement, timing, and relationships with clients that make the company a success. "He starts to believe his own press releases," one executive remarked. Arrogance makes him use more and more of the authority he has, with less and less influence, which is allowed to happen because the company is successful. The board of directors does not challenge this, because in a Go-Go organization, it is usually an internal board, or is composed of the founder's cronies or family members. The success is there. Everyone is making money. "Leave him alone; if we knew better, we would be in his place," and "We need him more than he needs us," are typical comments in Go-Go. The executive committee does whatever the founder says. There is no participative system in effect as yet.

Then mistakes begin to happen. The company starts to come apart at the seams, and people begin to question the founder's authority. The first to raise the flag of revolution against the founder, president or chairman, is (A)dministration, the person who has been hired or appointed to organize things, or the one who happens to have the finance portfolio.

A struggle for authority begins between the (E)ntrepreneurial types and the Administrative types, while the board watches from the sidelines. If the Entrepreneur gains final authority, the (A)dministrator is fired, and a new cycle of authority struggles begins with the new (A). If (E) does not gain final control, the board develops an axis with (A), usurps authority and squeezes out the (E) person. In Adolescence, when (E) comes under control, the executive committee comes to life and the board takes full authority.

In Prime, authority is with the executive committee and the board, and each executive knows the extent of his authority. There is delegation and decentralization of authority commensurate with responsibilities.

The difference between pre- and post-Adolescence is that authority is personalized during Infancy and Go-Go, while in Prime and successive Lifecycle stages, it is institutionalized and systematized. This institutionalization and depersonalization increases after Prime to the point that eventually, a person does not feel that he has authority in real terms.

This transition requires further explanation.

Management textbooks say that authority must be equal to responsibility, and vice versa. At first glance, this makes sense. How can anyone be held responsible for things over which he has no authority? Why should anyone have authority without a commensurate responsibility? Makes sense, right? Wrong! It took me fifteen years to realize this and to figure out why the textbooks are wrong.

I began to understand this while diagnosing companies. People repeatedly complained that they did not have the necessary authority to carry out their responsibilities. After a few years and several dozen companies, I started to wonder why I had never come across a manager who said that he had the authority equal to his responsibility. Is it possible that what is described in theory does not exist in reality? So I looked and looked, but could not find any person who would say, "Yes, I have all the authority I need for my responsibilities." I believe this situation exists only in a dead organization. Thus, what is prescribed in textbooks is highly undesirable! *Why?*

Let us see. To understand the following pages, the reader must fully understand Chapter 5; a review of that chapter is recommended.

Can we take a laser beam pen and produce a very thin-lined

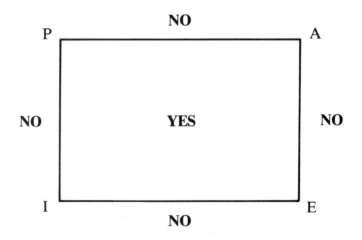

Figure 45: Static Definition of Responsibility

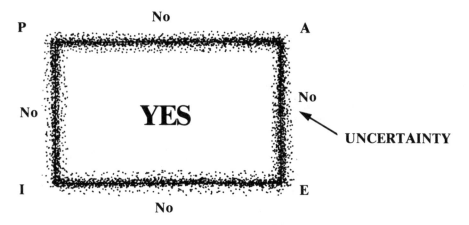

Figure 46: Dynamic Definition of Responsibility

square so that there is *absolutely* no question as to what is, or is not to be done, how we should or should not do something, when to or not to do something, and who should or should not do it? Obviously, it can not be done because there is always change. One cannot predict *everything* in advance and decide *everything* in advance. Thus, a responsibility has a point at which it is clear that a thing is an individual's responsibility, and the rest is not his responsibility. In between, there is uncertainty.

How should this uncertainty be handled? Let us look at a tennis analogy. In tennis doubles, the players always try to hit the ball to land between the opponent players. On a bad team, the area of uncertainty belongs to no one, each player will wait for the other player to make the play. On a good team, the area of uncertainty belongs to both players; they both might make the move for the ball, with one of them eventually responding.

However, both players going for the ball is *not efficient*. To make the system more efficient, should they draw a line in the middle of the court delineating *exactly* who is responsible for which part of the court? They cannot play that way. If they did, they would have to wait for the ball to land and then react to it. Obviously, that would be too late.

How does a Bureaucracy handle change and the ensuing uncertainties?

Back to the doubles tennis game analogy. Once it is realized there is an area that no one covers, and that it is inefficient to have both players try simultaneously to respond to that need, a new person is hired to handle that middle area. Nice, but what happens next? It is clearly evident that there are now two—not one—areas of uncertainty which no one claims as his responsibility. During the next budgeting period, a request is made for two more people to handle the new areas of uncertainty. This creates even more areas of uncertainty, so the tasks that call for more people multiply.

Eventually the court is filled with people. No one is watching the ball. They are all watching each other or they are stepping on each others toes; there are turf wars. Energy is spent not on hitting the ball, but in protecting individual turf.

The big question becomes: who is responsible for what? Some players retreat to the area most clearly identified as their own so they don't have to get involved in turf wars. Others try to cover uncertainties and in the pursuit, end up in someone else's territory, where they are accused of empire building, get ostracized and are sometimes forced to retreat. In the meantime, the balls are coming over the net but no one dares to lift a racket aggressively for fear of hitting someone else in the process. So the balls fly, and it's not until a ball hits a Bureaucrat square between his eyes that he reacts.

As the turf wars increase, perceived authority declines, the perceived responsibilities follow and decline in size. Someone above the court must fill the holes and take the authority to direct the game and call the shots. Thus, authority becomes increasingly centralized. People want to be told what to do. They would rather be precisely wrong, than approximately right. To give the Bureaucrat the benefit of the doubt, this behavior might stem from the nature of governmental requirements. Bureaucracies are constantly under scrutiny for waste and improper judgment. So it becomes more prudent to do the *wrong things right* than to do the *right things wrong*.[1]

The requirement of doing things right attracts the administrative type of personality who is risk-averse, and prefers form over

---

[1] The alternative of *continuously* doing the right things right, is reserved for saints; the alternative of doing the wrong things continuously wrong, is reserved for schlemiels, and neither are a resource for managerial talent.

substance. Being staffed by (A) personalities, however, reinforces the behavior of a Bureaucracy even further.

The mistake is that the Bureaucracy tries to minimize uncertainty and in doing so, it decreases flexibility. To minimize uncertainty, people try to define responsibility clearly. To make responsibility clearer when there is change, responsibilities must decrease and authority must decrease commensurately. Since it still needs to be managed, the system becomes increasingly centralized, responsibility and authority rise to the top. Minute, practically irrelevant problems flow all the way to the CEO. Since he is overwhelmed with decisions and responsibilities, real problems go unattended. Responsibility does not get dispersed, which makes the situation even worse, overwhelming the CEO even more, which means that even more problems go unattended. That is the process of dying.

People increasingly feel they are not responsible and that they have no authority. The time when they feel they have authority commensurate to responsibility is when they feel they have no authority and no responsibility, and that happens in a full-blown Bureaucracy, when there is no more change, when the square of responsibility stops moving, *and* so does the circle of authority. This happens when the organization stops responding to environmental change. And that means the organization is dead. We are fully in control when we are dead. To be alive means not to be in control over parts of our life. An experienced manager understands this—some things he can control, and some things he cannot; and in many areas he does not know whether he has control or not.

It is normal to have more responsibility than authority, or, to have more authority than responsibility. They cannot be equal, because both responsibility and authority change as the situation changes. Prior to Adolescence, authority is personalized; during Adolescence, it becomes depersonalized and institutionalized into the system. During Prime, authority is both institutionalized and personalized. After that point, authority is increasingly taken from the people who have responsibility, causing effectiveness to decline. People perceive their authority to decline to almost zero during Bureaucracy. That is why we find very happy people in Bureaucracies. There is no uncertainty, they just go by the book. Unhappy people are found in advanced Go-Go and Adolescence where organizational uncertainty is at its highest.

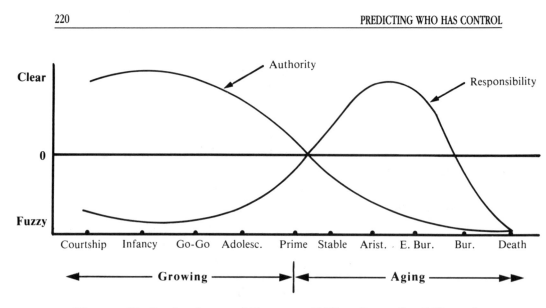

Figure 47: Authority and Responsibility Over the Lifecycle

THE BEHAVIOR OF POWER IN THE LIFECYCLE

In Courtship, power is meaningful because the founder is trying to build commitment. So any person whose cooperation the founder needs, and who can withdraw that cooperation, by definition has power. The founder tries to enlist these people to support his effort by making promises that he will later have to fulfill. This is how many people who may be of only marginal value to the general effort end up owning a piece of the action.

In Infancy, the founder maintains tight controls on the company because he does not want to lose control. He is like the mother wolf who rejects her cub if a human touches it. If the founder loses control at this stage, his commitment will evaporate and, subsequently, the organization will die in its Infancy.

With the birth of a company, power is transferred from the people necessary to start the company, to the people necessary to keep the company alive. This is a very interesting transition. Loyalties change. During Courtship, those people with power were outside the company. They were spouses, family members, bankers and friends. Once the company is born, the power is transferred to those who labor day and night to build the company. The founder's secretary becomes very powerful. The secretary practically provides the **(AI)** role to the founder's **(PE)** role. A good executive secretary, one whose opinion the founder trusts, is worth his weight in gold. He is the person who keeps the founder out of trouble by delaying the implementation of bad decisions, while waiting for the founder to change his mind. It is this so-called secretary with whom the founder confers as to what, when and with whom, to do anything. This secretary provides an important informational link to the founder keeping him informed as to what is going on. He is the political gauge who informs the founder on what is politically acceptable and what is not.

Other groups of powerful people are the sales managers, and buyers (if it is a retail distribution chain). The accountant is weak, and there is no marketing department to speak of. The weakness stems from the fact that **(E)**ntrepreneurship is centralized in the founder who makes all the marketing and financial decisions. There is no engineering effort to speak of either. The founder is still exploiting the technology which started the company, so there is no pressure for change yet. There is no human resources or personnel department because the company is small. Even if it is a large company, the importance of the personnel factor is minor in comparison to the importance of sales, which are crucial to the company's survival.

The founder might try to delegate sales and purchasing, if it is a marketing delivery organization. However, what he can not delegate are the financial responsibilities. He might not like the financial side of the business, but at this stage of the Lifecycle, whoever succeeds in maintaining a cash flow has power.

In Adolescence, power and authority are diffused. It is difficult to identify where the power lies. There is transition of authority and power from the founder to the financial people, and from the externally-oriented to the internally-oriented people. Thus, from Infancy to Adolescence, authority and power are not coalesced. Authority is centralized in the founder, while power moves around as dictated by the needs of the organization. During Adolescence, the founder has the authority while the financial systems person has power. Later, power and authority start moving toward each other. The two must coalesce before the organization can get to Prime.

In a healthy transition, the founder and the professional manager share the titles between them of chairman of the board, chief executive officer, president and chief operating officer. The founder might be the chairman, CEO and president, while the professional hired gun is assigned the COO role. In other cases, the founder might become the chairman, and the hired gun the CEO, president and COO. Sometimes the COO role is delegated to a third person. In any of these situations, authority and power coalesce. That is how the organization develops into Prime.

After Prime, authority and power are separated again; and as the organization slides into Aristocracy, power moves down the hierarchy and authority moves up, with the organization becoming increasingly centralized. The more systemically centralized the organization is, the more the vertical disparity will be between authority and power. Increasingly, there will be people who claim to have authority without power, and there will be people who exercise power while claiming to have no authority.

A split in authorized power can occur as well. This could take the form of an antagonistic union which was authorized to act for the employees, and which fights management with its authorized power.

In Early Bureaucracy where turf wars exist, the lines delineating authorized power are fuzzy. This phenomenon occurs because the responsibility squares are shrinking, requiring the authority circles to adapt in size. Since it is easier to scale down responsibility than to scale down authority and power, fuzziness occurs.

Peace and quiet reign when the authority and power circles are separated. Then there is authority with no power and power with no authority. There is peace and quiet because everyone feels paralyzed. Unions rely on management. Management relies on Washington. In Washington, the White House depends on Congress, and Congress is dependent on internal politics. Authority and power are diffused to the point where change becomes very difficult. Over the years, I have seen numerous examples of this.

A post office in Hawaii needed a machine to pick up sacks of mail on the receiving platform outside the office. The request required approval from Washington, D.C. The reply was slow in coming, but when it eventually arrived, the Washington people denied the request because such a machine could not stand in the snow outside the post office. As we know, it snows in Washington but never in Hawaii.

Another example of dysfunctionally centralized authority is

the Los Angeles Department of Social Services. This department has 15,000 employees and a $1.5 billion budget to spend on welfare. However, the director has only about $5,000 in discretionary funds at his disposal, and, a task as simple as moving a computer from one department to another require approval from a person so high up outside the DPSS organization, that such an idea was abandoned.

In Sweden, while trying to diagnose how to rejuvenate the governmental machinery, I asked the principals of the various Ministries (these are the top administrators under the cabinet members of the Ministries of Treasury, Foreign Affairs, Defense, etc.) to give me a problem they could not solve alone because they lacked the authority to do so. The problem they offered for analysis was to move a person from one Ministry to another.

Let us say that there is a need for a person in the Ministry of Foreign Affairs and there is an excess of people in the Ministry of Agriculture. A simple transfer cannot be made by the principal manager, who is the chief administrator of the government, the professional person under the Minister of the Cabinet who is a political appointee. Why? Because about 200 years ago, in order to limit the authority and powers of the king, each Ministry was organized as an almost autonomous organization. The center in common is the Cabinet. However, the Prime Minister is only a *primus inter paris*—first among equals—and has no authority over the other members of the cabinet. To further complicate matters, each Ministry has its labor union which has something to say on the subject of transferring people.

I found it would take the *CAPI* of 120 people—of a very high echelon—to change the law on transferring a person from one Ministry to another. This is paralysis. It is not strange, then, that the government grows in employees with no apparent growth in effectiveness.

THE BEHAVIOR OF INFLUENCE IN THE LIFECYCLE

In Courtship, influence is important. There is no authority to speak of, and power comes from withholding cooperation. In Infancy, authority takes over, power switches to the inside people and influence disappears. There is no time to talk; it is time to act! Influence takes time, and there is a shortage of that precious commodity. Thus, in an Infant organization, things are done with authorized power—without influence—in a dictatorial way.

During Go-Go, influence returns, but it is integrated with authority and power. There is *CAPI* in the founder; success makes people accept anything. Then the failure happens and influence is switched to the technocrats at best, or worse, it disappears altogether.

In Prime, *CAPI* is in the executive committee where management has both authorized power and influence. The company is successful in a systematic way. From the Stable phase on, influence increases at the expense of authority, which is being centralized. The centralization of authority means authority is declining for people in the lower echelons of the organization, who quickly discover that the only way to get anything accomplished is to use influence. That influence, however, is coupled with power, so what emerges is indirect power. That's when people behave nicely, but the focal person on whom this influence is directed acts scared. He acts not because he is convinced, but because he fears the repercussions.

When the next big breakdown occurs—loss of market and negative cash flow, which leads to Early Bureaucracy—authority is empty, influence is gone and power is the only source of energy left. This is war time; it is no time to talk or try to convince people. It is survival time and any tools or arms are considered legitimate.

CAPI OVER THE LIFECYCLE

CAPI measures controllability, strength and the predictability of an organization's behavior.

The behavior of *CAPI* changes depending upon where the organization is in the Lifecycle. In Courtship, who has *CAPI* is not important; we are in love. That is why during Courtship people are relatively promiscuous with control. Shares are given to people who are excited about the founder's idea, and who are willing to support the new organization. The founder is buying support for his dream. The day of reckoning comes when this promiscuous give-away of control endangers the founder's survival as the manager of the company. This usually happens during Adolescence.

Once the organization is born, *CAPI* is consolidated and is usually vested in the founder. If he has influence, which does not play an important role at this stage of the Lifecycle, authorized power is sufficient to achieve implementation. If the founder does not have *CAPI*, but only authorized power, this can become a source of crisis later on. When the organization moves into Go-Go, the more successful it is, the more arrogant the founder becomes and the more power he will use. The more power he uses, the less he listens to others and the more detached he becomes. The more he behaves that way, the bigger will be the mistake he will make which begins Adolescence.

The reason for this crisis is that the easiest component available is power. As the saying goes, "power corrupts, and absolute power corrupts absolutely." The more power the founder has, the more power he uses. So, nobody dares to challenge him about his decisions. Eventually, he will make some major mistakes which will endanger the organization and his own power within the organization.

In Adolescence, *CAPI* is erratic. There is a power struggle be-

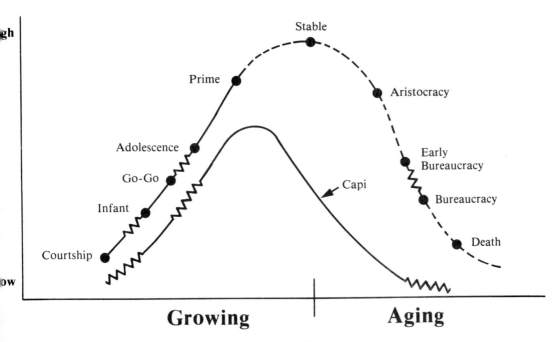

Figure 48: Capi Over the Lifecycle

tween the professional manager and the founder, between the board of directors and the family, and between the organization and the founder.

If the organization survives Adolescence, *CAPI* is stabilized in the system, and in the executive committee. This establishes a certain modus vivendi between the board, the executive committee, the founder, the stockholders, and the professional managers.

CAPI begins to decline after Aristocracy, because there is a conflict of interest between stockholders, management, labor and the technocrats. We will discuss how *CAPI* and control breaks down and why, in the next chapter.

CAPI is almost nil in Early Aristocracy and Bureaucracy, which explains why the right hand does not know what the left hand is doing. They try to subvert each other, and there are intramural civil wars. When *CAPI* is perceived as zero, the organization is brain dead.

10

The Causes of Organizational Aging ═══

What causes aging? A decrease in flexibility and an increase in controllability is a cause up to a point. The old organization will eventually have problems or diseases occur because the organization will lose control; *CAPI* will break down. Each interest group will pull in its own direction to the detriment of the total organization.

Flexibility and control are functions of **(E)**ntrepreneurship and *CAPI*. High **(E)** and *CAPI* make an organization flexible and predictable; organizational behavior is under control.

What affects **(E)**ntrepreneurship and *CAPI*?

THE BEHAVIOR OF (E)NTREPRENEURSHIP THROUGHOUT THE LIFECYCLE

Of the four **(PAEI)** roles, the most critical one for changing a culture is **(E)**ntrepreneurship. It precedes and determines the **(P)**erformance function because it is the long-term component of **(P)**. **(A)**dministration should be derived from the task which must be **(P)**erformed and since **(E)** drives **(P)**, **(A)** is derived from **(E)** also. In other words, *how* we do a thing must be geared to *what* we want to do, which, in turn, is derived from *why*—we do anything. *Who does it with whom*, and how—the organic *how*, the **(I)**ntegration role—should be derived the same way the mechanistic *how*—**(A)** is derived; from **(P)** and thus from **(E)**. An organization's values and philosophy

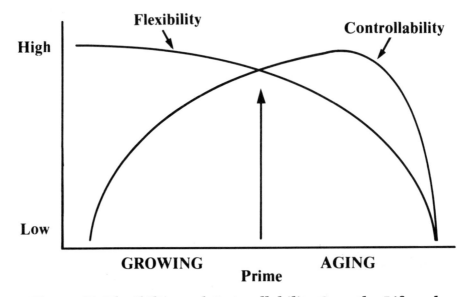

Figure 49: Flexibility and Controllability Over the Lifecycle

should be determined from its goals, its clients' needs, and from the technological requirements of satisfying those needs. Thus, the values of the Mafia are different from the values of a church. The bottom line of the this discourse is that as **(E)** changes in an organization, so does the organizational culture.

Let's try again to explain the importance of **(E)**ntrepreneurship in impacting culture. By now, it's easy to see that **(E)** affects **(P)**. **(E)** is the long-term **(P)**, so it is **(E)** that drives **(P)**.

Why would **(E)** affect **(A)**? It is **(E)** that retards the growth of **(A)** in the growing stages of the Lifecycle, and it is the disappearance of **(E)** which begins the demise of **(P)** and the uncontrolled growth of **(A)**. Thus, **(E)** drives the behavior of **(A)** also.

What about **(I)**? It is the same as with **(A)**. During the growing phases, it is high **(E)**, and thus high **(P)**, which retards **(I)**. In the aging phases, when **(E)** disappears and **(P)** declines, **(I)** must also decline as people start fighting for their individual survival.

Furthermore, **(E)** is the locomotive force of the organization. When commitment—**(E)**—is born, the organization is born. When commitment disappears, the organization becomes brain dead, even though parts of the organization may still be functioning.

Thus, we must focus on the **(E)** role to understand the Lifecycle curve. It is a vital sign, and must be monitored.

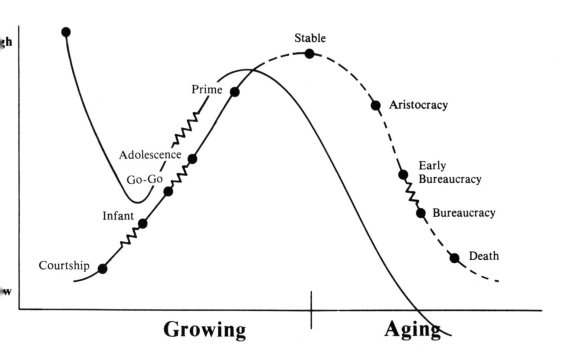

Figure 50:   E (Creativity) Over the Lifecycle

If we look at the following chart, we can identify the behavior of (E) on the curve.

The first thing we should note is that during Courtship, (E) is very high. There is a lot of noise, excitement, willingness to take risks, creativity, imagination and fascination with the possibilities. This behavior is functional because it propels the organization into the future. If there is no love affair, if there is no excitement, the first difficulty encountered could dissolve the commitment necessary for the birth of an organization, and the idea might be abandoned.

What happens when the organization is born and the risk is created? Excitement is high as long as there is no risk. When the risk is born, the (E) rapidly declines, because there is no time to think and there is no time to create. It is the time to get things done. This transition creates disenchantment. People begin to ask what happened. "Since we got this organization started, we don't have time to imagine anymore, to get excited, to get together. It is just hard work, day in, day out." This behavior is normal, because the organization must cover its risk. It must satisfy certain needs to meet commitments which were made in the marketplace and which the founder made to himself. It is time to deliver on those commitments.

If (E) stays dormant for too long however, the organization might die. Management needs a vision to maintain its interest, to keep its commitment and to ride out the difficulties of an Infant organization, which is hard work. If management does not get back to the dream, if it can't define what it is trying to achieve, then the Infant organization turns out to be hard work only, and management will eventually burn out.

It is mandatory to constantly maintain (E), at least latently, so that when the organization is finally freed from the cash pressure, when it's freed from the ongoing need to satisfy immediate demands and pressures from clients, suppliers and bankers, when the people have some time to think, the dream can come back to the surface of the organizational consciousness. When people start to dream again, that's when the organization moves into its Go-Go culture. At that stage, (E) goes up again, and the organization has the time to try new things. It has already proven that it can survive the difficulties of being an Infant.

What happens next? When the organization starts getting bigger, and making bigger mistakes, the need for (A) shows up. When the (A) role rises—the technocracy, bureaucratization, systematization, and institutionalization of the organization—the structure of who does what, when, and how, impacts the entrepreneurial spirit. At this point, instead of being the *channeling* energy, the entrepreneurial spirit is *channeled* by (A). People find that all the new rules and processes and forms about who decides what, with whom, and how, are constraining.

That's why the (E) curve between Go-Go and Adolescence, or throughout Adolescence before the organization gets to Prime, is erratic—zig zaging up and down. There is a tug-of-war between the founder and the organization. The founder wants to make the decisions, but he also wants to decentralize.[1] What develops is a syndrome where the founder wants to have his cake and eat it, too.

---

[1] Decentralization is the transfer of (E) down. Delegation is the transfer of (P) down. The founder wants to delegate, to transfer (P) down, but without a bounding (A), (P) equals (E) over time. Thus, de facto, he ends up decentralizing rather than delegating.

He says, "I want to decentralize. I want to institutionalize leadership in the organization so it's not necessary for everyone to come to me every time." "However," he adds, "don't you dare make decisions before you ask me first." Or he says, "make any decisions you want, as long as you are sure you're making the decision I would have made, if you had asked me." The result is a Catch-22 situation.

In the Adolescent organization the struggle is between (A) and (E)—a struggle between an orientation toward systematization, order and efficiency, and, an orientation toward growth, continuous change, and market penetration. It is a struggle between quantity and quality, flexibility and predictability, function and form. (A) provides the form, predictability and quality orientation; while (E) provides the quantity, flexibility and functional orientation. This struggle in orientation is obvious in the authority structure of the organization. The founder would like to restructure the organization, to have some systematization and some order. At the same time, he would like to dominate and control the critical factors of policy decision-making on finance, marketing, and product development.

Moving these discretionary powers from the founder into the organization and systematizing them into professional, managerial decision-making rather than entrepreneurial decision-making makes that struggle between (E) and (A) even more acute. The founder might say he is decentralizing and delegating, but he may not really be doing it. So, the people in the organization don't know if he really means what he says.

If the (A) and (E) roles are represented by two partners, it could cause the partners to split up. In that case, it is usually the (A) personality that remains, and the (E) personality that leaves the company. The entrepreneurial spirit is highly threatened at this point in the organization.

What happens in Prime? Between Adolescence and Prime, if the organization survives Adolescence, (E) continues to increase. (E) is institutionalized during Adolescence and, by Prime, it is in the system; it is no longer monopolized by any single individual.

The institutionalization of (E) means that entrepreneurial decisions are being made in a professional way. Information is accumulated, discussed as it relates to policies, guidelines and strategies, and decisions are carried out independent of any single individual and his idiosyncrasies. What happens after Prime? There is a loss of (E).

During Early Bureaucracy, when there is no (E) left, everyone starts looking out for himself. If there is any entrepreneurial spirit it's not applied for the benefit of the organization, but for the benefit of the individuals—sometimes at the expense of the organization. (E) begins to be squeezed out in Early Bureaucracy. (E) types are fired. On a social level, they get kicked out of a country, or leave as fast as they can get their hands on exit visas.

Factors Affecting the Existence or Loss of (E)ntrepreneurship in the Lifecycle

What is behind the changes to (E) throughout the Lifecycle curve and why do these changes occur? After working with large and small organizations for more than 20 years and testing this factor, I feel confident in saying that there are several primary factors that dramatically affect (E) in organizations. If we understand these factors, then we can take specific steps to deal with the potential problems before they become pathologic and endanger the organization itself.

The (E) spirit, both in an individual and in an organization, is the function of a disparity between desired and expected consciousness.[2] As long as a person desires more or better than what he expects, he is young. I learned in Sweden the difference between luck and success. "Success is getting what you want; luck is wanting what you got." When you desire or want more than what you expect, you are young, and rely on success, not just luck. You are not waiting for things to happen.

One day I told an acquaintance he was lucky that he was not overweight. He looked at me and said, "I work at it." Then I realized that I relied on luck rather than on success in being trim.

The day a person looks at the future and says "I like what I expect"—the day he accepts the expected, as desired—is the day he begins to get old.

There are four factors which affect the disparity between desired and expected, that can change the consciousness of an organization by directly influencing entrepreneurship. They are:

---

[2] $E = f\left(\dfrac{\text{desired}}{\text{expected}} - 1\right).$

1. Mental age of the leadership   } people factors
2. Functionality of leadership style

3. Perceived relative market share   } organizational factors
4. Functionality of organizational structure

These four internal factors are within the direct control of the company. There are, of course, also external factors which can strongly influence aging, factors such as the environment, technology, market and political changes. These external factors can cause an organization to accelerate its aging or even jump stages, which can happen in market deregulation. In general, coping with these factors requires that management use the same actions as it would for coping with internal factors. Only the timing and sequence of the steps are different.

Mental Age of Leadership

The first factor is the mental age of those who are the decision-makers in the organization. We are talking about those who control the organization, those who comprise *CAPI*; we are not talking about ownership. This could be related to ownership, but it doesn't have to be. Often management controls the organization, not the owners who are scattered and badly represented on the board.

What is the mental age of the people who set the tone and make the decisions in the organization? By mental age, I mean the disparity between desired and expected results in their own minds, which in turn affects the collective mind of the organization. Mental age is not necessarily related to chronological age. There are some individuals who are young at 50 and others who are old at 25. The question is, do they accept the expected as desired or do they want the desired to be different from the expected. The difference is not expressed only in quantity. It could be that they don't want more quantity, just more quality. But they must want *something* more, either quality or quantity. If they don't want more quality or more quantity, they are aging. They accept things as they are or worse, as they are going to be.

If the mental age of the people in control of the organization is such that they accept the expected as the desired, then the organization starts to age. It ages because there is no drive and no impetus for change within the organization—which begins at the center of control by those who make the critical policies and decisions.

Perceived Relative Market Share

The next factor that can affect (ε), is the perceived relative market share. *Market share* is the percentage of all clients who have a certain need to be satisfied, to whom the company is selling. In business language, it is the company's share of total sales of similar products that satisfy the same need. What does *perceived* mean in this context?

A company can go to 100 percent market share or 0.001 percent market share overnight without changing revenues. Market share depends on what is put into the denominator, on what reference market is picked. A company can have 100 percent market share by defining their market as being *only* those people who buy from them. It is like hiring a person in a political bureaucracy. The people making the appointment know whom they want to appoint, but the law says that they must search for candidates. So they define the task with characteristics that only their candidate has. "This job calls for a person, born in East Galina, 38 years of age, educated at West Galina High School, who graduated in 1967." How many people are there who are 38 years old, graduated in 1967 from West Galina High School and who were born in East Galina?

The same thing happens with market share. A company can have any desired market share, depending on market definition. It can easily be the largest, biggest, best in the world at something— its leaders need only find out what it is that only that company can do well. For instance, one of my clients is the largest, privately-owned, computerized, multi-media alarm company in the world. The point is that whatever market share companies believe they have, is only a *perceived* market share.

Relative market share refers to a company's share of the market versus the share of your largest competitor. Now let us assume a case where a company has a perceived relative market share of 2. That means, for instance, that they have 35 percent of the market and the next largest competitor has about 17 percent. Will it make the company competitive or complacent?

Being the largest, biggest, best in anything is like being the champion in sports. A challenging competitor is necessary to stay in shape. When a company's leadership believes that it doesn't have to compete to satisfy the perceived needs of its clients any-more—when they believe they have a captive audience that will come to them—it hurts the entrepreneurial spirit and the desire and propensity to adapt to a changing environment. The company expects the customers to adapt to the company, rather than the company should adapt to the changing needs of the customers. The organization arrives at this stage when it believes it has the majority of the marketplace; that it dominates the marketplace and that its perceived market share has peaked. The leadership begins to believe they cannot get any additional increase in the marketplace, because the cost of getting an additional percentage is higher than the value returned.

Those who make decisions in the organization begin to think: "This is it! We've made it! We are there!" This attitude can do irreparable damage to the creativity of the company. They have forgotten that when they get to the top of a mountain, there is only one way to go, down.

Being a champion can make a company complacent. The way to stay in condition, to stay at the top, is to always have a strong challenge. Dominance of the market is a goal that should not be savored longer than one night of celebration. New visions must be sought. The market must be redefined, which introduces new competitors into the picture. The horizons must move as the organization moves, or their eyes will look lower and lower until they see only the tops of their toes. And then they stop moving altogether.

Functionality of Leadership Style

The third factor that affects (E)ntrepreneurship is the functionality of leadership style. What does this mean? As the organization changes in its Lifecycle, different styles of leadership are needed. There is an interplay between followers and leaders. We know it from history and political science—people deserve the leaders they get. Tell me what kind of system you have and I will tell you the kind of leadership it calls for.

What kind of a leadership is desirable at each stage of the Lifecycle? If the organization needs a certain consciousness, what is the functional leadership to provide that consciousness? Leadership means that the leader provides a dynamic process that takes an organization from one level of consciousness to the next one, from one place on the Lifecycle curve to the next one. In other words, this is someone who is capable of taking a company from

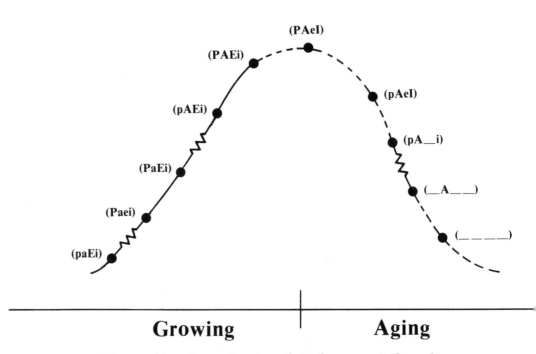

Figure 51:   Organizational Styles over Lifecycle

one set of problems to the next. He can resolve the problems of yesterday, while preparing the company for the problems of tomorrow.

Let's go back to the Moses analogy. He took the Jewish people from the problems of Egypt to the problems of Canaan. Leadership doesn't mean taking a system from a stage where there are problems to a stage where there are no problems. It means moving to the next level of problems, to the next generation of problems. Healthy leadership means that the next generation of problems will be more complicated and more sophisticated than the current problems. Thus, the organization grows. You are as big as the problems you contend with.

During the Courtship stage, the founders are dreaming about what they are going to do. A leader emerges who is going to lead the organization into Infancy. What does it mean to lead the organization into Infancy? Who is going to make that birth of risk occur? What kind of a leadership style is functional at that stage? Would it not be dysfunctional if the leader's style emphasized administration or (A)? Of course. Because an (A) would constantly say "no, no, no." Nothing would be born; the organization would never get started. What kind of leadership would enable the organization to be born, to coalesce that spark, to take the plunge, to take the risk, and make it happen? (**P**)erformance, (**A**)dministration, (**E**)ntrepreneurship or (**I**)?

It will be a (**P**) person. This is usually the person who says, "I'm putting in the first $5000 and I'm taking the risk first." This is the person who says "All right, let's go, let's do it, *I'm* ready." It is someone who is a doer, because for the organization to be born, it takes a real commitment. Someone who is going to *do* is needed; someone who is going to set the tone of *doing*, and provide a behavior model for an *action*-oriented organization.

During Courtship, the people in leadership positions are usually the dreamers and the theoreticians—the creators of the organization. When the organization is born, what very often happens to these ideologists? They are shoved aside. Then the action-oriented, hard-nosed doers take over. Doing, not talking, is what is necessary for the organization to survive Infancy. A desirable leader is the one who can both dream and do, because his vision will allow

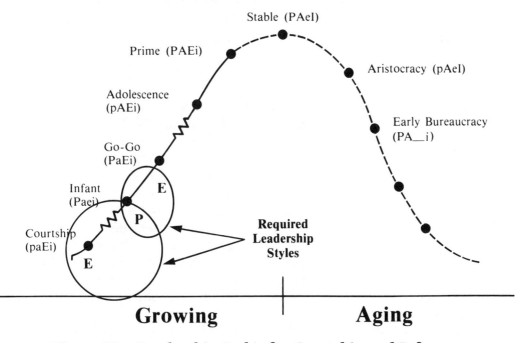

Figure 52: Leadership Styles for Courtship and Infancy

the company to emerge from Infancy much faster. Even so, the doing requirement is primary. The necessary style for movement into Infancy is the **(p)** style.

The leadership style reflects the next organizational style on the lifecycle. The leader with his style models where the organization should be going next. That's why the person is a *leader* and not a follower. That is why a leader could often outpace the people he leads.

Modeling the next stage of the life cycle provides functional leadership only in the growing stages. In the aging stages the leader has to model the previous stages or his leadership accentuates the decline of the organization. That makes the role of leadership even more difficult because one has to swim against the stream while in growing one only has to swim faster than the rest of the organization.

This explains why leaders of growing organizations have no empathy for functional leaders of aging organizations. They do not understand why it is taking so long, why the caution. They do not understand that swimming against the stream is politically more dangerous than swimming faster than the stream but in the same direction. In an aging organization, leadership has to make painful choices and still survive politically. In the growing stages, less painful decisions are made and less politically vulnerable is the leader (except for adolescence).

What kind of leadership is needed in a Go-Go company that doesn't have the cash crunch, and has begun to dream again? Look back at the Lifecycle chart. What is needed now is an **(e)**, because a move back into the creativity and dreaming mode is desired. Classically, the **(e)** function will be provided by the founder. Thus, there is often a founder with a **(pe)** style; he is doer/dreamer or a dreamer/doer. He can throw a hand grenade into the factory to start a fire, and then, as the fire starts, run in to put it out. As soon as the fire is extinguished, he throws the next hand grenade. He forces the company to grow by leaps and bounds by creating difficulties and then managing those difficulties. These founders are hard-working dreamers. They are arsonists and firefighters. It is crisis by management, rather than management by crisis.

In the Adolescent stage, the organization must be organized, systematized, and stabilized. At this point, quality is more important than quantity. What is the desired leadership? A bias toward

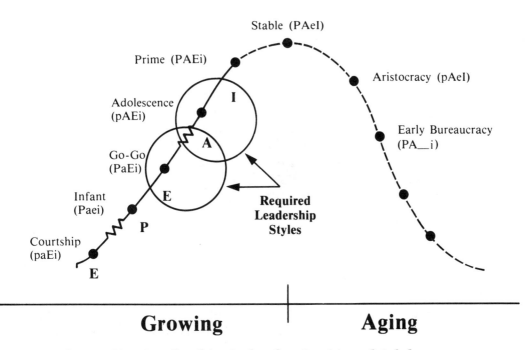

Figure 53: Leadership Styles for Go-Go and Adolescence

administration or **(A)** is important. This stage is where the difficulty in leadership transition usually occurs. The transition from Go-Go to Adolescence requires a switch from **(PE)** leadership style to **(AE)** style. This spells trouble. First, **(A)** is an altogether different animal than a **(PE)**. **(A)** is slow, thorough, analytical and risk-averse. This style pays attention to the details. **(PE)** is fast, and not concerned with details and risk-taking. The two leadership styles are incompatible. **(E)** wants his subordinates to be at work before him, and to leave after he does. However, because nobody knows when he will arrive at or leave work, the subordinates' behavior is erratic at best. The **(E)** types expect their subordinates to be on call at all times.

    (A) has a totally different style. He arrives at and leaves work on time. That makes **(E)** feel cheated; he considers **(A)** not sufficiently loyal to the company, he thinks that **(A)** is not trying hard enough. **(E)** shoots from the hip; **(A)** likes to think things over. **(E)** decides first and thinks later. **(A)** thinks, and then decides. **(A)** feels like he must walk behind **(E)** with a shovel all the time to clean up the mess. **(E)** on the other hand, feels that **(A)** prevents him from playing in the sandbox, and doing as he pleases. There is an obvious clash.

This clash can be somewhat alleviated if the person hired to provide leadership has the right style. What is needed is **(pAEi)**, not just an **(-A---)**. **(A)**, alone, will probably become deadwood under an arsonist **(--E-)**, and although he might survive personally, it will be at the expense to the company, when he becomes deadwood, **(----)** because he cannot fulfill the role the organization needs.

What is needed to link **(E)** and **(A)** is new leadership of the **(AE)** type. Those are the pain in the neck styles. They are excellent as consultants but unless they can change their styles, they are not good real-life managers.

Whether people can change styles or not must be tested in the field.

There are two options:

1. See if the **(PE)** founder can change his style to become **(AE)**; or
2. Replace the **(PE)** with **(AE)**; promote the **(PE)** founder to Chairman of the Board, and put **(AE)** in the Chief Operating Officer position

The difficulty of managing an organization during its transition from Infancy to Adolescence, is that the leadership in an organization must either change its style, or the leadership itself must be changed. Managing an enterprise is not a marathon race; it is a relay race. An organization must transfer leadership from one person to another, if the individual leadership cannot change styles as the conditions change.

One factor that can cause an organization to age occurs when leadership is not transferred functionally at the right point in time on the organizational Lifecycle. During Infancy, a big **(PE)** is needed, someone who is an aggressive dreamer/doer, who can *make visionary decisions quickly and generally on his own*. During Go-Go, someone who is organized and systematized, who can clearly articulate directions so that the *organization can make competent decisions*, is needed. It is no longer a one-person show. Thus, a systematizer, an **(AE)**, is needed. The danger, however, is that once a certain leader is successful, he becomes entrenched in his position even after he is no longer fulfilling the needs of the organization. **(PE)** won't make way for **(AE)**, and **(AE)**, once entrenched, won't yield to the next style needed.

It becomes even more acute if the change is from **(PE)** to **(pAei)**, because **(A)** becomes entrenched and there is no pressure to get him out. If we look back to the organizational Lifecycle description, we can see that there is no pressure to change leadership in Prime, Stable or Aristocracy. In Prime, everything is fine. In Stable, the problems are only latent. In Aristocracy, the company is liquid with good balance sheet ratios, and the Finzi-Contini syndrome does not allow people to express their dissatisfaction with the complacency. There is calm before the storm, there is no pressure to change leadership.

The **(A)** leadership style becomes dysfunctional, because it no longer offers what the organization needs. The leadership style needed after Adolescence, when the organization is moving into Prime should have an emphasis on **(I)**. Why **(I)**?

In Prime organizational cultures there is **(P)**, **(A)** and **(E)**. The structure is good and the right people are in the right jobs. The role of leadership in this case, is to hire the right people, to integrate the desirable conflicts that will emerge from a correctly structured

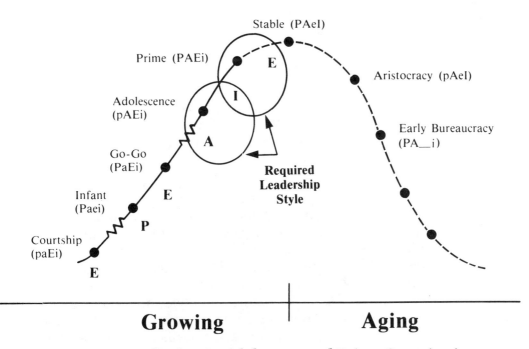

Figure 54. Leadership in Adolescent and Prime Organizations

organization, and to give them direction on where to go. It is necessary to have a leader who emphasizes the (I) role.

The necessary styles of leadership at any point in the Lifecycle, are the styles necessary to move out of the organization's current stage, and into the next stage. During Courtship, the organizational culture requires a leadership that dreams, and then gives organizational birth. It must be (PaEi), so it can to give birth and be action-oriented without losing vision. During Go-Go, (E) is needed going in, and (A) is needed to cool the Go-Go tendencies so the organization does not overload itself. The functional style is (pAEi). During Adolescence (A) is necessary to move in, but the company is riddled with conflict which must be dealt with; however (I) is necessary to move into Prime, so the functional style for Adolescence is (pAeI).

If moving into Prime requires an increase in (I), when the organizational culture begins to lose (E), leadership must provide for it, thus the leadership style necessary to remain in Prime is (paEI).

Leadership Styles

Courtship	PaEi
Infancy	PaEi
Go-Go	pAEi
Adolescence	pAeI
Prime	paEI
Stable	PaEi
Aristocracy	PaeI
Early Bureaucracy	Paei
Bureaucracy	?
Death	?

The reader should note that the required leadership style is dictated by the organizational culture and that during the growing stages, the culture the organization is moving *into* dictates what the necessary functional style is. After Prime, the leadership style needed is not what the organization's culture is going to develop into, but, just the opposite. The leadership style should be the one that will retard that development. Thus, since the organization is losing (E) from Prime on, the organization needs an (E) leadership to retard that development and provide for that deficiency.

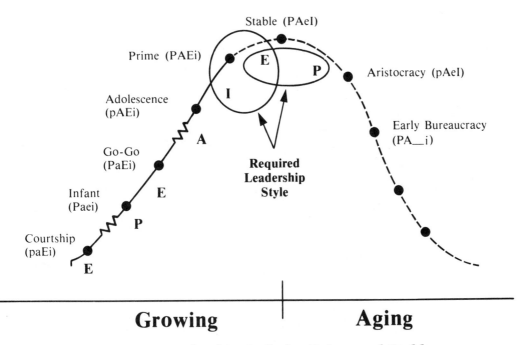

Growing | Aging

Figure 55: Leadership Style for Prime and Stable

A leader in Prime should be a person who is a **(paEI)**—a states-man. He is someone who sees the big vision and can integrate the people who fill the **(P)** and **(A)** roles to follow that vision.[3]

When the organization moves out of Prime, flexibility, **(E)** is lost. Thus, the kind of leadership necessary to retard this develop-ment is one that provides **(E)**. Because **(P)** is lost during Aristocracy, the functional style to retard deterioration in Stable is **(PaEi)**. This **(PaEi)** style is different from the **(PaEi)** style of an Infant organiza-tion. This stage requires a professional manager with the style of an entrepreneur. He must be a professional soldier, not a guerilla leader. He must make decisions *and* have a vision for a large organi-zation. This is a significant distinction, because often an organiza-tion that is losing flexibility will merge or acquire a Go-Go with the explicit goal of acquiring the Go-Go leadership. The organization soon finds that the Go-Go leadership does not have the political maturity to manage a company in the Stable phase where it is riddled with internal political realities.

---

[3] Adizes: *How to* . . . for a description and discussion of management styles.

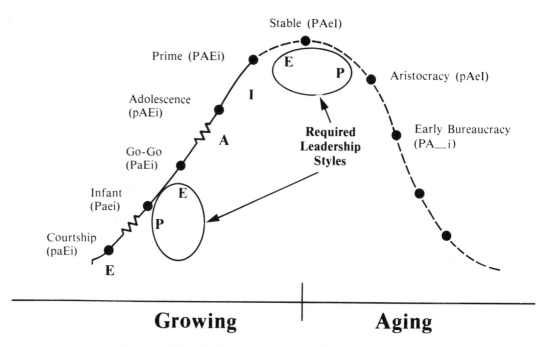

Figure 56: Infant versus Stable Leadership

Looking again at the leadership style called for, it is evident that in Infancy, if we present the style in four dimensions and according to the priority that is needed by the organizational culture, we get **(PaEi)**. **(P)** is first, for going into Infancy, **(E)** second to provide for moving into Go-Go, **(A)** is third, to provide for the long run of Adolescence. **(I)** is the least called for, unless the company takes the very long view, and in that case the style will be **(PaEi)**.

During Stable, **(P)** is the most important role in retarding the deterioration of Aristocracy, which means losing **(P)**. Next in importance is **(E)**, the loss of which caused the decline of the organization into Stable. **(I)** is third in importance in stopping the organization from moving to the next stage of the Lifecycle, Early Bureaucracy. Thus, the necessary style is somewhat different than the style of Infancy. The Stable leader has to be significantly politically oriented than an Infant leader: success at one stage of the life cycle does not guarantee success at another stage.

In Aristocracy, the company is in trouble. It does not need only **(E)** anymore. What it needs is **(P)**. It must get back to the basics, and right away. Back to hard-nosed decisions. Back to block-

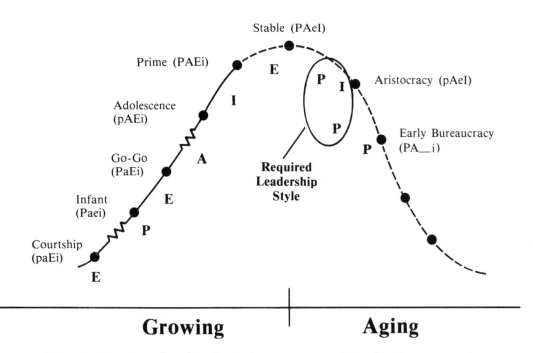

Figure 57:   Leadership in Aristocracy and Early Bureaucracy

ing and tackling. The organization must identify what business it is in and what value it has for its clients. It must get close to its clients and pay attention to the *why* and *what* more than the *how*. It must derive the *how* from the *why* and *what*, rather than let the *how* dictate the *why* and *what*. In the next stage (**i**) will decline too. People will probably desert the ship left and right. What is needed now is someone who can integrate, a coach who can uplift the spirits while making the painful transition. That is a **(PaeI)** style.

For Early Bureaucracy, there is a typical mistake made in failing organizations owned by government, or those being national-ized. The government does not appoint a **(P)** to lead the organization out of their difficulties. Instead, an **(A)**dministrator or an **(i)**ntegrator is usually appointed because the company was not nationalized to *increase* unemployment, but to save employment. The task given to leadership is to save jobs, not the company. What happens? Instead of rejuvenating the organization, the **(A)** and **(i)** now create a bigger bureaucracy which accelerates the decline of the company, and if the organization is big enough, the decline of the country.

What can age an organization—cause it to behave pathologically rather than normally—is leadership which is not functional to the needs of the organization according to where it is on the Lifecycle. In Stable, Aristocracy, and later stages, the organization keeps relying on (A)s when it needs (P)s and (E)s. The members get (A)s because in the declining part of the Lifecycle, the culture acquires the leadership that reinforces its existent culture. So, they get the wrong leadership at the wrong time. Often, it cannot be changed or controlled from within, and by the time it is tried, it's too late. The company is in such deep trouble that change in leadership is too little too late.

Functionality of Organizational Structure

The next factor to affect creativity in organizations is the functionality of its structure. Organizations are often structured so as to behaviorally inhibit the entrepreneurial spirit. Look at the example of a simple organization that consists of the following departments.

Notice that the departments are drawn on different length legs. This difference reflects basic differences in the orientation of each department. Those departments with long legs have a long-term orientation; those with short legs have a short-term orientation.

We can use the four (PAEI) roles of management to describe the basic orientation of each of these departments. For example, what should be the orientation in (PAEI) terms, of a typical sales department? Sales are closely oriented toward satisfying customer needs i.e., (P)erformance, and satisfying these needs efficiently,

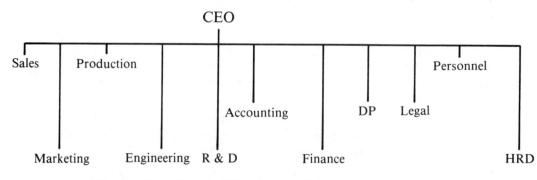

Figure 58: Typical Functional Organization Chart

which is a function of **(A)**dministration. Therefore a sales department should have the **(PAei)** style. What should be the style of the marketing department? Marketing is also oriented toward customer needs, **(P)**erformance, but in the context of developing creative solutions to satisfy the needs of tomorrow: **(E)**ntrepreneurship; so it should have a **(PaEi)** orientation.

The accounting department is a story in itself. Obviously **(A)** is the primary function, but **(E)** is also necessary. Why **(E)?** It is not **(A)** for **(P)** which means organizing to better serve clients' needs. That is the functions of sales, **(PA).** It is not **(AI)** which is a system of accounting that reflects the culture. What is left is **(AE),** but why? The following joke can make the point.

A small company was looking for an accountant. Three candidates applied and were asked "How much is two and two?" The first candidate, who had just passed the CPA exam, like most inexperienced technicians said, "Four! No question, no doubt about it! Four!"

The second candidate worked for many years for one of the top, large auditing firms. His answer was, "I have to call the home office first."

The third candidate was a graduate of the University of Hardknocks; he was streetwise. He half closed his eyes and asked, "What do you have in mind? Are you selling or are you buying?"

He was hired, and rightly so. For accounting to be an information system rather than a data system, accounting must know what management has in mind. It should be **(A)** of **(E)**, which means it should provide control of the company's direction. "Are we going into or getting out of the New York market"? Each question requires totally different information. In many companies accounting is bookkeeping. They work de facto for the IRS, not for management. Management gets data but no information. That happens because accounting is not brought into the management team. They are neither the driving, nor the driven force. They just produce reports, which reminds me of another anecdote.

Two people are in a balloon flying over the countryside. Clouds come in and after some time they are lost. Flying around, they finally see an opening among the clouds. They start descending, and on the ground they see a person. They shout to him.

"Hello, where are we?"

"In a balloon!" he yells back.

Frustrated, one says to the other, "That guy down there must be an accountant."

"How do you know?" asks his partner.

"Because he gave us accurate, precise information—totally useless!"

The same desired **(pAEi)** orientation of accounting should apply to the legal counsel and data processing departments in an organization. Each one of them, in order to perform its function adequately, must first ask, "What do you have in mind?" This question is a good test to check whether the organization has a lawyer or just a highly paid legal secretary.

Here is how it can go. Give a newly written contract to a lawyer with the request that he tell you whether or not to sign it. If he says "Fine, I'll call you in the morning"—fire him. Anyone with legal training can check if a contract is legal or not. That takes only memory to know all the rulings, precedents, and laws. What you want is not a lawyer who tells you "why not" but one who tells you "how yes" to accomplish what you want.

For that, the lawyer should have pushed the contract aside on his table, and asked: "Before I read it, first tell me, what you have in mind. What are you trying to achieve?" This lawyer will check, not only the legalities of the contract, but whether and how it will achieve your goals.

The same rule applies to computer people. If they take an assignment to determine which computer or system to buy before they check what and how the organization is going to use the computer in the future, then they are only salesmen of computerized typewriters and calculators, and not the type of people who will truly computerize a company.

Similar analyses of the other departments will produce the **(PAEI)** orientations shown in Figure 59.

In the normal course of events in most companies, how do these departments get along with each other? Which departments typically will have and should have, lots of disagreements and conflict?

Sales versus Marketing

Production versus R and D and Engineering

Accounting, Legal and Computers versus Everyone

Personnel versus Human Resources Development

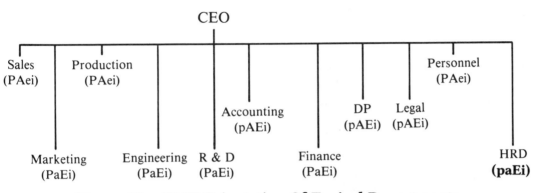

Figure 59:   PAEI Orientation Of Typical Departments

Why do these units have trouble getting along? What is the nature of their conflict? The first typical mistake in analysis is to attribute it to the people involved. Sales accuses marketing of not understanding the realities of what they face in the market. The sales department works hard to implement a pricing/product strategy, and as soon as it is working, along come the fat-cats from corporate headquarters to change it. Marketing on the other hand accuses sales of resisting change, of dragging their feet. "Salesmen, you know, aren't that smart. If they were, would they be on the road all day?"

Production and engineering are also at odds. Engineering wants to constantly change the technology, to update it. What does production say? "Come back next year. Don't mess up our production schedule. We are measured by our productivity and manufacturing costs; your changes *might* work in the long run but they *sure* make a mess and retard our goals in the short-run."

So, engineering is upset. "There is resistance to change from these small-brain production engineers. They have their eyes set on their own belly buttons. Heck, if we didn't push, they would still be working with a spinning wheel."

So, the organization tries to resolve the personal issues, rather than the structural issues. The frequent solution is to send someone from sales to head marketing, or someone from production to head engineering, so "those guys up there know the realities we face before they make their decisions."

Of course, this doesn't work either, because if the person maintains his sales—(**PA**)—orientation in marketing, the company loses (**E**). The same goes for the production person in engineering. If, on the other hand, the person changes his orientation from **(PA)** to **(PE)** he is accused of being a traitor, a turncoat, by the unit he came from.

Another manifestation of mistaken attribution to the problems, is to attribute the conflict to style rather than structure, to believe that a person or persons are not team players. So the cry goes "We need a team player." Out goes one player and in comes another. What happens next? If the new marketing guy heard his predecessor's marching orders, "be a team player," and tries to fit in, he can't exercise pressure for change, as he should. Who sets the tone now? Sales. The same thing happens in engineering. It is the production department that is the driving force. This solution does not work over the long run, the organization has team players but as the **(PA)** orientation dominates, the **(E)** orientation is lost.

The most frequently used solution to avoid these conflicts is to unite the conflicting departments. This produces a streamlined organization.

What's wrong with this structure? Sales is **(P)**-oriented, short-term and results-oriented. Marketing should be **(E)**-oriented, long-range, entrepreneurial, viewing and analyzing. When sales and marketing are put together, which orientation will win? Is it the **(P)** or the **(E)**? Is it the short-run or the long-run? The answer is obvious: the short run; the sales-orientation will win. Thus, when marketing and sales are put together, marketing ends up doing statistical analyses of how well the salesmen sold, or preparing sales brochures or sales collateral material. And they call this marketing. The marketing name is a misnomer. It is not marketing because the bonuses, the orientation, and the pressure are for selling, not for marketing.

The same thing occurs when production and engineering are put together. It is still called the engineering department, but what

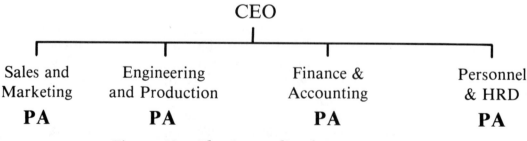

Figure 60:   The Streamlined Organization

engineering is probably doing now is maintenance. They are oiling and repairing the machines used for production. It's (E) being dominated by (P); the short-run driving the long-run, rather than vice versa. This means hardly any (E) is left.

When human resources development is put under personnel, a similar phenomenon occurs. The personnel department, although trained in (I) and aspiring to provide (I) for the corporation, is by and large in the (A) business. Frequently they do the dirty laundry for management. They fire, displace, perform salary administration, administer personnel evaluations, selection and labor negotiations. It is the (A)dministration for (P)erformance, when (P) means productivity. It is not strange then that labor, by and large, does not perceive personnel in the *human resources development* business, but rather as the long arm of management. So, when personnel comes in with ideas for job enlargement, job enrichment or participative management, what does Labor say? "Aha! This is a new trick to make us work harder for less money. No, thank you."

Personnel is frustrated. They *want* to develop people. They *want* to be humanistic and motivated. But they are accused of being manipulative. They are looked upon with suspicion. "Those bastards smile a lot; but they're wishy-washy soaped fish—you can't catch them. They wiggle right out of your hand. But don't turn your back. They stab you before you know it."

Putting an (EI), human resources development (HRD), under personnel will kill its (EI) function. It will be subordinated to the (PA) function of personnel. HRD people end up on the low part of the totem pole, ensuring that the coffee is warm and the refreshments have arrived for training sessions. They lose their (EI) functionality.

Another mistake is putting finance and accounting together. Finance is to be understood as investment analysis, treasury function, management of resources and use of funds. Accounting is to be understood as the controller's function: accounts receivable, accounts payable, and general ledger bookkeeping. By putting the two together, a very dangerous situation is created. The company creates a delayed reaction syndrome. The company skips a beat, like an arrhythmia of the heart. Let me explain.

Accounting's role is to be a pain. It should be and frequently is, precisely wrong instead of approximately right. They return a request because a signature is in the wrong place, *and it should be that way*. They are the guardians of law and order and a company needs this, otherwise the company loses systemic control. But that does not make accounting people popular, does it? They are accused of being bureaucratic, unresponsive, and closed-mouthed.

Now, let us look at a scenario where a certain product line is doing poorly. In an executive meeting where the problem is analyzed, will marketing suggest dropping the line? Most probably not, because they are the ones who suggested it in the first place. Instead, they will ask for a higher advertising budget, they will try to increase, one way or another the budget of the marketing mix. They will promise something and keep the product alive a little bit longer.

Will sales try to kill the product? Not yet, because their incentive systems are based on sales quotas. So they will suggest lowering the price. They will attribute the problem to lack of collateral, prices being too high and the incentive being insufficient.

How about production? There is no vocal objection here yet either, because their production plan incentives include this product line. So, they will probably ask for another piece of machinery— "if we only had that machine, we would improve the quality of the product, then it would sell."

Personnel is not geared to kill it either. It might lead to some reduction in labor force, and that spells trouble on the horizon for them. It should be noted that each department is interpreting the corporate problem through its own interests. Their solutions are derived from their local orientation.

Who, besides the CEO, is interested not just in market share, sales or production, *unless it produces profits*? It should be the vice president of finance. He should be looking at return on investment . . . period! If the internal cost of capital invested in this product line is higher than the return on investment he should say, "Let's do something else."

If accounting and finance are in one division, the attempts of finance to kill a weak product line might be rejected with the following remarks: "He's head of accounting, he always says NO, so what else is new?" If we would have let these bean counters manage this company, we would have been dead a long time ago!"

Several more months or years pass until it is not in the interest of marketing, production, or engineering to have the product line. Then, an axis develops and the CEO acts. Please note that in my experience, no CEO acts totally alone without consulting his top subordinates. What they tell him to do is colored by their interests, and their interests stem from the organization's structure.

When marketing and sales, production and engineering, personnel and human resources development, finance and accounting are united, where is the only place in this organizational chart that a true **(E)** orientation could still survive? Only at the top. Even then it is a maybe, because it depends on where the company is on the Lifecycle, and whether the leadership is functional. It could be a **(P)** or an **(A)** or an **(I)** at the top. In that case, a complaint will be that the organization is stymied, slow to react to market forces, and that there is no real strategic outlook. So, the organization hires someone to be a strategic planner.

Here is how it looks.

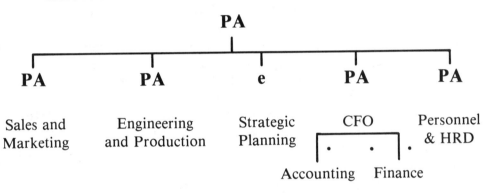

Figure 61:   The Net Impact on "E" for the Streamlined Structure

You cannot make a submarine fly by appointing a very qualified pilot to look through the periscope.

Sometimes when an organization hires someone to change the direction of the company, and he can't, because the company is structured wrong, they send him to Harvard to study some more. That won't help, unless the purpose is to make him even more frustrated than he already is. It won't work to send our pilot to an advanced school for pilots to learn how to navigate better. He's asked to fly a submarine!

Please note: *Structure causes strategy and not vice versa*.[4] There

---

[4] This is in disagreement with the famous treaties of Alfred Chandler. In my view, strategy *should* determine structure, but present structure determines present strategy. See: Chandler, Alfred B. *Strategy and Structure: Chapters in the History of the Industrial Enterprise* (Cambridge: MIT. Press, 1962).

is no use in trying to have a strategy for a submarine to fly. You must change the submarine to an airplane and then strategize in what it should do. Structure causes behavior, structure causes strategy and not vice versa. If one wants to change behavior, one must change the structure first. No new strategy can be implemented until a new structure is in place.

What should the new structure be? For, that, we need a strategy, don't we? It is a chicken and egg problem, that I have solved. (See Chapter 12.) The bottom line is that there is no use bombarding a (**PA**) *structure* with (**E**) *people* and consulting reports. It has little if any impact, and is a waste of money.

So why do people do it? It is *easier* to train someone at Harvard, hire a strategic planner to sit, smoke a pipe, write reports and get an ulcer; it is easier to pay BCG a million bucks for very competent recommendations, than to go through the pain of organizational, structural change. It is not money that bothers management. It is time, the political wars, and the fear of the political repercussions of change that cause the pain. "Once you free the genie from the bottle, who knows who will survive?"

Structure affects strategy because structure reflects the relative self-interests, and the interest structure will impact the emerging strategy. Structure causes behavior, and if the structure rejects (**E**), it can become the fourth factor contributing to the loss of (**E**).

I can't resist making a side comment as we are discussing structural causes of behavior. I get frustrated reading newspapers and magazines. Here is an example.

For years, I have been watching the struggle between the United States National Security Council and the State Department. From the day the NSC was established, there are reports of infighting between these two governmental agencies. Smart people like Dr. Henry Kissinger headed them both, so there was no fighting on the surface, and it made him very powerful because he controlled the units that developed *and* implemented foreign policy. When the two agencies were split, it caused competition between the two heads as to who makes foreign policy, and it has been a continuous struggle, and will be until the structure is changed.

To clarify why the conflict exists, I wrote an article which was published in the *Wall Street Journal* on the op ed page. I include it here in its entirety. (I am adding the (**PAEI**) jargon, which did not appear in the article, so that the reader can follow my reasoning.)

THE INTERNAL CONFLICT OVER FOREIGN POLICY[5]

Richard Allen's recent departure from the National Security Council should not make us lose sight of the fact that the conflict between the NSC and the State Department and the rest of the bureaucracy for that matter, has existed since the NSC was established. It would profit us to analyze the nature of this ongoing conflict so that whoever is next sent into the NSC director's job doesn't get burned, too.

There will always be conflict between those who conceive change [(E)] and those who implement it [(PA)]. The same conflict that existed between Mr. Allen and Alexander Haig existed between Zbigniew Brzezinski and Cyrus Vance. The same conflict existed between Henry Kissinger and William Rogers, and it also existed in the Kennedy administration with Walt Rostow and Dean Rusk.

The nature of the struggle is the same as that which should and does exist between production [(PA)] and engineering [(E)].

At its inception, the State Department was expected to make policy [(PE)] and carry it out [(PA)]. But with the centralization of decision-making, due to telecommunications and jet travel, the foreign-policy decision-making process [(PE)] moved away from the ambassadorial level and subsequently up into the State Department, and eventually it was centralized in the White House. Since State is now left primarily with the implementation role, [(PA)] it functions very much like a corporate sales department.

To allow the president to make complete and well-rounded decisions, the small, high-level, NSC was established. We can read in the memoirs of both Mr. Kissinger and former President Richard Nixon that the president did not rely on State to make and change foreign policy. For that he used the more flexible group at the NSC. Thus the National Security Council functions much like a corporate marketing department, [(E)]. It abstracts the information that the State Department, among others, has accumulated in the field and analyzes the data to make long-term policy assessments, which the president can accept or reject.

If State were responsible for making foreign policy, the NSC would be reporting to that department, rather than to the president. Thus the role of the State Department has changed from

[5] Adizes, Ichak, "The Internal Conflict Over Foreign Policy." *Wall Street Journal.* December 22, 1981.

foreign-policy *making* to one of *contributing* to the policy-making.
Mr. Haig, who is much more organizationally aggressive than
Mr. Vance, claims that disagreeing with him is tantamount to
disagreeing with the president. Since Mr. Haig believes he makes
foreign policy for the president, he thinks his view-point should
dominate the decision-making process. But those times have
passed. Mr. Haig can only recommend policy to the president.
This means he must compete with the alternative recommendations of the president's adviser on national security.

Unfortunately, since reporters are as befuddled as Messrs.
Reagan, Haig and Allen as to the nature of the conflict between
State and the NSC, there is said to be a rift over "who should
make policy for the president—the National Security Council
or the Department of State?" This is precisely what the media
continue to ask, and it is precisely the wrong question. The
answer as to who speaks for the president on policy should be
obvious. The president speaks for the president.

The conflict between the two departments is a conflict of
complementarity. It is natural, desirable, functional and should
be expected. The conceptual orientation of the NSC **[(E)]** and
the concerns over foreign-policy implementation of the State
Department **[(PA)]** will almost always be in conflict and should
be. The responsibility of the president is to listen to both view-
points and make a judgement. But if, as in a business organization, he tries to resolve the conflict by "integrating' the long-
range view into the short-range contingency, the short-run outlook will dominate and the long-term perspective will be lost.
The present danger is that the large State Department bureaucracy will dominate the small, NSC think-tank group. This is
dangerous for President Reagan, because information from that
source will also dominate.

Mr. Haig's misunderstanding of the new reality of who
makes foreign policy is the crux of the current conflict. *That
Mr. Haig's personal management style does not fit his organizational role exacerbates the problem.*

Since the proper role of the president's assistant on National
Security Affairs is not fully comprehended, Mr. Allen was caught
in a "Catch-22" situation. If he and his staff fulfill the mission
for which they were established, namely, independent long-term
policy planning, then conflict is deemed divisive and undesirable. This is a serious misunderstanding.

The conflict between the NSC and the State Department
will always remain a highly desirable conflict. For the creation

of an intelligent foreign policy, this conflict must be recognized, tolerated and legitimized. The NSC needs to be equal and not subordinate to the State Department. News reporters must realize that differences between the two do not mean that the United States is pursuing inconsistent foreign policy. What is important is that the president remain consistent, not whether his advisers disagree.

Reporters misinterpreting the conflict will say it reflects badly on the president to have his advisers fighting. This only compounds the difficulty of the president's decision-making process.

It is conceivable that this conflict will be resolved with Mr. Haig winning the power struggle. If he does, I predict that this win will turn *into a loss for Mr. Haig in the long run*. In a centralized system the president will continue to make the final foreign-policy decisions, not the secretary of state. The president eventually will want to make different decisions than the State Department, in its concern for bureaucratic implementation, will be willing to support. Thus the clash which is now between the White House and the State Department. Such a confrontation can only be *detrimental to Mr. Haig*.[6]

The NSC is supposed to provide the (**E**) function for the president, and the State Department should provide the (**PA**) function. There is and should be conflict between the two. How should this conflict be resolved? The president should listen to both and then make a judgement. The State Department should not dominate the NSC and claim monopoly on foreign policy, and the NSC should not take the State Department's role of implementing decisions—(**PA**)—which is what caused Irangate to happen.

What should be the style of the head of the NSC? In my opinion, (**EI**). He should make his recommendations, and not necessarily agree with any of those proposed by others. The mistake is to expect the NSC head to be a team player. If the head of NSC is active, he is accused of not being a team player. So they bring in a team player. This team player is then accused of assuming too low a profile and of making insignificant contributions. No one can win as head of NSC because the role is not clearly understood.

The conclusion one should derive from the above is that *United*

---

[6] Note the date of the article. It predicted the fall of Alexander Haig as Secretary of State by six months.

States will have no clear foreign policy until it structures its government to have one. I did not say the president of the United States does not have, or will not have a clear foreign policy. I am saying that the president's *administration* will have no clear foreign policy until it is correctly structured to deliver one.

The person most frustrated by this situation must be the president. I heard presidents Jimmy Carter and Gerald Ford being independently interviewed during the Young Presidents' Organization University in Hawaii, 1982. On one question they both answered the same question the same way, without knowing what the other had been asked or answered. The question was: "What was the most frustrating experience of being the president of the United States?" The answer was, (paraphrased): "The frustration of not seeing your decisions implemented; the difficulty of getting policy carried out."

The recommended practice in structuring companies is to structure them in a way that encourages and nourishes the role the organization needs most. Thus in growing companies, (A) functions should be structured and have a V.P. Administration in charge of Accounting, Personnel, Legal and Data Processing. In aging organizations, (A) should be split and (E) united, have a V.P. in charge of Marketing, Finance, Engineering and HRD. But never, never, never should Marketing and Sales, Production and Engineering, Finance and Accounting, Human Resources with Personnel be structurally fused.

The Problem Of Organizational Colonialism

Until now we have diagnosed a structure of a simple profit center organization. A multi-profit divisional company faces an additional challenge, which I call organizational colonialism. An organization can be described in its totality with a single Lifecycle curve. However, this curve is really the average behavior of each component division or department in the company. The trouble with an average behavior is that it doesn't accurately represent the real situation. A person with one foot in boiling water and one foot in freezing water does not have a comfortable 70-degree average temperature.

Companies are composed of units, departments, or divisions where each is on a different location on the Lifecycle curve. It is not unusual to find multi-profit divisional companies with profit centers that are in Infant, Go-Go, Prime and Aristocratic profit centers. Typically, these entities are organized in the following hierarchy.

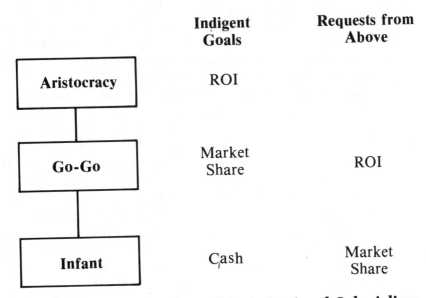

	Indigent Goals	Requests from Above
Aristocracy	ROI	
Go-Go	Market Share	ROI
Infant	Cash	Market Share

Figure 62:   The Problem of Organizational Colonialism

The reason this is so frequently encountered, is that Aristocracies like to take over Go-Go companies. It gives them growth they can't otherwise achieve. Go-Go companies have Infants under them because Go-Go companies are promiscuous; they start businesses easily. This type of structure however, is susceptible to a problem.

The phenomenon of Infants reporting to Go-Go organizations, and Go-Go organizations reporting to Aristocracies, I call *organizational colonialism*. The problem with organizational colonialism is revealed by analyzing the inter-relationships between units in terms of needs and appropriate measures of performance.

What is the goal of an Infant organization? To break even, to get enough cash to survive. It is fighting for cash. It needs cash constantly and always demands, "We need more capital." This is usually annoying to the Go-Go, because the Go-Go says "What, more money? We gave you some four months ago. When will you stop asking for more? Furthermore you are not growing at the rate we are used to. We grow 35 percent a year and you have not achieved that rate. Why should we give you more money?"

What does a Go-Go want? Sales and sales growth is the goal they impose on those reporting to them. Moreover, Go-Go organizations also need capital for their own growth so they are not inclined to share. What does Aristocracy want? Dividends. Return on Investment. Instead of giving, it is taking. It wants to milk the calf not just the cow. So the Aristocracy milks the Go-Go and the Go-Go kills the Infant by denying it resources. I call it colonialism because the unit above is imposing its *own* goals that reflect *its* place on the Lifecycle on the unit it dominates, ignoring the goals of the unit according to its own Lifecycle position.

What can happen is very interesting. All of the organization goes under. All the components that enable rejuvenation and growth are available, but the organization is structured in a way that the different units impose non-functional demands on each other, and all of them suffer. The goals that are imposed on the organization under each parent are not functional to the child's stage in the Lifecycle curve. The demands are only functional to what the parent wants, and it is using its power to impose its desires.

To summarize, the mental age of those in control of the organization, the functionality of the leadership style, the perceived relative market share, and the functionality of the organizational structure are the four factors that impact **(E)**.

To diagnose an organization, look at its behavior. That should point to a place on the Lifecycle. Then analyze. Is **(E)** personalized in the leader, or is it systematically provided. If it is personalized, the organization is pre-Adolescence. If it is systematized, it is post-Adolescence.

Is **(E)** sufficient, as measured by the rate of change and needed or proactive change to environment? If is it declining, check the above four factors and see which of them contributes to the existence or demise of **(E)**. It should confirm your hypothesis about the location on the organization Lifecycle and its causes.

We will discuss how to deal with the decline in **(E),** and how to rejuvenate it, in the next part of the book, after we discuss how control affects location on the Lifecycle curve.

Factors Affecting "Power Politics" (*CAPI*) In The Lifecycle

There are internal and external forces that explain why *CAPI* behaves the way it does throughout the Lifecycle.

CAPI can break down for internal reasons. It can break down because of a breakdown in family relations, if it is a family business, or because of other divergence in interests. The external forces could be political—the government gets involved and makes new rules or guidelines that affect control of the organization—such as transferring power to the workers. This action is carried out in many countries. The workers are brought into decision-making positions without the politicians understanding the managerial repercussions. Management then must negotiate with subordinates over subjects which previously were exclusively a managerial prerogative. Decisions get stymied, entrepreneurs leave the country, sending their capital out first. (That's what happened to Peru, for instance, in the 1970s with their industrial communistic experiments.) When *CAPI* is broken, the organization ages because it loses control and the ability to make change efficiently.

CAPI Over the Lifecycle

We have already said that prior to Adolescence *CAPI* is with the founder. He is usually a dictator. But, if he is fully in control, why is organizational predictability low? It should be high. The answer lies in the fact that prior to Adolescence *CAPI* is personalized, it is vested with the founder who is usually a big (**E**). He provides an unopposed, continuous change. It is predictable that the organization will behave unpredictably.

Since the founder calls all the shots and is in control of the organization, he is usually arrogant, dictatorial, and authoritative. He makes decisions in a non-participative way; he makes them intuitively. There are no articulated strategies; one seldom understands his decisions. Thus, the situation is that the organization is not under control, although the founder has control.

The lack of organizational control stems from the lack in (**A**)— systems, rules, and policies—that give a backbone of predictability to the company and control the founder as well. In Adolescence this backbone is developed and the organization moves to Prime where it is flexible *and* predictable.

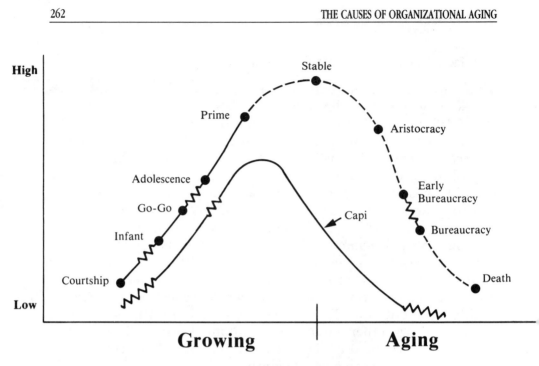

Figure 63:   Capi Over Lifecycle

Control from Adolescence and beyond is systemic rather than personal. Incrementally, from Prime down, the system is stronger than the individuals who constitute it. That is why a structure can cause the loss of **(E)**, which explains the increase in organizational predictability and loss of flexibility.

When *CAPI* breaks down, when interest groups split in several different directions the organization is predictably stale. No one group alone can direct change in the organization, and since each group has different interests, it is difficult to coalesce and affect change. Eventually, when the form is barren and yields no desired function, a breakdown will occur. The system will die, and a new one will emerge from the ashes.

Which internal factors can cause the break in *CAPI*? Here are some possible suggestions.

Prior to Adolescence, one must look at who controls the company and what their individual goals are. In a healthy, growing company, the founder is in control and his interests are to make the company survive Infancy. In Go-Go, usually the goal of those or the one in control is to have fun, to have a personal sandbox to play in. All other interests are under control, whether it is his family that is making demands, or labor which usually is not yet unionized.

In Adolescence, there is a split in interests. (A) is risk-averse; (E) wants growth. If (A) wins, interests that are risk-averse dominate and the organization drifts into premature aging. If (E) dominates, the organization moves back into the Go-Go stage. If (A) and (E) move together, the organization moves into Prime. (To learn what will make them work together, see Part IV.)

In the Founder's Trap, the self-interest of the founder dominates at the expense of the interests of the corporation. His need to be in control, to satisfy his own ego, prohibits the organization from developing self-control. No one else can play in the sandbox.

Members of the executive committee and the vice presidents of such an organization exhibit premature, personal adolescent behavior although they could be middle-aged or older. They laugh a lot, giggle, fight, complain about each other and go to "Papa" for judgments and decisions. However, they don't take any responsibility for the things they are complaining about. They expect Papa to acknowledge their complaints and solve the problem *for* them. Their major complaint, and frequently their hostility, is toward Papa. In this case Papa is not necessarily the Founder, the person who actually started the company. It is the person who made it grow during Go-Go. There is a love-hate relationship between the founder and the subordinates. They want him out and at the same time they can't manage without him. At this point, the organization can get stymied and there will be little, if any change from internal sources until the founder passes away or the company is sold.

In the Family Trap, the situation is even more serious. The split in interests can take many forms. As one Brazilian executive told me about his fight with his brother over control of the company, "It all started when I took his duck away when we played in the bathtub 30 years ago."

Sibling rivalry is one cause of losing *CAPI* in the Family Trap. Usually, the older son gets the reigns of management. The younger son, who might be more aggressive, resists his brother's control. (There is a rule that determines which style a child will have depending on his birth sequence, and the style of his parents. By and large, firstborn children are not (E)s if the father was an (E). The father burns the (E) behavior out of the child. Usually (E)s firstborn, in my experience, has (A) tendencies. The second child is usually an (I); and finally the third child can afford to stick out, and be an (E). Obviously this is not an ironclad rule.) The hierarchy of leadership by birth sequence is not necessarily accepted by the children who are born later. "This is not a royal succession," they claim. "Why him and not me?"

Another source of breakdown in *CAPI* is that family pride can dominate rational managerial thinking. To maintain control, members of the family are prohibited from selling stock. Voting stock, for instance, is in a trust where the patriarch or matriarch have control over the trust. So the children clip coupons and have no way to affect what is going on. Except that children grow and patriarchs die. Then the untrained children start fighting with the professional managers over money. There is no Papa to keep them in control and chaos results because professional management can't act professionally under those conditions. Some of them quit, and the family squabbles over who will take over. Ego trips and personal interests dominate at the expense of the organizational needs. (This analysis applies mainly to the Western world. In the East, my experience is that they accept birthrights, thus making succession there, in *CAPI* terms, more stable.)

In Prime, the interests are coalesced. Management is managing a coalition of interests—stockholder's interests for returns on their investments, management's own interests in growth and labor's interests in security. The company is not under the control of an individual, but of a plan, a strategy that unites and reflects the different interest groups.

After Prime, diversity of interests begins to occur again. The stockholders separation from management which occurred in Adolescence was a desirable event. It produced Prime. But such separation has increasingly negative implications later on. Management becomes more self-interested than owner-interested. Such self-interest is not only at the expense of stockholders, it becomes increasingly at the expense of labor also.

In Aristocracy, the organization can afford the split in interests because each one is milking the company, and since it is fat, there is plenty of milk. The spark that breaks the peaceful coexistence occurs when there is no more fat. Then, instead of carving up the organization, they start carving up each other.

The first to lose are the stockholders who see their investment dwindle; then the firings start and Labor loses. Eventually, management is fired; they are usually the last to lose.

To verify where an organization is on the Lifecycle, ask who has control. (I am not referring to ownership, but to behavioral, managerial control.) Is it an individual or a system? If it is an individual, the organization has not yet reached Adolescence. If a system has control, it is past Adolescence. Is there a commonalty of interests of the groups that comprise *CAPI*? If yes, the organization is in Prime, or maybe Stable. If there is no commonalty of interests that comprise *CAPI*, the organization is past Prime. Has the fighting started? If not, the organization is in Stable or Aristocracy. If yes, it's Early Bureaucracy.

The breakdown of control can also be externally caused. Government legislation can decide what and how things are done, and thereby change the rules of the game. In Scandinavia and Germany, workers' representatives must be on the board of directors. That can lead the organization over the Adolescent hump into Prime, and if management does not know how to handle the diversity of interests, right into Aristocracy.

Japan is in Prime because management behaviorally, rather than legally, tries to optimize the interests of labor, ownership and management. Other places in the Far East—such as Malaysia, Hong Kong and Singapore—are still battling the Adolescent stage, and frequently falling into the Family Trap, which in those cases, is not as dangerous as in the West. In the Far East, members of the family still accept the hierarchy by birth, so *CAPI* is not yet broken. In the West, family feuds are more common. As Easterners are westernized, unless they develop formal systems to maintain **(1),** they will suffer from the same managerial diseases that the West has.

Part IV

HOW TO CHANGE ORGANIZATIONAL CULTURES

Introduction to Part IV

In Part I, we described what happens at each stage of the corporate Lifecycle. In Parts II and III, we provided the tools that explain and predict the behavior of an organization during its Lifecycle and what causes growing and aging. With that understanding, we can make a diagnosis not only by observing the organization's behavior, but also by analyzing the causes that brought it to its Lifecycle stage. By analyzing those causes, we can better distinguish between normal and abnormal problems, and then provide therapeutic interventions that can propel the organization through the Lifecycle into Prime.

As I have warned in the Introduction to this book, growing and aging are *not* caused by size or chronological age. There are "old" young companies and "young" old companies—young companies that have been in existence for 100 years, and old companies that have existed for only five years. There are young companies doing ten billion dollars in sales, and old companies doing five million in sales. Whether an organization is young or old depends on how flexible and controllable it is.

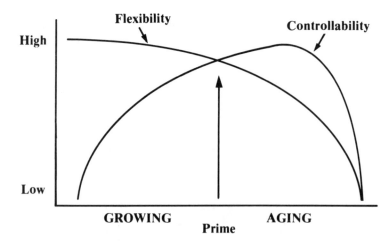

Figure 64: Flexibility and Control Over the Lifecycle

268

To further understand the diagnosis of the corporate Lifecycle, we must understand what affects the flexibility and control curves.

Flexibility is the function of the (ε)ntrepreneurship role. The more (ε) an organization has, the more flexible it is.

Control is a function of *CAPI*, which is a function of the diversity of interests. If there is a high diversity of interests, the organization is paralyzed, and it loses control.

Chapter 10 analyzed what affects (ε) and *CAPI*. In Chapter 11, which introduces the therapeutic part of this book, we can begin to understand how to affect these factors and facilitate the organization's move into Prime. Chapter 11 tells the theoretical underpinnings to the therapeutic model. Chapter 12 is an overview of the organizational therapeutic sequence, while Chapter 13 is an overview of the contingency therapy—how the treatment should differ depending on the location on the Lifecycle.

11

The Theoretical Underpinnings ====

HOW THE THERAPEUTIC SEQUENCE DEVELOPED

In 1967, I conducted my first consulting job. When I look back, I want to bury my head somewhere and wait for the memories to disappear. My client was a branch of an international firm that was having difficulties penetrating the local market. So they asked me, a newly-minted PhD in Business from Columbia University, New York what to do. I looked at the company's market and at their product and gave them advice: Cut your price here. Do marketing research there. Change your marketing outlook. It was basic Marketing 101, but I felt quite cocky about my advice. They listened, agreed with me, paid the bill and then nothing happened; or to be exact, very little happened. I was very upset. What incompetents! They can't apply a good idea when they see one, I thought.

I went on to my next consulting assignment, and, to be sure that I wouldn't have the same experience—to assure that my great ideas would be accepted and implemented—I requested to work for the CEO. The organization agreed. So I studied the problems and made my recommendations, which in this case required structural changes. And this time, I stayed around to see that my recommendations were implemented. That's when I realized why good ideas stay ideas, and why there is resistance to change. People do not individually see the change as being good for them personally although I, as a consultant, saw it as being good for the company. So they drag their feet. I requested that I become the executive vice president, threatening to quit if I didn't get the appointment. I wanted to be *sure* that my recommendations would be implemented. They agreed.

That's when I really got into trouble. I discovered corporate politics. If I pushed someone, he would push back, and the question became who had what to lose, and how fast. I was stirring the frying pan and in fact, I was in it. I fought and achieved more than the first time, but at a cost to the quality of my life.

Then the next opportunity for learning came about. I started a program for managing fine arts organizations—museums, theaters, symphonic orchestras, ballets, and operas. I received a grant from the Ford Foundation to study the field. At that time in 1969, there was no training program in this field, and nothing was written or known about it. I was the first to tackle it, and there was a lot to learn. I realized then that management theory is based on business experience, mostly in manufacturing, and that artists can't be managed in the same manner as blue collar workers.

Management is a dirty word in the arts. It is synonymous with exploitation. You must manage *for* the artist rather than *the* artist. But how do you do it? I found that the closest field would be educational management or hospital management. Deans or chairmen of departments in universities or hospitals should not *manage* the faculty, they should manage *for the* faculty. I discovered that management is a complementary task. It takes an art administrator and an art director working together to make a great theater.

Skip ahead to 1973. I was invited to be a Visiting Fellow for the Center of Democratic Institutions, Santa Barbara. This was the highlight of my intellectual life. At the Center, seven permanent fellows and three visiting fellows met around a table daily from 11 A.M. until 12:30 in the afternoon, to discuss a paper, usually presented by someone of leading intellectual ability in the world. Presidential candidate Eugene McCarthy presented a paper, as did leading philosophers from both sides of the iron curtain. This was an intellectual think tank if ever there was one. Another visiting fellow who served at the time was Edward Goldstucker, the theoretical father of the 1968 Czechoslovakia uprising, Alexander Dubcek's theoretical leader.

But the Center was in trouble. It was going to die. The president of the Center, Robert Hutchins, was the leading spirit and he was gravely ill. There were serious doubts that the Center could survive after he departed. So I offered my consulting abilities and they accepted. I thought long and hard on what to do. I wrote a report. Everything I wrote proved, over time, to happen. Nevertheless, none of my recommendations were implemented. This time, however, I could not say that management was incompetent.

Robert Hutchins was a phenomenon. At the age of 23, when he graduated from Yale Law School, his professors elected him as their dean. His term papers influenced the thinking of the Supreme Court. At age 26, he was elected president of the University of Chicago. World leaders came to confer with him at the Center, and I was a witness to it. He could not be incompetent. Nevertheless, all my predictions came true and all of my recommendations were sound. In spite of his intellect and capabilities, he did not build a legacy that would carry the Center after he died.

I became concerned. Something was wrong, but what was it? Talking with other professional consultants I realized that what I had encountered was an industry-wide problem and not just *my* problem. All consultants complain that their recommendations get filed away, even if they were submitted to the CEO or the board of directors. Then I realized that this problem of implementation exists in other fields as well. In medicine it is called compliance. The patients do not necessarily follow the prescriptions given. In the weight loss field it is called follow-up. The common denominator is that in order to produce change in behavior, more is needed than a prescription, a consultant's report or a recommendation, which are all one and the same.

So I looked into psychotherapy and worked with David Shapiro. It was then that I figured out how Shapiro achieved change. Basically he made *the client* do the work. My mistake in the past, typical of consultants, was that *I* had taken responsiblity for change *from* my clients as consultants typically do. I should have felt responsible not *for making the change*, but for making *them* responsible for making the change. How?

In David Shapiro's book *Neurotic Styles*,[1] I discovered that peo-

---

[1] See: Shapiro, David. *Neurotic Styles*: Forward by Robert P. Knight, (New York: Basic Books, 1983).

ple have repetitive patterns to their psychological problems. Each person is an individual with his own unique idiosyncrasies; however, people nevertheless fit a pattern. I thought about my consulting experience and I saw patterns there also. I discovered mismanagement styles as a diagnostic tool. I found why and how people mismanage and, that organizations have predictable patterns. I began to understand these patterns, and started to develop a theory and practice on how to effectively deal with them.[2]

First, I realized that I had to make the client accept responsibility for the change. That first step I call *Syndag*—synergetic diagnosis. Why synergetic?[3] Because the clients, as a team, make their own diagnosis of what is going on and what must be done about it. The *CAPI* group from the client organization belongs on this team. They are those who have authority, those who are needed for implementation, and those who know the subject.

Once a climate for change is created, the organization can proceed to solve the problems. It started the process of change but how to follow up on it?

Skip ahead to 1975. My "Model T" practice was applied to a company called CBI in Atlanta. I had been practicing there for three years. My theories produced more than average results. Today, they still practice the theories and the process. After my experience with CBI, I was invited to treat the parent company, Equifax Services.

I repeated the process of Syndags and organizational restructuring, but it had a limited effect. The energy force for change had fizzled out. I learned then that it is not enough to produce start-up energy for change; one must continually feed the energy source, or it will dissolve. So I divided my treatment into modules, each with an energy-creating component. When the old energy is depleted, a new module with an energy-generating phase must be started.

I tried my new energy theory with the Domino's Pizza organization between 1978–80. They had tremendous success using my process, and still send 30–40 people a year for training at the Adizes

---

[2] Adizes: *How to . . .* , op cit. is a result of this thinking.
[3] I know that *synergistic* is the proper word here, but I want to communicate synergy and energetic (energy) or synergistic energy. Thus, I created Synergetic.

Institute. The company rose from $150 million to $1.5 billion in sales in ten years.

I developed 11 steps called *phases* that produce organizational change (see Chapter 12), and started learning what sequence to use, and how to switch from one to another. With CBI, I could keep the energy for change with Phases I, IV & V but then it stopped. I tried to implement team-building as Phase VII, but I could not do it. The sequence was wrong. So I changed the sequence and put Synerteams as Phase II. At Equifax, I learned that Phase III was in trouble. The proper sequence is, I, II, III, IV, and V.

My next client was Northrop Aviation. I implemented Phases I, II and III. It worked, but not for too long. The energy stopped and I had to try again. Domino's Pizza was next. Phases I, II, III, IV, V, VI. Yes, it worked, but then Phase VI had problems. Louisiana Coca-Cola Bottling Company was the next client. With a supportive president, Richard Freeman, Jr., we went all the way—Phases I through XI. This sounds simple, but it took 20 years of trying and learning.

There is no way I can present the entire process in a book. Training a person in this methodology today takes between five and seven years of part-time, on-the-job experience and internship training. Then, the graduate realizes how much he really does not know. I, feel I know more *and* less than I knew in 1967 when I began; now I really know how much I do not know.

There are many intermediate experiments which helped me put the sequence right. At API, an alarm company in Los Angeles, the sequence I used was: Phase I, II, III, IV, V, XI. Again, I could not do VI after XI. The flow of change was wrong. So Louisiana Coca-Cola Bottling in New Orleans was my first proof that a total change in culture can be produced; that a company can go from almost divorce in pathological adolescence all the way to Prime.[4]

Success Rate

I am often asked how long the change will last, and what is the success rate of the methodology. Looking back at my clients, I would

---

[4] The company was sold and I have no information as to what happened to the company, since then.

say the success rate is 100 percent or zero percent, depending on how you look at it. Change is like gardening. If you work at it, the weeds are taken out and the flowers will bloom. If you *do not maintain* the garden, the weeds will overtake the flowers. The companies that did not continue changing their new cultures, those that said "Thank you, now let us get back to work," were like untended gardens that eventually go back to weeds.

It is difficult to change organizations. It is like tending the gardens. When you relax, the culture goes back to the weeds. But why the regression? Why don't flowers grow naturally? Why the weeds? And who says that weeds are weeds and not flowers? Maybe it is the flowers that are the weeds? In other words, who appointed me the judge of what is the "right culture" and what is the wrong culture of an organization? Again, I had quite a few sleepless nights.

Then I realized that I had the tools to define health and pathology. Is there an argument that a company should make (**PAEI**) decisions, and implement them, for which *CAPI* is necessary? Healthy management = f (**PAEI**; *CAPI*).

Anytime one of the (**PAEI**) roles is missing, a mismanagement style of leadership will repetitively occur. And if one of the roles is missing in the organizational culture, typical problems will recur (see Part I of this book). If the company succeeds in developing the missing role over time, that is a normal development and if not, it is pathological.

I had a deterministic theory that could discriminate between flowers and weeds—between health and pathology. The role of management is to control the development of the organization throughout the Lifecycle. If management can not do that, an external therapist is called for.

Did the change remain? Did the people in the organization continue practicing Adizes? Were the companies successful over time or were they like the model companies in the book *In Search of Excellence*[5] that, by the time the book was in its new printing, were not excellent anymore?[6]

Organizations experience entropy. (See next section of this

---

[5] Peters, Thomas J. and Waterman Robert H.: *In Search of Excellence* (New York: Harper and Row, 1982). 360 pp.

[6] "Who's Excellent Now" *Business Week*: (November 5, 1984) p. 76

chapter.) If they are not managed, they get sick, the weeds take over the flowers.

It is interesting to note that the ratio of building to destroying is at the cost of building. What took me three years to build, could be destroyed in three months—a new president comes in who does not understand the methodology and the new culture of mutual respect and trust that was so carefully nourished goes out the window.

If the market changes and there is pressure to survive, (EI) orientation goes down and (PA) orientation takes over. I hold an annual International convention to nourish and replenish clients and practitioners "batteries" as the (P) pressure slowly kills off their (EI) dedication. If the company eventually goes to the weeds, why do it? I worried about that, but a friend of mine who is a medical doctor, helped me realize my excessive expectations.

"Ichak," he said, "in the end, we all fail (i.e., people die), there's nothing wrong in doing the best you can in the meantime."

And the methodology does succeed in the meantime. After a year usually 40 percent of the problems a company identifies in the Syndag are gone, solved, as judged by the participants in the Syndag who contributed those problems in the first place. 40 percent are better. Only 20 percent of the problems are at status quo. Rarely are any worse. Companies have fantastic rates of growth and profitability. Turnover of personnel is stabilized. The rate of innovation goes up. Morale is up. In general, there is significant improvement.

World-wide companies that practice Adizes get recognized as some of the best managed companies in those countries.

Who is the Client?

What about a company whose management invites me to help them out with their "garden," but what that person wants me to do is not necessarily for the good of the organization? "What should I do," I asked myself. "For whom do I work? Who is the client?" I discovered that I represent the people, not management.

In court many times we see the people versus XYZ or the prosecutor represents the "unborn child." Who are those people?

An organization has the right to exist. Its rights are distinctly different from those of the owners, management, labor, customers, or anyone who constitutes or uses the organization. I have experienced numerous occasions where all of the above were destroying the organization. Management, for instance, was looking for ego aggrandizement rather than making prudent business decisions. Owners frequently exploited the organization, milking it or putting a lid on it. Labor fought changes, protecting its own interests; clients did not care about the organization's needs, they cared about their own needs.

So who is this organization I am working for? If it is not management—if it is management that needs changing—is it the board that I am working for? Not either. The board is frequently the mirror of management, which also needs changing. It is not stockholders, who in public companies use it as an investment, and their commitment to the company is limited exclusively to its ROI success.

My mistake was that I was trying to *personify* the client. I was looking for a person just like many people look for God as someone who has a long beard and white hair and sits somewhere with zoom binoculars to watch what we do.

An organization for me now is like God in the Jewish prayer book, it has no body and no image. It is a system. In the legal world, an organization is a legal entity (Inc. or LTD, or A/S, depending on the country) independent of the partners that constitute it. The rights of such an incorporated organization are protected by law and a violation of those rights, even by the people who established it are against the law. I believe it does not need to be incorporated to have rights, to exist. It exists because it *exists* or to rephrase the philosopher René Descrates, who said, "I think, therefore I am," an organization *is* because it *does*.

So whom do I represent when I work for the organization? I work for the organization's ability to satisfy clients' needs in the future. It exists for those clients who are not born yet. The organization has the right to exist not only now, but in the future, too. The kid has the right to grow and move into Prime, and anyone who curtails, distorts, or impairs that normal healthy growth needs treatment.

Many times in performing organizational therapy, I make this point clear. As I listen to the *CAPI* group talk, I realize that everyone explains the organization's needs in terms of his own needs. They are all (management, labor, technocrats, the board, owners) trying to use the organization for their own needs. The mistake I used to make was to take the organization's side and argue, and get attacked in the process for my efforts.

That's when I learned how to use the frying pan, without being fried in the pan. So, I began adding a chair to the group's circle (there are no empty chairs in my process) and in front of that chair I put the name of the company (everyone else has his name card in front of him). Then I point to the empty chair and ask "Who is that?" Once they realize that I truly mean for them to assume that the company is sitting there, I ask them what it would want. If it could speak, what would it say? Oddly enough, people understand this, and start seeing that the organization also has needs. It is a baby that can't talk, but if it is not treated correctly, sooner or later it will cause problems.

Where is the Practice in Its Development Now?

By 1980 I had the 11 phases, the interventions for cultural change, worked out. Six of the phases were written into detailed manuals and I trained other people to perform them. To be certified in the Adizes methodology, people had to pass exams and do internships. I use contracts so people take the training and certification seriously. The other five phases were written into general guidelines, and I've begun training people in those phases too. Over the next few years the entire process will be documented. Now there are more organizations in addition to Louisiana Coca Cola Bottling that have gone through the 11 phases. Villares, a $1.5 billion company in Brazil that was in the pathological part of Adolescence is now in Phase XI and edging into Prime.

By 1983, there were several dozen certified Adizes full-time facilitators practicing the methodology in ten countries. Manuals were translated into different languages. We gained experience on how social culture impacts the process of change. Also, I could see how other people learned and were practicing the methodology. I learned in return what I could not take for granted, what I assumed was obvious, but was not. (In Serbo Croation the word for "teach" is literally the word for "relearn." Through teaching and training I relearned my own theory and practice.) By and large, I have learned that social culture and political environment do not change the theory. (PAEI) and *CAPI* are theoretical foundations that apply everywhere. Only the interpretation is different. The *CAPI* group is different in Malaysia where family ties are tight and the founders reign, than in Israel where everyone feels he was born to be president.

The main difference in the process of change is not the country, the language, the size of an organization, the culture or even the personality traits and management style of the leadership, but rather the specific location of the organization in the Lifecycle. The sequence and speed in completing a phase must be tailored to an organization; the speed and sequence of treatment must be adapted to reflect the particulars of the client; depending on its location on the Lifecycle.

I also realized that the therapy of cultural change was well-established and repeatedly successful for organizations in advanced Go-Go, Adolescence, simple pathological Adolescence, Prime and Beginning Aristocracy. The methodology was still weak for large Aristocracies, Early Bureaucracies and Early Go-Go organizations. For organizations with 300 to 1,500 employees, the methodology was good. We could practice change successfully. In smaller organizations, *CAPI* was *very* personalized in the founder, and his style would over-dominate organizational behavior. Thus, changing the organization would necessitate changing this person's personality, which means personal therapy must occur before any organizational therapy could occur.

In larger organizations or organizations that are more advanced in the Lifecycle, there is something called organizational dynamics. By changing the organizational culture, we could also change the founder's behavior. It was not so easy in small companies. The driving and the driven forces change places. Prior to Adolescence, the driving force of the organization's behavior or culture, is leadership. After Prime, it is the culture which drives the behavior of the leader.

Lifecycle	Driving force	Driven force
Infant and Beg. Go-Go	Leader's style ⟶	Organizational culture
From Adolescence To Aristocracy	Organizational Culture ⟶	Leader's Style

So, for those cases where a person's style drives the organizational culture, I added a psychoanalyst, Dr. Ivan Gabor, to the Institute staff. His challenge was to change the individual's style without doing years of analysis and therapy. He found a way to deal with the person, not in order to change his personality so he could function optimally in any situation, but only as much as is necessary to enable the organizational culture to change so that the driving and the driven force can change places or at least work side by side.

I developed my theory and practice on how to change large organizations while I was working as a consultant with the Bank of America, the largest organization I have attempted to change. It required a full-time commitment, and in order to give that, I had to give up my tenured professorship position at UCLA.

Bank of America was an organization of 89,000 employees, $120 billion in assets, its location on the Lifecycle was a deep Aristocracy in premature aging. It had bad loans in agriculture, real estate, oil and third world countries. No matter how much better the organization operated, it still looked bad. The operational profits were going up every year, but the bad loans wiped them out with one sweep. "While we are worrying about gathering peanuts, the elephants are stepping on us," said Al Osborne, senior vice president, credit. This was a major challenge of changing positions under fire. It took three years to make a change. Bank of America went as far as Phase V, changed its structure, positioned itself to compete as a Financial Services organization, and not just as a bank; but time ran out. (A case study would require a book length treatment well to be written, in due time.)

The next bureaucratic organization we undertook was the Los Angeles County Department of Children Services. With 3,500 professionals, it took two years to complete Phases I, IV and V. We are still learning how to speed up change in bureaucracies.

By and large, there are now about 400 companies worldwide which use, to different degrees, the methodology. There are about 75 Certified Adizes professionals who practice and exchange know-how.

That's the history. Now let us proceed to the theoretical underpinnings of the 11 phases; the description and goals of the 11 phases; and then to the specifics of what to do to an organization at each stage of the Lifecycle.

The Theoretical Underpinnings

When we speak of an *organization* whose *culture* needs *changing,* what are we actually speaking about? There are three components to the above sentence: organization, culture, and changing.

Up to now, I have described organizational cultures. In the next section, my goal is to present how the change should be accomplished. But before I do that, we must talk about the "organization" that needs to change its culture. What is an organization?

An organization is a system of interdependencies to satisfy needs. The interdependencies are intra-and-inter-people, physical components, economic variables, legal, political and social forces, technological factors, and other variables, which we frequently neither understand nor can identify. Everything somehow impacts everything else that impacts the organization in some way and to varying degrees. These interdependencies have a focus, which is to meet certain needs that can be satisfied only through certain interdependencies. Those needs change over time, and the clients served by those interdependencies change over time. When there is no need and thus no client, there is no interdependency necessary and the organization dies. The organization is born when the need is potent enough that someone will "manage" the interdependencies to satisfy those needs. How these interdependencies are handled is called *management.* Culture consists of networks of meanings which are expressed in organizational behavior. These meanings of organizational behavior change due, partly to changes in lifecycle stages. Some behavior is normal, while other behavior is stymied in its development; that is called abnormal. The problem is that there are infinite interdependencies within a system. The question is finding out what to work on?

I discovered that an organiztion has three *main* subsystems, and how we balance those three subsystems can change the culture. Those subsystems are the *authorance, teleological* and the *reward* subsystems.

Authorance is composed of seven subsystems: authority structure, power structure, influence structure and the combinations of authorized power, indirect power, influencing authority and finally *CAPI.*

Authorance is the total possibilities a person has, organizationally and managerially, to cause someone to do something.

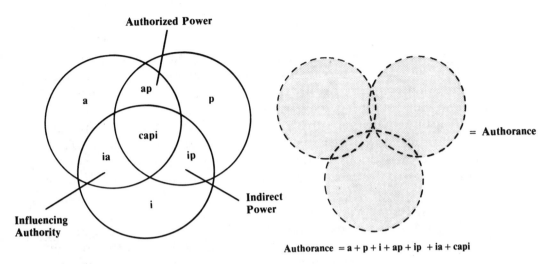

Authorance $= a + p + i + ap + ip + ia + capi$

Figure 65: Authorance

The teleological subsystem is the one that deals with purpose: why we do what we do. *Telos* in Greek means purpose. Here, we focus on the mission of the organization, its clients, the changing environment, goals, derived objectives and tasks. The teleological subsystem has four subsystems to it: client interface (E), transformation (P), finance (A), and human resources (I).

The reward subsystem deals with the variables which motivate people to carry out a task. It has two subsystems and each subsystem has several variables, which in themselves could also be systems. One is *extrinsic* rewards—the rewards which people want but whose

Figure 66: The Teleological Subsystems

value is determined by external forces. These are not tied to the task and responsibility that a person has to perform. There are two types of extrinsic rewards: $Re_\$$ and Re_{np}. $Re_\$$ are salary, fringe benefits, bonuses, profit sharing, and other economic returns. Re_{np} are the **n**on-**p**ecuniary rewards like status symbols, titles, insignia, size and location of office and a key to the executive washroom.

The other reward subsystem is *intrinsic*. Those rewards do not require external verification for their perceived value. They are derived from doing the task. If the task is eliminated, the source of the rewarding experience is removed. Intrinsic rewards have three types $Ri_{(task)}$, $Ri_{(potency)}$, $Ri_{(mission)}$.

Let us study rewards in more detail.

$Re_\$$ = A person does not have to perform a task to feel rewarded, as long as he is given a salary or bonus. But how much that money is worth depends on what he believes others are getting for a comparable task, and what that money will buy.

The money and how much it is worth, must be evaluated through an external verification mechanism of the task and the person who was paid the money.

Re_{np} = **N**on-**p**ecuniary rewards also need external verification of their value. A desk covered with glass has no meaning in the US, but in Turkey, it means that the individual is an executive with status and position. Plush wall-to-wall carpeting has no meaning in Turkey, but it has a definite meaning in the US. The value depends on what symbolic meaning those symbols have on people, and what the giver of the symbols wants to communicate. Re_{np} does not need a task or responsibility to be rewarding. It needs people to recognize it.

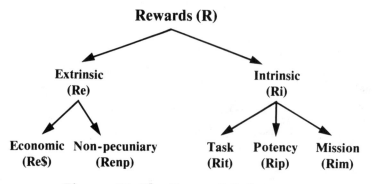

Figure 67: The Reward Subsystem

If a person is given the title of vice president and a special parking space, but no one is supposed to know about it, the secrecy eliminates the reward because extrinsic, non pecuniary rewards (Re_{np}) provide a hierarchy that must be communicated.

Intrinsic rewards are a rewarding experience even if no one knows about them. They exist as long as the task is carried out. Ri_t is the intrinsic rewards derived from performing a task. "I like what I do. I work here because I like my work." It is a function of how well the task, and the responsibility matches the personality makeup of the person performing the task.

Ri_p is the intrinsic reward derived from a sense of **potency**, from the perception that a person has that he can do something, even if that something is not necessarily something he likes to do. The fact that it can be done is rewarding.[7]

Ri_m is the reward derived from the sensation that a person is advancing to a **mission**, to a higher-level goal of longer range than the immediate task performed.

It is interesting how I discovered this Ri_m reward. In 1970, I was invited to lecture and consult in Peru, which at that time was attempting to establish a worker's participative system (industrial communities)—a variation of the Yugoslav self-management system. As I was presenting this model to the President's commission on industrial communities, a participant said, "your model is too capitalistic." I was taken aback because I thought that my theory was apolitical. To explain his insights, let us go back to a scenario of my lecture and please note the word that was repeated the most.

I was saying: "The various rewards are: Am I getting: 1) my pay ($Re_\$$),
2) the recognition I perceive I deserve (Re_{np}),
3) do I like what I do (Ri_t), and
4) do I derive pleasure from the fact that I can master, control something I can do (Ri_p)?

I am obviously exaggerating the simulated lecture to make the point, but the participant caught it. The most repetitive word I used was "I."

"Are the Vietnamese fighting because they get paid well ($Re_\$$), or because they get a non-pecuniary rewards recognition in showing their wounds (Re_{np}), or is it intrinsic rewards from the task (Ri_t)—

---

[7] Ri_p = f (*CAPI*/authorance/task)

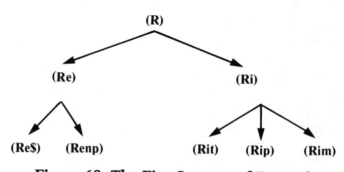

Figure 68: The Five Sources of Reward

they just like fighting, or is it intrinsic rewards from potency (Ri_p)—
they derive satisfaction from beating their opponents in the field?"
he asked.

The obvious answer was that none of the above applied. They
were fighting because they believed in their mission. People go to
war, kill and die for what they believe in. The capitalist approach,
as the Peruvian general interpreted it, is too *self*-oriented, not enough
society-oriented.

So Ri_m (intrinsic rewards from mission) went into my model.[8]

How do the rewards differ? Extrinsic rewards provide a perception of reward only by their rate of increase. As a constant, they
have a very limited, let us say, a two-week long motivating impact.
Thus a salary increase is great for two weeks, then the employee
wants more. The same happens with titles or other non-pecuniary
recognition. They have limited life spans. To keep a person motivated one must continually give more. I remember my experience
as a youth leader in a childrens' camp. To keep the noisiest kid
cooperative, I had to give him a title and make him my assistant
(part of the establishment). But that was good only for a few days.
Then I had to invent new titles and new recognitions, feeding the
little monster with attention to keep him quiet. Intrinsic reward,
on the other hand, is nourished each time a task is performed.

---

[8] For more about the above, see Chapter 5 on Authorance and its components,
and videos, audios and manuals at the Institute. The Teleological subsystem needs
little amplification for the purpose of this chapter. A three-hour videotape, produced
and marketed by the Young Presidents Organization in New York and the Adizes
Institute in Santa Monica, goes into depth about this subsystem and how to develop
it correctly. There is also an 80-page manual about the reward subsystem available
for students at the Adizes Institute.

To understand these five sources of reward systems, let us look at what will happen if only one reward is granted to the exclusion of the other four.

$$\cancel{Re_\$} \quad \cancel{Re_{np}} \quad \cancel{Ri_t} \quad \cancel{Ri_p} \quad \boxed{Ri_m}$$

What kind of calling or profession will people have that the only source of their motivation is $Ri_{(mission)}$? Their salary or recognition is low or stable and thus it is not a source of motivation. The task in itself is not rewarding, neither is the sense of potency because often they get murdered. The answer is a missionary. What propels them is the Mission. It is the mission of converting non believers to believers and saving souls that gets them to sacrifice their life.

$$\cancel{Re_\$} \quad \cancel{Re_{np}} \quad \cancel{Ri_t} \quad \boxed{Ri_p} \quad \cancel{Ri_m}$$

How about $Ri_{(potency)}$ as the exclusive source of motivation? Who is motivated by Ri_p? I think the answer is the bureaucrat. Look at a small time *aparatchik* behind a desk. The salary is meaningless. He might have an increase in salary fixed to inflation or to something else. It was motivating only when the fixing of salary increases was announced. From there on it is dreadfully the same. Recognition? He gets none. He is considered a small fry office clerk. The task is menial, boring, meaningless, and repetitive. Mission? What mission?

So, if this human being behind the small window derives any pleasure, any sense of satisfaction, it is probably by making people wait in line, in refusing to accept a form because the customer did not sign it *exactly* where it was supposed to be signed, or by sending people back and forth ten times before he will approve something. The only source of gratification is the sense of self-importance he derives from the potency the job offers. (I distinguish between what the job is and how the job is done—issuing licenses for instance, which can provide Ri_t and—the method of issuing licenses, which is Ri_p).

Look at customs inspectors at airports. Try to question even a little bit of their authority and see what happens. If there is pleasure to be derived from the job, it is from having the authority to check whatever they please. (They have been using some $Ri_{(mission)}$ lately in their effort to stop drug trafficking).

$$\cancel{Re_\$} \quad \cancel{Re_{np}} \quad \boxed{Ri_t} \quad \cancel{Ri_p} \quad \cancel{Ri_m}$$

How about $Ri_{(task)}$ as an exclusive source of rewards? That will be the solitary, elusive artist who never displayed his art or published his work. He enjoys writing or painting and that is it.

$$\cancel{Re_\$} \quad \boxed{Re_{np}} \quad \cancel{Ri_t} \quad \cancel{Ri_p} \quad \cancel{Ri_m}$$

The next is exclusive Re_{np} (**re**wards, **e**xtrinsic, **n**on **pecuniary**). This is the cheap politician. The income is fixed or perhaps low. The task might be grinding. As a cheap politician, he has no mission except the desire to be re-elected; there is no higher goal. He is not a statesman. Statesmen worry about the next generation; politicians worry about the next election. Many elected politicians do not feel a real sense of potency in being able to make change. Thus, $Re_\$ = 0$, $Ri_{(task)} = 0$, $Ri_{(potency)} = 0$, $Ri_{(mission)} = 0$. What is left? The title, the recognition, the name, the applause, in other words— the ego trip (Re_{np}).

$$\boxed{Re_\$} \quad \cancel{Re_{np}} \quad \cancel{Ri_t} \quad \cancel{Ri_p} \quad \cancel{Ri_m}$$

Who has no organizational mission as a motivating force, has a menial, repetitive, boring task, has no managerial potency; that is, who is fired if he flexes his muscle? Who gets no recognition, is considered to be a loser, and at the bottom of the barrel? The only thing he gets is a paycheck. The majority of our society: It is the average worker on the line.

Why is it strange then if workers unionize or hold wild cat strikes? That gives them some sense of $Ri_{(potency)}$. Why is it strange that they request salary raises? That is the only source of growth they are allowed to have. Is it not human to want to grow?

Why is the Japanese worker so diligent and hard working? Is it because he was born in Japan, or is it because all five sources of reward are being utilized? He gets profit-sharing which means that $Re_\$$ varies and is thus motivating.

There is (Re_{np}) too. It is a family culture where people get recognized or punished according to their contributions.

The task might be the same as everywhere else, but the $Ri_{(potency)}$ is different. The Japanese have participative management, an employee can and does impact what gets done. He is asked for his opinion. As the company grows, he grows; since he is there for life and the company is loyal to him and expects the same in return, that gives him a sense of Ri_m.

The Japanese worker is like a car running on five cylinders, while the western worker is running on one cylinder, the worst one. The Westerner needs constant fixing, because the motivating span of his reward system is very short.

Accountability Fit

Why Authorance, Task and Reward?

We are trying to predict behavior, right? We are trying to change behavior, right? Behavior is determined by inputs and outputs. The input is the person's behavior. The throughput is what happens within the organization. The output—how people and structure interact—is organizational behavior. How the structure (authorance, task and reward) behaves, I call accountability. A person is accountable if he *knows* his task, has the *authorance* to carry it out and gets the expected rewards. If all people are accountable, the organization performs better than if otherwise.

Now, let us put the three subsystems, *Authorance*, Teleological, and Reward together. Envision a responsibility as a rectangle. Assume the vertical lines can be measured in units. What are those units and how does one measure them? It is the same as the marginal utility concept in economics. It is highly subjective. The only thing important is that 2 is double of 1 and thus 2 units of responsibility are twice as much responsibility as 1.

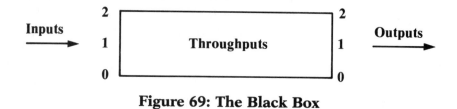

Figure 69: The Black Box

The box is now the famous black box from systems theory. On the left we will have input and on the right, output. Inside the box are the throughputs.

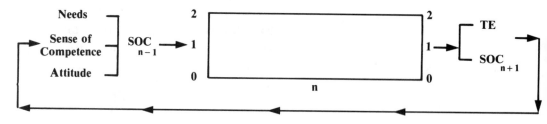

Figure 70: Inputs and Outputs—Sense of Commitment (SOC) and Task Effectiveness (TE)

The input is SOC, Sense of Commitment. A person has a sense of commitment to do a job, to carry out a task, a sense of responsibility, at Level 1, let us say. Where does this sense of commitment come from? First from his attitude, which is derived from past experiences in this or any organization including the family.

He asks himself, "Was I given a job I can do? Can I trust the organization? If I deliver the expected, will I be rewarded?

Some people have negative attitudes. The expected task of them is at Level 1, but their commitment is lower because the individual's attitude could be, "They always give me what cannot be done, and even if I do perform, I do not get commensurate reward, so why bother?"

Another factor impacting sense of commitment is the sense of competence. Does the person perceive that he has the competence to do the task?

The last factor is need. Does the person perceive that the task will gratify a basic need? That need might be for achievement, which motivates (**p**) people, for control which motivates (**a**) people, for creating and building something new, which motivates (**e**) people, or for affiliation, which motivates (**i**) people.

The sense of commitment as an input is the function of need, sense of competence, and attitudes. How they interrelate impacts a person's sense of commitment to a task.

On the output side, there is (SOC_{n+1}), sense of commitment n + 1, the sense of the person's commitment after gaining some experience, and after trying to carry out the task that impacts his new attitude, his new sense of potency and his new sense of need gratification, depending on whether those needs were reinforced or deprived in the process.

Now let us look at the throughputs. What happens in the black box, the organization, which impacts the experience the person will have?

There will be three dots at Level 1 (See Figure 71): the center dot depicts the level of responsibility expected; that will be identified as *T*—the task. The left dot, also at Level 1, depicts the authorance the person perceives he has. On the right is the reward subsystem, the amount of rewards an individual perceives he is receiving.

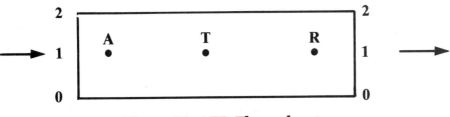

Figure 71: ATR Throughputs

Now let us take the letters ATR and the location of every dot communicates the respective subsystem to be analyzed.

Here is the first chart:

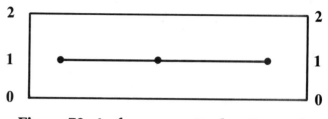

Figure 72: *Authorance* = **Task** = **Reward**

What this chart communicates, is that this person was given responsibility for a task at Level 1, he had commensurate *authorance* to carry it out, and he perceived that he received commensurate rewards. Will the person act responsibly? Will he carry out the task? What will happen to his sense of commitment after the experience?

If the three subsystems, task, reward and *authorance* are of the same size, at the same level, I claim that there is an accountability fit. In other words, the person can be held accountable. He is not responsible yet. To be responsible the person must be committed to his accountability. A person is responsible to Level 1 when he can be held accountable to Level 1 and is committed to Level 1.

What a person can be held accountable for depends on the fit between the subsystems. If the subsystems do not fit, if the person has a task of 1, a perceived reward of 1 and authorance of 0.5 what will happen? It is not difficult to predict that the person will do as much as he can which is 0.5.

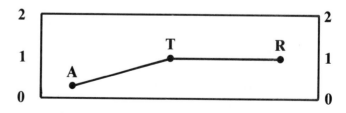

Figure 73: *Authorance* < **Task** = **Reward**

Let us look at several cases.

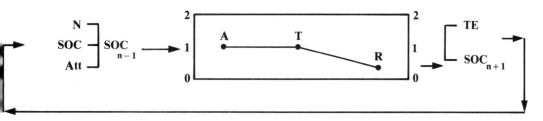

Figure 74: Case No. 1: SOC $_{n-1}$ = A = T, Rewards = 0.2

What will the effectiveness be of the person with the Figure 74 experience and what will be his future sense of commitment?

I claim that since the person is committed, say he just joined the company, he will try to complete the task. In the short run, the responsibility will be 1 and task effectiveness will be 1, but what will happen to the person's sense of commitment (SOC_{n+1}) over time? It must decline, because the person did not perceive himself as being rewarded adequately. So there will be a deterioration in his post-experience sense of commitment. To what level will his sense of commitment decline? To whatever level he believes he is being rewarded for, 0.2.

What about the next person?

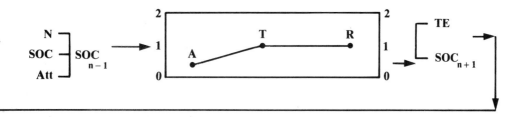

Figure 75: Case No. 2: SOC_{n-1} = T = R, Authorance = 0.2

Eventually, his commitment will lessen. Although he is expected to perform 1 and is receiving commensurate rewards, he can accomplish only as much as he has authorance for. So, he will fight in the short-run to get more authority, more influence and even use some power. In the long run, he will only do as much as he can do.

What about this?

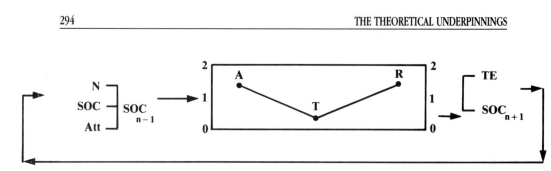

Figure 76: Case No. 3: The Spoiled Kid Syndrome

I call this case the bosses' spoiled child syndrome. The owner or boss brings his child in to work for daddy. Being the CEO-in-waiting, perceived power and influence are very high. Furthermore, the kid gets plenty of rewards because he is the owner's offspring; however, he is not expected to do much. Daddy wants to run the show. The child in our example is committed to do more than he is expected to do, and will try to do more, only to be discouraged from doing so. Eventually, if the child does not quit, he will do only as much as he is expected to do.

What happens when:

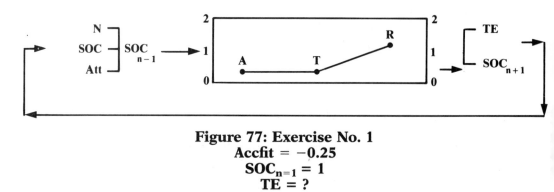

Figure 77: Exercise No. 1
Accfit = −0.25
$$SOC_{n=1} = 1$$
TE = ?
$$SOC_{n+1} = ?$$

Here is a person committed to doing a task at Level 1; however, one of the subsystems is at 0.25. In the short run he will try to do 1 (TE = 1), but his sense of commitment will have to decline.

Which factors will cause the sense of commitment to decline? First his attitude will change. If that does not bring his sense of commitment low enough, his sense of potency will decline. I have seen PhD's—top students in their class, with fast-track minds—

start to wonder about their worth after they have had some disastrous experiences working for a messed up organization. The accountability misfit was so great that they lost faith in themselves.

If the decline in the sense of potency is not sufficient to reduce the sense of commitment, the decline in needs will decrease the commitment. The person will "retire," while still on the job. "I do not need to achieve, or to control or to affiliate," he will say, as he resigns himself to accept the world as it is and to just get by. The three factors do not decline linearly. They decline simultaneously, with different rates of decline. The same thing happens when the sense of commitment grows. The components that affect it (attitude, sense of commitment and needs) do not grow at the same rate, although they grow simultaneously. First, attitude changes noticeably, then the sense of potency, and then the basic needs.

Whenever ATR is not in balance, there is a negative Accountability Fit, and the number in front of the negative symbol is of the lowest subsystem. For purposes of predicting behavior, that is the subsystem to which the person adapts.

Let us exercise.

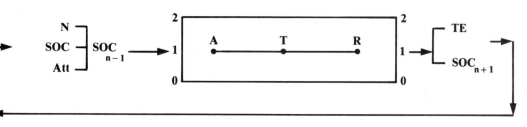

**Figure 78: Exercise No. 2: $SOC_{n-1} = 1$ and Accfit $= +1$
What will be $SOC_{n+1} = ?$ TE $= ?$**

The person with the Figure 78 experience will do his job and TE will be 1; SOC_{n+1} however will be more than 1. The person will ask for more—more responsibility, more authority, and more rewards. The experience he had was positive. Thus, he will want to grow and will ask for more responsibility.

The Dynamic Model

There is a catch though. Accfit $= 1$, is a theoretical situation. *Authorance* does not always fit *exactly* the task and *exactly* the rewards. These three subsystems vibrate, which means that if anyone is ever happy and content *all the time*, something is wrong. Life means that one day a person feels he is on the top of the world—he knows his job, he can do it, and the rewards are not bad. Then it changes. The next day a component of the task emerges for which he has no *Authorance*, or he has it, but it is composed not of *CAPI*, but of influence. Furthermore, someone next door got a bigger bonus, and guess what happens. Accfit declines, and he starts wondering about his commitment.

Organizations experience entropy. They are very sensitive mechanisms, and get out of tune like a car does. The task changes due to the demands of the external environment. Not everything can be predicted and spelled out in a task definition. A job description is like a guideline, it should not be a legal document.

Authorance changes even if authority does not (which, however, it does). Power changes because it is perceived power. If an employee is needed less or more, it impacts his sense of power. Influence changes also. Changes in the situation and people cause influence to change.

Perception of extrinsic rewards also changes. $Re_\$$ changes because the external world is used to measure value changes. If the price of something increases, an individual may start perceiving himself as being underpaid. If his neighbor gets a raise, he feels underpaid.

The perceived value of non pecuniary extrinsic rewards (Re_{np}) also changes with the environment.

The intrinsic reward derived from performing a task (Ri_t) has components that are rewarding and components that are undesirable. Not every task can match exactly the personality, tasks and needs of every person ($Ri_t = f(n/_t)$).

Intrinsic rewards derived from accomplishing a mission $Ri_{(mission)}$ are not always motivating either because they deal with the long run. Sometimes that long-run goal is evident; sometimes it is elusive.

Rewards for being potent are not fully motivating all the time because they are a function of how much *CAPI* a person has for the task ($Ri_p = f(CAPI/\text{task})$. If the task changes and *CAPI* changes, then by definition there are days he believes he *can* control the world and there are days he feels controlled by the world.

Entropy is a fact of life. The role of management is to provide negative entropy—provide for bringing the Accfit into balance, knowing well that it will get out of balance nevertheless. It is like taking the car to the garage for service, even though it will get out of tune again.

What keeps people committed for the long run in spite of the fact that Accfit is always a misfit in the short run? Hope. Hope that tomorrow there will be a forum to air grievances, that those grievances will be heard, and that things will work out in the future. In what sequence should the tune-up be done? Should the people with a negative attitude, who are not committed to the mission be fired? Yes, if Accfit is $+1$. No, if Accfit is negative. Bringing new people into the organization won't make a difference in the long run, unless we change the throughputs.

If the Accfit is changed, sense of commitment (SOC) will slowly climb. To make it climb faster, we can bring in new people and change the Accfit at the same time, which is what one of my clients does. That is how in eight years making successful acquisitions, he went from \$12 million in sales to \$700 million in sales, and without loosing any equity.

At what sequence should the throughputs be tackled? Obviously the task should be the first to be stabilized, because it is the driving force for authorance and rewards. The degree of authorance needed depends on the task and the intrinsic rewards are derived from the task.

Authorance should be the next subsystem. Reward is the last subsystem, because it changes by itself as the teleological and authorance subsystems are stabilized. The intrinsic rewards are derived from the task which we already stabilized. Thus, mission and task-intrinsic rewards go up by virtue of matching responsibility to task, and people to task. By designing the *Authorance* structure participatively, non-pecuniary and potency rewards (Re_{np}) and Ri_p) grow.

At the end we deal with $Re_\$$. Thus if a client comes to me complaining that morale is low and there is a high turnover of personnel and that he would like me to design an incentive system and he usually refers to money, what should I do? I tell him to wait. Redesigning the reward system is the last thing to do, not the first. (See Chapter 12 for how the eleven interventions change the accountability fit.)

Goals of the Methodology

The Adizes methodology for cultural change has four goals which I try to achieve simultaneously. The first goal is to solve abnormal problems, those problems that management has tried to solve but could not. Those are the problems that the organization should not have in light of where it is in its Lifecycle; those problems are not going to disappear on their own.

The second goal is team-building, which is not a goal in itself but a means to the first problem solving goal, the better the team-work, the stronger the *CAPI*; the stronger the *CAPI*, the bigger the problems we are able to solve. Goal 2 converts quality into quantity—the *better* the team, the *bigger* the problems it can solve.

Goal 3 is individual style enrichment which is a means to goal 2 above. In order to build a better team, people must change as individuals as well. Quite a few people are not team players. They do not have the self-discipline, nor do they like to follow the team discipline necessary to be team players.

The Adizes methodology attempts to enrich their managerial styles. I do not pretend to change people, but I can smooth their edges, so that they can work with others. That means increasing the threshold level of the **(PAEI)** roles in their style. I can not remove zero. For that, individual therapy is necessary whether it is done with a therapist or in a group therapy. The methodology is not group therapy for an individual, it is organizational therapy. Thus if a person's style is **(PAei)** and **(pAeI)** is needed for the task or the organization's place on the Lifecycle, the Adizes methodology can help the person make that change. The more enriched the style is, the more flexible the person is in his style, the better are the ingredients that constitute the team, and the easier it will be to achieve Goal 2 of team building. Subsequently, it will be easier to achieve the ultimate Goal 1, which is organizational therapy: cultural change and solving abnormal problems.

Goal 4 is cognitive managerial training. It is not enough to change style. Well-meaning but incompetent people can produce disasters. Thus, we need knowledgeable people to make knowledgeable decisions.

Goal 4 supports the achievement of Goal 3, which supports Goal 2. They all act together to achieve Goal 1.

How do we do this SIMULTANEOUSLY?

Management = f (**PAEI**;*CAPI*) is the starting point. All of the 11 interventions have a common denominator; I try to achieve this formula in each case. Each phase is done with a team that has *CAPI* over the task of that phase. Then members of the team are *assigned* tasks that fulfill the (**PAEI**) roles. Look at the example below:

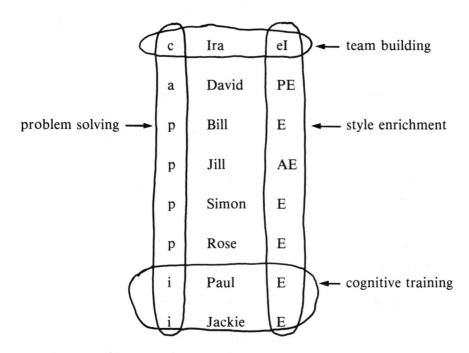

David had authority over the subject for discussion. He was given the (**P**) role, which means that he has the responsibility to see that the team finishes the task as assigned by the deadline, and that the team's decision is implemented. He was given a manual and trained as to what he was supposed to do, to ensure that decisions were not only made, but also implemented. David chose the team members, those whose cooperation was needed to correctly implement the decision—those who had power. He chose Bill, Jill, Simon, and Rose. Then he chose those whose know-how he needed to solve the problem knowledgeably. They were Paul and Jackie.

In this group, it was determined that Jill had the least (**A**) tendencies in her style. So she was given the (**A**) role, which is to pay attention to all the details of the team work, including updating absent members of the team. The rest of the team was to give ideas as to what to do, how to solve the problem. They served as (E)s.

It should be noted that negative energy is being converted to positive. Those who could sabotage the decision in its implementation—those who had power—Bill, Jill, Simon and Rose, were asked for their opinion on what should be done. We have had numerous cases where members of the team decided by themselves against their own self-interest because it made sense for the good of the company.

David then chose Ira to integrate the team. Ira was chosen because of, and not in spite of, the fact that he had no authority, power or influence. He was chosen because he had no biases. Ira went through five days of Integrator's training and then the team started working.

The four goals are achieved in the team. The team can solve the problem because it has *CAPI*. Ira will integrate and build the team. Paul and Jackie have influence because they are knowledgeable about the subject and teach the team what they know. Thus, all the four goals are achieved.

Ira developed (**ı**)ntegration, David (**p**)erformance, Jill (**a**)dministration and the rest of the group (**e**)ntrepreneurship. But the same people were also members of different teams. On another team David was (**ı**), Ira was (**e**), Jill was the (**p**), and Rose might be the (**a**). So, we developed style enrichment.

What about other methodologies?

Look at training programs for problem-solving. Because they are based on cases and boiler plate exercises, it is the trained participant who must make the transition of knowledge from the exercise to reality. Because he usually has no *CAPI* to solve the problem,

	SHORT RANGE	LONG RANGE
ORGANIZATIONAL GOALS	1. SOLVING PROBLEMS	2. BUILDING TEAMWORK
INDIVIDUAL GOALS	3. MANAGERIAL SKILLS TRAINING & DEVELOPMENT	4. INDIVIDUAL STYLE ENRICHMENT

Figure 79: Simultaneous Goals of the Adizes Methodology

he can't do it alone. The people whose cooperation he needs to solve the problem most probably did not attend the same course. Thus, the knowledge he attained is usually not applied.

Team-building training courses assume that better-trained people become better team players. I question that because what people really want is not team-building, but problem-solving. If problems are not solved, the team-building process suffers. Some of my most depressing professional experiences have been working with Aristocratic organizations who have gone through lots of organizational development training. Terms like "mutual respect," "mutual trust" and "team work," evoked cynical remarks or total apathy.

Style enrichment is fine, but unless it solves some problems, it will meet the same fate as team building.

Last, but not least to be criticized, are management training programs. These programs have very little impact on organizations because they train individuals. *CAPI* is the key to change. Training *individuals* to be better managers has a very limited benefit. If the goal is to have more knowledgeable people, fine; but a better manager won't change the organization unless it is in Go-Go or Infancy. By and large, Infant and Go-Go organizations do not send their management to executive training, because there is no time. The people who go to those programs are the Aristocrats although they can't make change by themselves, no matter how knowledgeable they are. The best that can be expected from them is that they can articulate well what is not happening, and why it's not happening.

Now, let us look at a short version of the 11-phase change interventions and how they relate to the theoretical underpinnings above.

12

The Eleven Phases of Managing Organizational Change ====

THE PROCESS OF ORGANIZATIONAL THERAPY

There is a sequence of activities or interventions that must take place in an organization if it is to move from one phase of the Lifecycle to another. Additional steps may be required if the company has some specific problems.

The steps utilized depend upon the organization's location on the Lifecycle. Therapy consists of a series of assignments (phases) that the organization is given to work on. The theoretical framework determines who gets the assignments, the sequence of the assignments and the allowable completion times. The classic surgical solutions for organizational change are occasionally used, and new management is integrated into the existing structure as needed. However, this action is more of an exception than a rule.

There are eleven basic steps or phases within the Adizes methodology which are designed specifically to produce organizational change. These therapeutic processes must be applied to a certain sequence and with the proper amount of emphasis to produce the desired results. The treatment is analogous to that given by a medical doctor. The curative drug must be prescribed in both the proper dosage and at the proper time. Healing drugs can do damage if improperly administered.

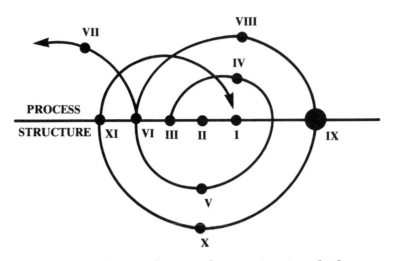

Figure 80: The 11 Phases of Organizational Change

First let's take a look at the eleven phases; we'll discuss how they're applied to each stage of the Lifecycle subsequently.

We should notice that there is a major difference between the upper and lower parts of the sequence. The upper half of the figure is for those phases that impact the process of a company. With these phases, we intervene to change the way the organization behaves, meaning the way management behaves, and the process of decision-making as it *should* be. The phases in the lower half of the chart impact structure or the institutionalized way things are accomplished. As an analogy, process is how the water flows in a river. The structure is provided by the river banks. As the water flows it affects the river banks and the river banks affect the water flow, which means that in the long run, process affects structure, and in the short run structure affects process. A total 11-step intervention program is designed to intermittently and repetitively affect process and structure until both are changed as desired.

The program is set up in modules. When energy in one module begins fading, the organization loses interest in pursuing change. Then a new phase is introduced, so that at a selected point in time, surges of energy are created in the company to propel the organization through the next difficult process of change. The modules are I, II, III; then IV, V, VI, VII and X; and finally, VIII, IX, XI.

This method is a practical, disciplined and comprehensive approach to assisting businesses in solving their problems while enhancing their management practices and the role of participatory management within the organization. It is based on the demonstrated principle that people working together in complimentary teams can solve bigger and more complex problems, and can produce more meaningful organizational changes, than individual managers working alone.

The *Adizes* ℠ synergetic method differs from traditional management consulting methods because it does not go in as a consultant in order to change an organization. The *Adizes* Associate is not an outsider with answers in specialized areas of expertise. Rather, he instructs and leads the members of an organization through a series of processes designed to assist them in discovering their own answers and implementing their own solutions. Although the method has a prescribed procedure, the sequence, timing and level of effort expended by the company on each step is carefully tailored to its unique needs. Each step focuses on a distinct organizational or managerial requirement, with the entire process developing into a program that produces optimum company productivity and profit performance. The methodology achieves deep and potentially lasting results by cascading cultural change throughout the organization.

The Eleven Phases Of Change

0	Conceptual Foundations	Introduction to the Adizes concepts
I	Syndag*	Organizational Diagnosis—a systemic audit of the organization and its managerial process
II	Synerteams*	Team building for functional problem solving
III	POC* structure	Implementation, follow up, and starting a structural bottom-up channel of communication
IV	Synerscope*	Mission definition
V	SynOrDes*	Departmentalization—organizational structure
VI	SynRAS*	Responsive accountability systems
VII	Cascade	Cascade I–VI to lower organizational levels

VIII	Peak performance	Identify opportunity for excellence and stretching
IX	Resource Allocation	Allocation of scarce resources whether financial, human or physical
X	Parallel Structure	Top down and bottom up structure
XI	Reinforcement system	Design of gain sharing for stakehold-ers

* Copyrighted service names of the Adizes Institute.

I do not count 0 as a step, because in itself, it does not produce change; it is introductory in nature.

I. Syndag

The first phase in the methodology is a detailed diagnosis called *Syndag*, an acronym for synergetic organizational diagnosis, which reflects that the diagnosis is conducted as a team process requiring the active involvement of those people who constitute *CAPI* in a company. Experience has shown that the impact of this group diagnosis on the behavior of the company is much greater than that which can be achieved through individual interviews with the same people.

In this phase we impact both process and structure. We analyze what can be improved in the process of decision-making and in the structure, and make a complete managerial audit of the company so that its energies can be directed toward the resolution of the root causes of problems. In doing this, we use the involvement and commitment of the *CAPI* group.

A comprehensive diagnosis is crucial to the long-term success of any program to improve an organization's performance. The data gathered in the diagnosis provides a complete profile of the company's needs which can then be used to tailor the overall program to meet the organization's unique requirements. The specific objectives of a Syndag include:

- A *detailed* identification and analysis of the major areas for improvement within all parts of the company, to include an analysis of the root causes of those problems.

- A *detailed* strategy for the arrest, relief or resolution of those problems, including: identifying which problems will be solved by individuals, which by teams, how the teams should be composed, and when the problems will be solved.
- Legitimizing the need for change in the organization and creating an energized atmosphere of mutual cooperation and teamwork to get the job done. Syndag provides a sample of the Adizes methodology, which illustrates that problems can be discussed and solved with mutual trust and respect.
- A new perspective on the business of management including the inevitability of conflict, why it is necessary for healthy organizations, and how to harness it.
- A plan of action for the future that is backed by the power and commitment of the key managers.

An accumulation of all the potential improvement points within the company puts the handwriting on the wall. It gives management a clear picture of the reality they face. We want to make the previously implicit desire for improvement explicit. While illustrating that things do not have to be bad to get better, we raise the consciousness of the company so that they can move out of the current equilibrium into a new equilibrium, one that is better suited to change. Through this diagnosis we legitimize the need for change and create the energy necessary to make a difference throughout the entire organization.

This is done by identifying where the organization is on the Lifecycle, how it got there, and what it needs to do in order to move to the next desirable stage. A Syndag can be used to diagnose a company *only* when the company is committed to a long-term change process. This restriction is made because the excitement and energy created by the Syndag, coupled with the participant's expectations for substantial organizational change, can become dysfunctional to the company if senior management decides not to proceed.

I have also developed a short Syndag for those companies which do not want long-term commitment, just a diagnosis. But these are variations of the therapeutic process, and not covered in this book.

II. Synerteams

After the organization's problems and the reason for their occurrence are identified and analyzed, the next stage is to compose and train the teams needed to solve the first-priority problems identified in the diagnosis. This team-building exercise is important because most of the problems identified in the diagnosis are not problems that are easily solvable by individuals. The most difficult problems in organizations require cooperation between several individuals, and the required teamwork doesn't easily occur in organizations. *CAPI* must be coalesced. Problem-solving teams comprised of individuals with conflicting opinions, perspectives and interests are extremely difficult to manage. The skills to manage these teams must be introduced to the organization, because they are not skills normally well-developed in most managers. The Synerteam phase is designed to provide special skills and hands-on experience to the managers working with problem-solving teams. This is a very task-oriented phase because the teams are learning while resolving the priority problems identified in the diagnosis. Skills developed in this step include:

- What it takes to make a good decision.
- How to *predict* if a decision will be implemented.
- When and how to compose a team to solve a problem.
- When *not* to use a team to solve a problem.
- Why conflict occurs in groups and how to make constructive use of it.
- The difference between decision-making, taking and accepting.
- How the *Adizes* process for problem-solving enables a manager to resolve tough issues in an *effective* and *participatory* way.

III. POC—Implementation Follow-up and Start of a Bottom-up Structure

In Phase I, problems were identified and agreed upon, thus eliminating second-guessing. In Phase II, members were trained, and teams were composed to solve the functional priority problems. The next task is to start building a new structure parallel to the existing organizational structure. This new part is an **(EI)** structure, and is designed to identify and solve problems for which individuals do not have *CAPI*. In this phase, several changes will occur.

1) Synerteams, when they run out of *CAPI*, have a source to obtain it so they can finalize their assignment. This retards the undesired by-product of participative management called management by committee—groups of people with assignments and no *CAPI*.

2) The process of change produces anxiety. Will it work? Does the president really want to change? Can the people really handle their assignments? Everyone has his own bag of anxieties evoked by change of status quo. Those anxieties must be addressed, or people rationalize in a hurry why the change won't work, and begin to say, "we better stop while we're ahead and it does not get worse."

In psychotherapy, this is the phase where the patient must undertake responsibility for his own treatment. In jogging this is the famous "wall" that the runner wonders if he should stop running. In weight loss, it is the point where the dieter starts developing theories why the diet is harmful and why he should stop it and look for another diet another time. This is the point where, if resistance to change is overcome, change will be institutionalized. In Phase III, both structure and process are impacted.

Phases I, II and III are the warm-up stage, where people learn to trust and respect each other. They learn to identify problems together, and to solve them together. Now the team is ready to tackle tougher problems.

In Phase I, the organization learned to diagnose problems together. Once this is accomplished, they can go deeper into the cultural change begun in Phase I. Deeper, in this case, means more heat, and more conflict to work on because it is harder to solve a problem than to analyze it. In Phase II, people learn that functional problems in marketing, production, quality control, sales, etc., *can be* solved.

An example is Northrop Aviation's F-18 fighter plane. Northrop used the Adizes methodology to produce its own results of cultural change. Since Infancy, the organization had focused on two-engine planes. It was more than a rational decision; it was almost a religion. During the Syndag, this was picked as a very significant item, that should be solved by a Synerteam. Within six months of having

CAPI and knowing how to integrate and harness conflict a decision was made to produce a single-engine plane, the F-18.

Phase III goes further in managing conflict. People learn the difficult maneuver of exercising upward leadership to activate the higher-ups in the organizational hierarchy, to get the authority needed to solve problems that a particular manager is responsible for. In Phase II, managers practice how to enlist the support of peers and subordinates. It is more difficult, but just as necessary, to learn how to enlist the support of one's boss, his boss, or the boss of bosses, and other top management to whom one does not usually have access. That is Phase III.

By the time the three phases are finished, there is a real sense of control. At this point, the organization can look at its goals and structure. To attempt it before this point would be like planning to climb Mount Everest with people who believe they can't get out of bed.

Phases I, II and III create a "yes we can" climate. The employees at Equifax in Atlanta, Georgia, when this module was finished, put up a banner: "For a change, we can make a change." Bank of America employees reacted similarly. Its branches had their own banners: "Yes, we can do it." In this module, the organization learns to identify, analyze and solve functional problems without a witch hunt, without personal attribution of fault. We focus on what is wrong that must be immediately solved, and how to do it, rather than who did it wrong, when it was done wrong and why someone else did it wrong.

what not *who*
now not *when*
we not *they*
how not *why*

IV. Mission Definition

Phase IV, which is to define the mission of the organization as a team process, starts by defining the rock. Phases I, II and III were for learning to work together with mutual trust and respect. Now we put those skills to work to change the organization. Where is this company going? Again note that this involves "we" as a team, rather than departments working individually with a staff unit integrating the final product into a corporate mission. This is a visualization process where *we* jointly discover what it is that *we* as the company want to do, so that when finalized, *we* support it and *we* know that it can be accomplished. A clear definition of the company's mission and scope of operations, as a team process, is the purpose of this phase. Included are analyses of:

1) The needs which are served by the business, and as those that can and should be served
2) Business capabilities in relation to those of competitors
3) The future environment and its likely effects on the business
4) The values of the company as a hindering or facilitating factor for adapting to change
5) The future opportunities and threats facing the firm

These five points look like the content of any typical consulting report but they are not. The content might be the same, but the process is different. It is not a mission *for* management. It is a mission *by* management. The end result of this phase is a one page summary which should never be more than one page. It reads something like this:

"We are in the business of _____. Since _____ and due to _____, thus, we will _____ so that _____ _____."

It is a clear, concise statement which is understood and owned by the *CAPI* group. In many companies, top executives carry a copy of this page in their wallets. It is a unifying document that focuses their thinking and facilitates improved communication.

Syndag creates energy by identifying what can, should and will be improved. By the time Phase III is completed, the first PIPs are old, and new energy for change is needed. Phase IV provides the energy through the process of visualization—what if, what can, and what should?

If syndag is a push away from the status quo, Phase IV, Synerscope is a pull toward a new status quo. The therapy is designed to be a push-pull change process that keeps the organization moving.

V. Definition of Responsibilities—Top-down Structure

In light of the mission, Phase V focuses on structure. Only when people know where the organization is going can they decide how to structure themselves in order to get there. Structure must follow mission. This phase is structured to redesign the organizational structure in such a way that it will facilitate accomplishment of the present and future mission requirements. Organizational functions and individual responsibilities throughout the organization are analyzed to determine if they are appropriate for the company's new needs. The structure is developed to facilitate the assignment of responsibilities and a clarification of accountability. The creative, planning functions—the **(EI)** functions—are identified and separated from the doing **(PA)** functions. In this phase, organizational colonialism is overcome, power centers switch, line takes control and staff recognizes its legitimate role. In this phase, the founder or his family are finally freed of the Founder's or Family Trap.

This is one of the most complicated phases in the methodology. Structure causes behavior and being a structuralist, I give special attention to this phase. To be certified in V, people must be certified in all the other ten phases first. This extensive phase requires a book by itself.

VI. Responsive Accountability Systems (SynRAS)

Now that the company has redefined its vision and structure, there is a critical need in Phase VI to address the following:

- Wind tunnel test of the new structure. Define and clarify responsibilities within and between units.
- Match these new responsibilities with appropriate levels of authority.
- Enhance the information systems so they document individual accountability for every dollar in and out of the organization, as well as other key indicators, in a manner that mirrors the new responsibilities in the new structure.

If these issues are not rapidly and completely addressed, the new mission and structure will not be implemented, and managers frequently cannot, or will not, feel accountable for their new jobs. In this phase, we redesign the information systems so they will fit the new structure and lead management to identify whether or not it is achieving the new mission. This process is critical because it encourages openness, sharing and cooperation of information rather than using information as a source of power. It is a managerial information system rather than an exclusive accounting information system.

VII. Cascade

Now that we have impacted the upper echelon of the company, Phase VII will cascade the methodology to the lower levels of the organization so that everyone shares the new language and philosophy, and it becomes part of the culture. This phase is critical to reduce alienation and separation between upper and lower management. It is also the phase where the Adizes technology is transferred, and we train and certify in-company people to function as facilitators of change and to pass on the Adizes process to lower levels of the organization. The client is learning to handle its Lifecycle by itself. We cascade those phases which were completed prior to this point—Phases I, II, III, IV, V and VI.

How different is this phase from other participative systems experiments? Participative systems are usually introduced to lower hierarchies of organizations. Top management's role is usually to approve of the experiment; they usually do not change their style, because they have no time for retraining. The result is a culture clash. Those above do not necessarily like the new culture introduced below them.

Management is not only at the top of an organization pyramid, it is also at the bottom of another pyramid. It has above it, competition, labor unions, customers, and other external pressures which it cannot control. Participative management introduces pressures from below onto top management, in addition to the pressures from above. It is not strange then that the more successful is a participative experiment, the greater is the chance it will be opposed by management. Thus, success is failure and failure is success.

In Adizes Phase I though VI, we build management teams at the top, and participative management at the executive level prior to cascading participation down. That means that we increased the number of people who feel responsible for the external pressures. We flatten the pyramid. As top management relates with each other and how they feel with their superiors, they are willing to proceed and feel participative with their subordinates.

VIII. Peak Performance Stretching

With a clear mission, responsibilities, authority and a sense of team work, respect and trust are improved. In a team process, all departmental projections are presented and then stretched to optimum

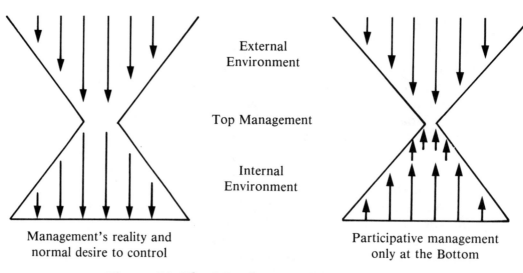

Figure 81: The Management Pressure Cooker

performance levels. In stretching we get the whole team to participate. People help each other with ideas on how to do better and
more. An analogy can help here. In order to truly maximize the
distance your hand can stretch you must first stretch your arm
and then your side, the upper part of your leg, then the calf and
finally your toe. The best that the hand can achieve is possibly
only with the support and active participation of the whole body.
The same is true with an organization. The whole company must
stretch in order to achieve the best that anyone can do.

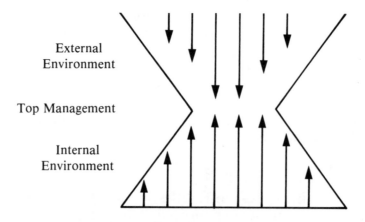

Figure 82: The Adizes Approach

Let us use a scenario to present this phase. The whole *CAPI* group is going to stretch.

We look at a typical sales budget. The first item is product A, which has a projected sales of $1 million. Question: "How can *we* (not you) make it $1.1 million in sales?" The reason we do not direct the question to the sales manager is that he has already tried his best and he came up with the $1 million figure. Now, it is the "we" time, not "you" or "he" time. The sales manager might say "If I could get the product faster, we could sell $1.1 million." Now, the question goes to the production manager, "what will it take to get the product faster . . . by the first of the month, let us say?" The answer might be, "Sales must give us more accurate projections on time." The sales manager is asked to comment on that and so it goes until no more improvements can be done, where no more stretching is possible.

A good budget is pages of numbers and even more pages of mutual commitments. People commit to getting the product out on time, to making projections on time and to being accurate. This is not really a budgeting process, a process of resource allocation. What we are doing is stretching the entire system to find where the weak links are so that we can bring the system to optimum performance.

In this phase, after the stretching is completed, sharing and allocation take place. Let me explain this part in some detail.

At the end of Phase V—organizational stucture—we have an organization that is presented in colors. Green units are profit centers which derive their revenues from customers—external clients. Blue units are profit centers which sell their services or products mostly to internal clients at a transfer price that must be agreed upon. Yellow units are service centers which provide their products or services at fully loaded cost (no profit planned). Red units are cost centers that do not charge for their services, but their cost must be shared (not just allocated) by those who use the cost center.

I have a theory on how to determine colors of units and how and why to maximize one color at the expense of the others. Unfortunately, the theory is far too intricate for discussion here. All I am trying to say is that it is not as simple as I might be presenting it here for purposes of clarity.

In Phase VI (SynRAS), an information system was designed that will enable a follow up to ensure that each unit is performing at peak performance and following its goals according to its colors within its resources.

In Phase VIII, we stretch to that peak performance—everyone and every unit. Transfer prices are negotiated at this point, and it is decided who is going to pay the bill for the red units. In most companies this is usually decided by the accounting department. It is called overhead load or allocation. From previous chapters, it should be clear that when staff takes over from line, it is a sign of aging. Thus, in this phase, we call for freedom from the oppression of accountants. The Greens, Blues and Yellows get together with the aid of accountants who only provide opinion and information (when asked). The Greens, Blues and Yellows decide together what is a fair share of the cost centers between them.

Unbelievable discussions occur. There are services that cost centers provide that no one wants or needs. For instance, accounting provides reports that no one uses. When the line has to pay, and has the capacity to decide what it wants to pay for, the Reds think twice before they swell their budgets, because they will have to justify it to the clients, not just to the president.

The usual process we try to change in this phase is the practice whereby units, including cost centers, provide budgets which are analyzed by accounting or the budgeting department, using statistical or ratio analysis, and then approved by top management. Then the staff decides allocations and overhead loads that frequently make the line unprofitable, whether they want the corporate services or not.

How many times have unprofitable units been sold only to become profitable overnight when these corporate allocations were removed?

Phase VIII, I have been successful in making cost centers perform like profit centers. They perform very efficiently because they have to face their internal client, justify the service and listen to how their services are going to be paid. Millions of dollars have been saved at this stage of the therapy.

Warning! If the reader wants to apply Phase VIII alone and just bring his team together for such a discussion, it might fail and the conflict that will develop can damage the team-work he has. It should be noted that this Phase VIII follows phase VII where preparations in team-building and conflict-handling were accomplished prior to such a discussion.

Exercising the phases is like training for weight lifting. Each subsequent phase adds more heat—weight—than the previous phase. No premature handling of conflict is prescribed.

I am so encouraged by the results achieved in changing staff units' behaviors, that I believe government bureaucracies can be made to behave like business organizations, in spite of not having a profit motive. For a full test of this belief, we will have to wait until it is tested in a real, full-fledged bureaucracy.

When the sharing of red expenses is finished, management looks at the results. Do they like it? If not, then it is time for strategic planning. They analyze what strategic changes in resource allocation are necessary so that the desired results will be achieved. If they cannot achieve desired results by working better or harder—since they have already stretched to peak performance—a change in direction is called for. This is phase IX.

IX. SynREAL (Synergetic REsource Allocation)

Strategic planning can only now be attempted, because it is based on the right people having the right information as determined by the structure, and it is directed to measure the mission achievement. There is no point in attempting strategic planning if the information is biased by the distribution of power that was in the old organizational structure. It is difficult to look outside the company when you must constantly look over your shoulder to avoid being stabbed in the back.

This phase is designed to develop a long-range plan and create a strategic planning system for increasing product lines, market share, and profitability. The goal is to create a common vision of the company's future that has the key management's full support, involvement and commitment. In this stage, capital budget is prepared. In Phase VIII, the operational budget is made. Thus, by Phase IX, we have mission, structure, strategy and budgets.

X. Bottom-up Structure

While the top management group is going through Phases VIII and IX, the process of Phases I, II, III, IV, V, and VI is rapidly cascaded in Phase VII. By the time Phase IX is finished, we can plan how the total organization is going to practice all the eleven phases—who will do what, and where the training and certification of in-company people will be done. In this phase, plans are made to continue the Adizes process without external intervention.

Changing a culture is like changing a religion; all religions have reinforcement methods. Muslims pray many times a day and go to the mosque on Friday. Jews go on Saturday and Christians go on Sunday. Where people go to worship is different, but what is identical is that they all go and hear a sermon to reinforce their religions. It is not enough to convert and then stop practicing. The same applies here. In Phase X, a plan is made, determining when each phase will be introduced to each unit in the organization, so the process is integrated and it reinforces the process of continuous change. For instance, in the eight weeks that comprise January and February, if there are eight levels of units in the organization, all units must complete a diagnosis (Syndag). It starts from the bottom like a wave. In the first week, the level eights complete their Syndags and pass up the ladder to the POC above them, those problems for which they have no *CAPI*. During the second week, the same process repeats itself for level seven units which pass up and down PIPs, depending on where the authority for each PIP is. In the third week it is level six, and so on, until in the eighth week, corporate top management meets. They get all the problems from below that only they have the authority to solve.

During the Syndag, a plan is made as to which problems will be solved by individuals, which by teams, and when they will be solved.

Then in Phase II, during March, team-building takes place and functional problems are solved. We have developed a computer program into which all the problems are inputted, and authorized people can find out which units have which problems, who is solving them and when they will be solved. When there is a solution, the data bank can tell what the solution was and how it was accomplished.

This process is like a roto-rooter of organizational channels. There are no problems that must and can be solved *by the organization* that do not get acted on.

In April, the mission is made starting from the top and cascading and integrating it downward. Then in May the organizational structure is reviewed. It should be noted that this is a proactive process, not reactive. We do not wait until the structure has problems, to restructure the company. Every May, by the calendar, the structure is reviewed. It can be reviewed sooner than May if needed, but as a rule, it must be reviewed no later than May.

In June, the information system is reviewed. In July the system of stretching and sharing is undertaken. In August, it is resource allocation, and in September this same Phase X of how Adizes does and should work, is reviewed and improvements are made. Then Phase XI is reviewed and improved. By then, its January, and the cycle starts all over again.

XI. Incentive Systems

The last phase of the Adizes methodology establishes incentive systems. This is deliberately left to be the last phase because it is often the most painful. It deals with money, personal rewards, and recognition. The reward system (Ri_p, Re_{np}, Ri_m, Re_t) has changed by doing the other ten phases already. What is left to be done is ($Re_\$$). The goal of this step is to *jointly* develop incentive systems that reflect cooperation, team achievement, and that motivate people to perform in a manner that is consistent with the new mission, goals and accountabilities. The organization knows where it is going, and they have the structure and resources to get there. This is the stage where everyone will benefit from what is achieved by the corporation. Stakeholders are identified and a centralized system to reward individual, group, departmental and corporate achievement is designed.

Once the eleven phases are finished, what happens? We go back to Phase I, because in the meantime, a year has passed; new problems exist that require a new team, a new mission, and a new structure.

The goal is to institutionalize a continuously adapting process in the organization. We treat the organization like we treat a car. Why do we take a car to a garage and every 6,000 miles have it tuned? For preventive maintenance. The same thing should be true for an organization.

We don't wait until the problems become a crisis to solve them. In this system, if it is May, we must be doing reorganization or better, if we are doing reorganization, it must be May. We don't wait until the organization is a mess. Every May, the organization's structure is tuned. Every June, the information system is tuned. It's a continuous process of looking where the organization is going, how the structure is working and how to motivate the people. It's done in a deliberate and repetitive sequence.

The 11-phase Adizes method is significantly different than those used by traditional management consultants or behavioral scientists. Management consultants are typically content-oriented and emphasize the *what* of the decision to be made, and less how it was made. The implementation is less emphasized. Classic behavioral science interventions put more emphasis on *how* a decision is made, than *what* is actually decided. With Adizes, implementation is of primary importance and equal emphasis is given to both the *what* and the *how* of a decision.

In traditional consulting, the sequence is to define the mission and strategies, and then to design the structure. In Adizes, internal problems are identified first (Syndag), the sense of potency that change can be produced effectively is increased in the consciousness of the organization and then the mission is defined. Defining the mission without creating a sense of potency is equivalent to daydreaming. It is impossible to move into strategy. The structure is most probably inadequate, so it is likely that the strategy will reflect the constellations of power of the existent structure.

After the mission has been defined, the structure should be changed accordingly. With this new and better allocation of power, a new strategy can be developed.

Accountability Fit and the Eleven Phases

Phases I, II and III—diagnosis, team-building and functional problem-solving (the first module of change)—do not treat any of the three subsystems. They do change attitudes and promote a sense of competence. People realize they can talk about problems and will not be persecuted for it. They see that problems can be solved. Hope is established. People agree publicly that there is an accountability misfit and they start believing that change can occur. Their sense of commitment grows. SOC $_{n-1}$ goes up. Phase I creates energy for change; Phases II and III test and prove that the energy can be channeled to produce results. That sums the first module of the therapy.

The second module is next. After changing the sense of commitment, the throughputs can be treated, and the accountability fit can be fixed.

The first subsystems that can be treated and stabilized, are the teleological subsystems. That is where Phase IV comes in, defining the mission.

In Phase V, organizational structure is determined. This makes the transition from the teleological subsystem to the *Authorance* subsystem, because in this phase, each organizational unit's responsibilities are determined (in colors), as is who reports to whom. In Phase VI, authority and who has it is established. A system of accountability is developed, stating who is responsible for what, what authority that person has to carry out his responsibility, and how it will be measured.

During Phase VII, Phases I through VI are repeated through the cascading process. It continues the process of stabilizing *Authorance* because now power and influence are being worked on. In Phase VIII the stretching and sharing reinforces interdependence, and that finishes the stabilizing of *authorance*. Now, *authorance* must be equilibriated to the teleological subsystem.

This is done in Phase IX, when the new structure must decide to change direction, change its telos, test the new structure, and make adaptations to the structure. Phase X reinforces the process of continuous equilibriating.

While all these phases have been going on, the reward subsystem is not standing still. It is changing and rising on its own because

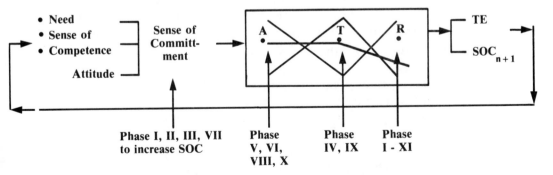

Figure 83: The 11 Phases As They Address the Teleological Subsystems

parts of the system—Ri_m, Ri_p and Re_{np}—are driven by the changes in the authorance and teleological subsystem.

Phase IV, defining the vision, increases $Ri_{mission}$. Phases V, VI, VII and X increase $Ri_{potency}$. Phase V and staffing it, increases Ri_{task}, because tasks are defined along PAEI roles, and staffed accordingly. Phases I, II and III, working in teams to diagnose and solve problems, increase $Ri_{potency}$. Role assigments within the team to spur style enrichment, increase $Re_{non\text{-}pecuniary}$. Workers can be team administrators and integrators. People are not stuck in only one role for many years. They act in different roles, perhaps they have managerial roles in a team, although outside the team they are workers and not managers. They are appreciated for their contribution and are told so.

The whole reward curve has been going up, except $Re_\$$. Now in Phase XI, it is time to fix that. If we tried to do it earlier all the frustration with the inadequacy of Ri_t, Ri_m, Ri_p and Re_{np} would be expressed exclusively through increasing demands for $Re_\$$. It would not only be expensive, but also futile, because $Re_\$$ has a short lifespan as a motivating force.

The eleven phases brought Accfit into balance. Phase X left a technology behind, and certified in-company Adizes people to continue the process of equilibriating. The organization has moved to Prime and knows how to stay there. Why is it in Prime, and why is Accfit in balance?

Because the organization knows its teleological subsystems. It knows where it wants to go, has a structure to get there (authorance), and there are extrinsic and intrinsic rewards for accomplishing the desired. Furthermore, there is a process to rediscover new goals, new structures and new reward systems. The organization changed predictably and can continue to change under control. That is Prime.

The eleven phases also impact the four causes to aging. Phase IV annually redefines the mission, which at the beginning treats cause 3 to aging, later preventing this cause to aging from developing.

Phase V and VI treat cause 4 to aging (the structural causes).

What can still cause aging are the personal causes like leadership style and mental age over which we have less control. My experience has been, however, that the Adizes therapy provides a centrifugal force: as the organization grows or rejuvenates, as the situation changes, the demands for leadership change too. Thus, this factor is treated too.

Bringing an organization to Prime and creating a system that keeps it in Prime is the goal of the methodology and it takes one to three years to accomplish.

13

Treating Organizations—A Contingency Approach

TREATING INFANCY

What happens and what should happen during Infancy? Results are emphasized and creativity is de-emphasized. Furthermore, there is a danger that the founder might lose his excitement. He might feel that except for the pride of ownership, he is getting little else. At this stage, the founder at least feels that he is in control.

In Infant organizations I strongly recommend an internal, rather than an external board of directors. It is important at this stage, that the founder gets emotional support. The organization most definitely needs legal and financial advice, which can be brought in from the outside. What is needed, but cannot be brought in from the outside as well as when provided from the inside, is emotional support. If lawyers and accountants are on the board, they may put demand on too much reality-testing and enforce it with their votes. They can flatten the enthusiasm to the point of aborting innovative projects and make the founder feel that he has lost control. Such people should act only as paid advisors.

The Infant organization needs constant close supervision in order to keep it out of trouble. It needs attention, nurturing, support, and protection from exposure.

Because Infant organizations have no system, they are constantly getting into trouble. All of their needs must be met almost simultaneously. The therapist must perform at least two functions for the Infant organization. First, he must give it a sense of reality; and second, he must help the organization get the resources it needs to make that reality happen. The therapist must make reality-oriented projections on cash flow and protect the founder from hiring mediocre people, and from sharing stock prematurely. An Infant organization should be made aware of how it can grow, and how to develop realistic expectations. Infant organizations are inexperienced, and they often make unrealistic commitments. Because their resources are slim, they are often overworked. As a result, they lose the grand view, and their expectations of what can be done are circumscribed by the limited world they are exposed to. Because Infant organizations are usually overcommitted to the insignificant and the unfruitful, they waste their resources on the trivial. Since the resources of Infant organizations are slim, to say the least, they exist from hand to mouth. Frequenly, they run out of working capital. The organizational therapist must hold their hands to help them overcome each crisis, and equally important, he must help them realize what they should *not* do.

Infant organizations are given assignments which orient them toward analyzing the environment, planning future cash flow needs, and forecasting sales, production, and staffing needs, but this should be done sparingly. Attempts to transform an Infant organization into a highly structured and specialized organization are usually harmful. Since the executives must often do all the work themselves, spending time on standard operating procedures would reduce the Infant organization's flexibility and productivity, and endanger its ability to survive in a highly competitive environment.

Some Infant organizations spend inordinate amounts of time on systems, or buy computerized systems before they are really needed. Others establish expensive headquarters before they can afford to. They should reserve such luxuries for the future. A founder of one such organization bought fancy systems, located the organization in a prime location, and established an organizational routine that severely restricted improvisation. The organization could not take the expense, and it lost its earlier strength, which included flexibility and adaptability.

The organizational therapist gives the Infant organization assignments which lead it to predict, analyze and schedule. Individuals are assigned these assignments because the organization is not big enough to afford teamwork. The deadlines are flexible, because the organization is overworked, and as long as it is on the right track, there is no real need to put more pressure on it.

The Infant organization may fail to develop its capacity for **(E)**, because the founder burns out. In this case, the organization becomes the Lone Ranger's trap. An owner works very hard but nets very little. Most of the organization's operating earnings go toward paying the interest on debts. The owner ends up working for the bank and his suppliers. He is often so busy that he is unaware of what the competition is doing. His prices may be far too low and he may be achieving sales success at the expense of profits. If the company goes bankrupt, the Lone Ranger's trap becomes a graveyard. Otherwise, it will die with the death of the owner or grow under new management. In any case, while the organization is alive, its owner works harder for less than he would have earned as an employee elsewhere. The only possible benefits for the owner of such an organization are independence and pride of ownership.

For the company to advance to Go-Go, the leadership style should be **(PaEi).**

The owner should be careful not to give away ownership and lose control. He should consider interlocking companies or legal structures where he controls the top level of a hierarchy. This allows many people to join the hierarchy and become owners at different levels, without the owner losing control.

Since Infant organizations are short on cash, I suggest that they do a rolling 16 weeks forward cash flow projections, which should be monitored weekly. Profit and Loss statements are an insufficient control system because they are usually on accrual and ignore loss of liquidity to accounts receivable and inventory. Thus, the Infant organizations must also monitor the turnover of inventory and receivables.

Adizes as a methodology has no therapeutic advantage in treating Infants. As a matter of fact, organizational therapy is not recommended to Infants because the methodology takes time, and that is what Infants don't have. In my experience, it has value only as a preventive methodology.

TREATING GO-GO

What should be done during Go-Go? (e) is high. *CAPI* is high, the company is doing fine and the Go-Go organization feels it can attack anything at any time. That's how it gets into trouble. Go-Gos make decisions they shouldn't have made, make commitments they shouldn't have made; they get involved in activities they know nothing or very little about.

What managers of a Go-Go organization must remember, is that they are on the brink of serious problems. They should prepare for the forthcoming move to Adolescence. They must get ready to institutionalize (e) and *CAPI*.

A desirable activity in Go-Go is to start developing teamwork. The organizations must develop (I)ntegration to create an environment that will not require as many rules when they get organized later on. If they build (I), the need for administrative systems can be reduced, because the integrative forces—the teamwork—will substitute for technocratic, bureaucratic and administrative solutions for institutionalization of the decision-making process in Adolescence.

The appropriate therapy for the Go-Go organization is to help it realize what *not* to do. This is necessary because the Go-Go organization tends to spread itself too thin and tackle too many frontiers at the same time. The first assignment that the therapist should give the Go-Go organization is to have it list all projects which are in the process of completion: those underway, those just being started and those being contemplated. Then the organization should be required to estimate the resources and time necessary to accomplish each project. The Go-Go organization is usually shocked to learn that it is planning to complete a lifetime of projects in one year. The sooner the Go-Go organization realizes it will have to set priorities, the faster it will focus and become more efficient. The organization must learn, experience and accept the fact that resources are limited and that given limited resources, the law of opportunity costs prevails. Doing one thing means one cannot do something else; and the cost of doing one thing is the price of not doing another.

This simple law of economics, known as the law of butter or

guns, was popularized by Paul Samuelson.[1] It usually comes as an unpleasant revelation to the Go-Go organization, whose members want to have their butter and guns too.

After the Go-Go organization has set priorities, it is given the assignment of establishing detailed objectives and guidelines. The next step is hand-holding to facilitate the implementation of the organization's plans. One must constantly watch to see how new assignments are added and make the organization realize when it violates its own priorities. The Go-Go organization is usually restless and jumpy.

The Go-Go organization is quite difficult to handle, and the therapist is always on the verge of being dropped because Go-Go people do not appreciate taking time off the firing line to think things through. The organization needs to mature. Its members are so excited with their results and their ideas that they do not want to hear any doomsday prophecies about the price that will be paid tomorrow for today's mess.

The members of the Go-Go organization are simply too busy to spend any time getting organized, and so they do not see the *short-term* benefits of such a time investment. Typically, the Go-Go organization rewards performers. Thus, it is contemptuous of administrative tendencies and shows little, if any, desire to have the external facilitator implement change. One simply must wait for such an organization to grow at its own pace. If, however, it cannot get organized itself and does not call for help from the outside, the organization can fall into the Founder's Trap.

The teams to which assignments are given in the Go-Go organization are small: two or three people at most. The assignments must be short and able to be done in a short period of time (thus, many small tasks have to be assigned in succession). This is necessary, because the people in the Go-Go organization do not have the patience for postponed gratifications. If they do not see immediate relevance and benefit, they lose interest and usually discontinue the treatment.

---

[1] Samuelson, Paul A. *Economics*: 12th Edition, (New York: McGraw-Hill, 1985).

Getting out of the Founder's or Family Trap—Institutionalizing (E) and *CAPI*

The difference between Go-Go and Prime is that (ᴇ) and *CAPI* are personalized in Go-Go, while in Prime, they are institutionalized in the structure and the process of management. In other words, they are systematized. If this systematization is correctly achieved, the organization can avoid the troubles of Adolescence.

Every organization has four subsystems: Client Interface, (ᴇ); Transportation, (ᴘ); Human Factors, (ɪ); and Financial Factors, (ᴀ). Each subsystem has a developmental (e) and a maintenance (p) component.

The subsystem which changes the client interface is marketing (eE); (p) of (ᴇ) is sales, engineering is (eP), when production (manufacturing or operations) is (pP), HRD is (eI), personnel (pI), finance (eA); and accounting (pA).

The (ᴇ) function is reflected in marketing, process engineering, human resources development, and finance.

The problem with Go-Go organizations, and what can cause the Founder's Trap, is that (ᴇ) is monopolized. The leader monopolized all the responsibility for making marketing, technology, financial and human resource decisions. The founder may be a genius in one or more fields, but he usually is not in all of the four subsystems.

Thus, if he is a marketing whiz kid, he will not let anyone else make financial, top management human resources decisions,

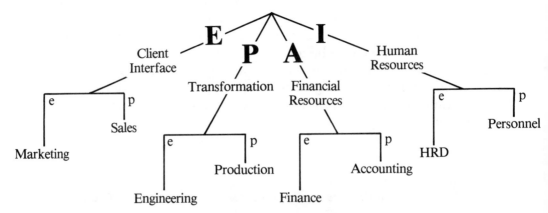

Figure 84: The Four Subsystems of Any Organization

or technological changes, because they are interrelated with marketing.

In Infancy, this monopolization and unification makes perfect sense. The marketing, technology, finance, and human factors are deeply interwoven; they are almost identical at this stage. Making a decision in one of these areas has instantaneous impact on the others. In Infancy, the Founder is experimenting and trying to identify, articulate and formulate success. Thus monopolization of the four areas is normal, to be expected and even desired. In order to institutionalize **(E)**, the four areas must be separated and transferred from a person into a structure—into marketing, engineering, finance and HRD departments—even though the founder will resist the delegation of authority for fear of losing control. The process of transfer is as follows: Phase I, IV, V, VI, XI; then II, III, VII, VIII, IX, and X.

During Syndag, the problems are identified, diagnosed and a plan of action is made. The group agrees on where they are on the Lifecycle, and that they need to institutionalize (E) and *CAPI*.

In the next therapeutic session, Phase IV, mission is defined and form is provided. The group agrees what the priorities are, and an agreement is made as to what business the organization is and is not into. During this process, communication is cleared, and mutual trust and respect grow. This is the time to begin to restructure the organization.

First, the **(P)**erformance functions—sales and production—are structured to reflect geography and product lines. The **(E)** areas are not touched until **(P)** is fully stabilized. Then the four **(E)** functions are legitimized. All **(P)** and **(E)** departments are put under the founder. But, it soon becomes clear that there is too much for him to do. He has a choice to delegate **(P)** or **(E)**. Most probably he will delegate **(P)**. If he does not, he must be encouraged to do so. If he still does not, the therapist should not proceed. He should let the founder manage **(P)** until he develops trust in his subordinates. When the founder is willing to delegate **(P)**, a COO is appointed to run the **(P)** functions, while the **(E)** functions continue reporting to the **(E)** person.

Before **(E)** is delegated, the **(A)**dministrative function must be institutionalized. Accounting, quality control, legal, and data processing are established separately from **(P)** and **(E)**. They are in service of the president to control **(P)**.

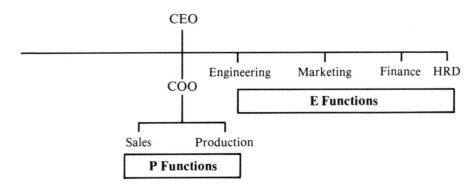

Figure 85: Go-Go Treatment, Bringing in the COO

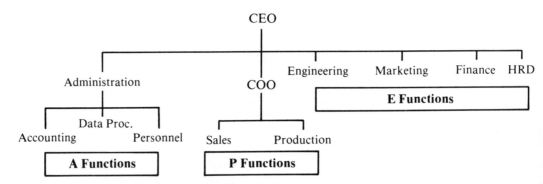

Figure 86: Balancing P, A, and E

The founder needs integrated **(A)** to provide counterbalance to the **(E)** which locomotes him. [In Go-Go, I unite **(A)** and separate **(E)**. In the aging stages, I separate **(A)** and unite **(E)**.]

The founder is still in charge of all **(E)**. Only after he develops trust in **(P)** and **(A)**—which is done through Phase VI where an accountability control system is developed—are we ready to go to the heart of the problem: decentralization of **(E)**.

The first department to be established is the one the founder is *least* interested in. It is usually finance if he likes marketing or engineering and product development. Then, the next one to be established and decentralized is the next one he is the least interested in, and so forth; but all departments still report to him.

The next step is to create and institutionalize the corporate executive committee, where the COO, CAO, and four **(E)** department heads sit. The president presides, but we draw up a calendar for the whole year to ensure that meetings do take place. Agendas are established and a rule is made that no decision is a decision until it is in writing. Minutes are taken at every meeting, and assignments are given. The why, what, when, who and how of every project are determined.

The executive committee members are taught the Adizes process of decision-making, in which they learn to make decisions as a team. Thus, institutionalized *CAPI* is developed and the relative independence of the (E) departments is established. Contentions and conflicts are legitimized and functionally channeled. Next in phases VI, VIII, IX budgets, control systems, and strategic plans are developed as a team process freeing the organization from exclusive dependency on the Founder. In phase XI, incentives are articulated, systematized and established as a system. By the time the structure is right and the people are working as a team with plans, controls and incentives, (E) and *CAPI* are institutionalized, the company is in Prime and the Founder is off the hook without losing his company.

The Problem of Premature Delegation in a Go-Go

One hears repeatedly that the founder's main problem is that he does not delegate. In the Go-Go organization, if the founder does not delegate, he will fall into the Founder's Trap; but the treatment for this problem is not easy to apply. If the organization is in Infancy (where the founder works even harder than he does in the Go-Go stage), delegation is not only unpalatable to the founder, it is dangerous to the organization's health.

In Infancy, delegation is not desirable because the unlimited dedication to his creation is what keeps the founder going. At this stage of the organization's life, asking the founder to delegate responsibility might threaten and alienate him from the organization and reduce his commitment to the organization. Furthermore, it is difficult to delegate nonprogrammed decisions, because decisions which will serve as precedents are being created at this stage. Delegating these decisions is equivalent to decentralizing, which for an Infant organization means passing control from the founder to someone else. This is almost impossible because the organization has no managerial depth. Typically, a founder will question the consultant who recommends delegation by asking in an irritated voice, "Delegate? Fine! But to whom?"

Delegation of the founder's functions should start at the advanced stages of the Go-Go organization, when there are too many tasks for the people to do. The founder should not feel that by delegating he is giving away all the fun (control). Furthermore, when approaching the Adolescent stage, administrative systems are being planned, and programming is underway. The healthy Go-Go organization needs policy-making—what *not* to do—which is tantamount to decision programming. The more programmed the decisions, the easier it will be to delegate without losing control.

Thus, the validity of the recommendation to delegate, often given to small, busy managers, should be analyzed in light of where the organization is in its Lifecycle. The timing is crucial if the treatment is to succeed.

TREATING ADOLESCENCE

How do we handle Adolescence? Look what's happening in Adolescence. There is a compounded difficulty. (**E**)ntrepreneurship and *CAPI* are in transition. Form and function are competing, and form is winning. The danger is that the founders might get a divorce from the organization. The undesirable impact on the organization is that (**E**) gets squeezed out, and the organization ages prematurely.

What must be done in Adolescence? The sequence of phases is essential. If the sequence is not followed, it usually does not work. First, after Syndag (Phase I), obviously, we must start team-building (Phase II) to free the organization from the founder. There is a tremendous dependency syndrome from which the organization must free itself. We want the founder and the employees to feel that, "we *can* work together, we *can* make decisions together, we are not exclusively dependent on the founder."

Once people feel more comfortable together and are making decentralized decisions, the next thing to do is to define the mission (Phase IV). Where is this organization going? Usually, only the founder knows, and that's written down on the back of an envelope, or it is in the founder's head. We have to share that vision. What is the dream that the rest of the organization can understand and share? Sometimes the founder does not know what the mission is or he cannot articulate it. He operates with an intuitive sense that he cannot spell out. Furthermore, the Go-Go organization is usually divergent in its thinking. It goes in many directions simultaneously. This supports centralization of decision-making. The result of it is that everyone is dependent on the founder because only he knows what the right direction is at any point in time.

Thus, after building a team and a climate of trust and respect, the mission needs articulation. Once the team knows where the organization is going, they can restructure the organization. Since (A) is the endangered role, they must build a strong (A) structure. Appointing a vice president of administration and shaping the CEO role, is the goal. Then (E) must be institutionalized. Up to this stage, (E) is usually monopolized by the founder. He probably monopolized marketing, technology, finance and human resources decisions, although by and large, the founder is unlikely to be competent or even interested in all of these goals. He simply wants to control the strategic discretionary decisions.

The institutionalization of (E) is done structurally by establishing organizational units in the above four areas, starting with the area the founder is least interested in. If he is a marketing whiz kid and least interested in finance, finance should be the unit to be established, and a chief financial officer gets hired. The area in which the founder is most interested, is left to report to him.

Now the team has teamwork, a mission, structure which protects (E) so that the team can transfer the (E) from the founder downward, and they are ready to move the founder to become chairman of the board or chief executive officer. A new leader can then be brought in with the title of chief operating officer.

During Adolescence, the organization must transfer leadership from a (PE) to a (PA) so the timing and the sequence must be right. If (A) is brought in before the company has a structure and a mission, the new leader is like a pebble in a shoe. Anytime the organization moves, the (A) says "No." But no one understands why.

The organization goes crying to the founder with "He's messing it up, he does not know us."

"I knew it," the founder says, "nobody can do it as well as I can," and he fires the (A). The (A) should be brought in only after the organization knows where it is going and it has been articulated so that the people share a direction and after there is a structure. By then there is teamwork and relative independence from the founder and the new leader can be brought in to manage and will be able to relate to the founder.

Next, the organization should change the information system? Why? The information system in a Go-Go is usually ad hoc, built up over time according to people and situations, and usually it does not reflect where the organization is going. Instead, it reflects where the organization has been. It also does not reflect the informational needs of the new roles in the new organization chart. If the organization does not change the information structure at this time the restructuring will erode. This happens because the structure, which is authority, power and influence, will act according to the information. If people don't have information, the organization doesn't have the power or authority to decide. The organizational structure that was created will be eroded and finally, eliminated. Thus, the Adizes therapist will refuse to restructure the company unless he can work on three things: 1) who reports to whom, 2) about what, and 3) for what, which means incentive systems. The organization must work on all the three subsystems if it is to change a structure. He might change the mission (phase IV), the responsibility structure (phase V), the information system (phase VI), and incentives (phase XI). The new ATR must be in balance if the new "structure" is to work right. The treatment is similar to advanced Go-Go but not identical.

The Adolescent organization is somewhat schizophrenic. It wants stability, yet it also wants an escape from the mess of development, the superficiality of projects, and the despair of getting involved in useless, expensive investments. It therefore seeks to establish policies, routines, standards and systems. At the same time, however, it wants to keep the freedom of irresponsibility, of trying out untested methods. It wants to set as many records as possible.

The therapist is caught in a double bind in such an organization. If he facilitates stabilization and systemization, some members resent him. If he does not systemize, other members will resent him. Hardly anything the outsider does will be accepted gracefully by the *whole* organization. The Adolescent organization is a pain in the neck. The therapist must have enormous patience to deal with it. He must maintain a very delicate balance between flexibility and systemization. He must change direction and assignments rapidly and with good timing.

For example, he may follow an assignment about future planning with an assignment about the system necessary to implement future planning. While maintaining optimum tension between structure and process, the therapist should help the organization focus on the desired results, and on the process for achieving them. Thus, the schizophrenia of the Adolescent organization is, in a sense, resolved by treating the process and the desired outcomes simultaneously.

When the Adolescent organization clearly identifies and achieves commitment, it becomes a Prime organization. If an Adolescent organization is incapable of such focus, it can become either arsonous or rigid. It becomes arsonous if it loses all interest in systemization. It gets involved in too many projects and fizzles out. If it loses (E), it becomes rigid and disappears since it cannot adapt or produce results.

The assignments for the Adolescent organization are usually given to a multidisciplinary group (from production, marketing and sales), so that there is an adequate balance between (A) and (E). The therapy leads to commitment to (P).

Strict deadlines are necessary. Leniency permits organizational schizophrenia to play a bigger part than it should. The therapist is tossed from (A) to (E), becoming the victim of their incongruence.

PRIME

What do we do in Prime? The Prime organization usually does not ask for external treatment. In their collective consciousness, managers do not sense a need. They feel they are doing fine. However, this could be the beginning of the end. The company is going down but usually people do not see that. In Prime, they feel as arrogant as in Go-Go, except that in this case they have a good reason to feel confident. Everything is fine. They are doing very well. Profitability is good. Market penetration is good. They are the best and why should they change? Prime is the stage where the decline begins. In this stage, they must take proactive preventive measures or eventually, they'll need to take reactive measures. It's much cheaper to do it up front than do it later.

What should be done? The big worry is losing (E). They must not allow the form to take precedence over function. Form and function should be of equal importance. The Prime organization

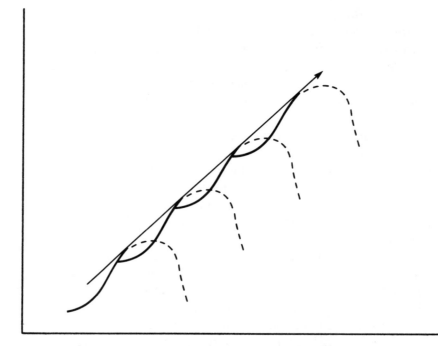

Figure 87: Spin-Offs for Prime

can nurture (**E**) by decentralizing, spinning off satellites from the organization, and creating a new Lifecycle curve. By doing these spinoffs repeatedly, by experiencing continuous rebirths, they are not allowing the organization to become Stable.

What happens to an organization with decentralization? Look at the figure below.

The modern organization can be pictured as a triangle struc-

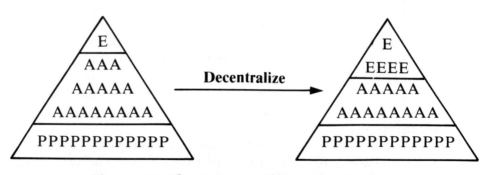

Figure 88: The Impacts of Decentralization

tured in layers. The (P)s are at the bottom; they are the people who produce the results for which the organization exists. The administrative process (A) is in the middle, which is the role of those who supervise and ensure that the desired result occurs. This function is for systematizing and watching for deficiency. At the top are those who set the direction—(E). The top has the highest discretionary powers in the organization. When they decentralize, what happens to the line which separates (E) from (A)? With decentralization, that line is pushed down. That means that the administrators of yesterday must become the entrepreneurs of tomorrow. They need to convert (A)s into (E)s.

Decentralization is different from delegation. Delegation is concerned with systematizing something and transferring it to someone else. Decentralization is more than just simple delegation; it is transfer of discretionary powers. The more decentralization, the more stimulation of the entrepreneurial spirit in the organization.

Prime is the right time to decentralize. Decentralization in Go-Go can be dangerous, because good control systems and an articulated mission are missing. Decentralization can generate an out-of-control disaster. Decentralization can start in Prime, because by then, the people know what they're doing, have some control over it, and have some structure to see to it that it happens correctly. Decentralization is a proactive vehicle for retarding aging through stimulation of (E).

The therapist's assignments involve identifying boundaries for decentralization. This includes simulating the new organizational structure (so that individuals feel comfortable about the new system) and training management (so that it can perform the new tasks). The groups to whom these assignments are given consist of those people who can be expected to lead the new profit centers. The deadlines for the completion of the assignments are neither stringent nor lenient.

There is usually no problem with managerial transplant in the Prime organization. Since the pie is continually growing, the employees welcome newcomers. The Prime organization is therefore the best candidate to buy other companies or to be bought by them.

If the Prime organization does not decentralize, it will slip into Stable. This can happen as management grows older, market share grows larger, and the structure becomes more complex. The Prime organization simply becomes too heavy.

Decentralizing and Avoiding Organizational Colonialism

As discussed in the analysis section, the efforts of decentralization and acquisitions often end up creating a problem called *organizational colonialism*. Infant and Go-Go companies end up reporting to a Prime or Aristocratic company in the following structure.

The demands of the parent units are not functional to the capabilities of the offspring. Aristocracy requests return on investment from Go-Go, while Go-Go wants to invest for increased market share. The Infant wants cash, which Go-Go controls, since the Infant is not getting as much market share as it is. Through these dysfunctional demands, the Aristocratic company destroys the growth potential offered by Go-Go and Infant organizations.

An organizational structure should be like an extended family. If we were to take a picture of this structure, the grandfathers would be in the middle, their children in the back, and all the little kids in front. Applying this analogy, the Prime or the Aristocracy would be in the middle, with the Go-Go not under the Aristocracy but adjacent to it. Infants and Prime units would be the same. This way, the individuality of the organization is protected by not superimposing the demands of one on the other. The goals are different for each unit. The Prime creates new Infants. The Aristoc-

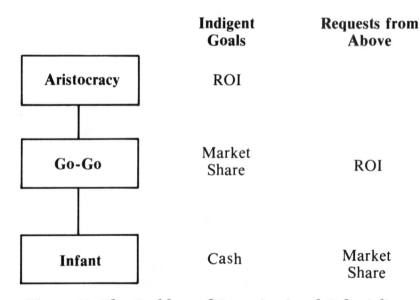

Figure 89: The Problem of Organizational Colonialism

racy finances the Infants, and the Go-Go finances itself. Now there is a family.

What does it mean, family? Everybody has his own goals and there is an *interdependency* between them. Prime creates new ventures; Aristocracy finances those ventures, and the Go-Go organizations grow on their own. Eventually, the Infant becomes a Go-Go, the Go-Go becomes a Prime, and the Prime becomes Aristocracy. While each unit might be aging, the totality does not.

What exists is a portfolio of units like a portfolio of products or stocks. There should be a portfolio of business units, each at different stages of the Lifecycle. As some age, others are born, and there is an interdependency which keeps the whole family functional.

The Organizational Family

There should be concern about the leadership of this organizational family. What style of leadership should head this family? The style of the leader and the organization's place on the Lifecycle should match. An Infant organization requires big **(P)**s and **(E)**s as managers. As the organization moves from Infant to Go-Go, it doesn't have to change leadership. What is needed is someone who can take the organization from Infant to Go-Go to Adolescence.

Aristocracy is a different story. Now, a **(PA)**-type to milk the organization and get money for the other organizations to grow, is needed. This is assuming they're dealing with an Aristocracy

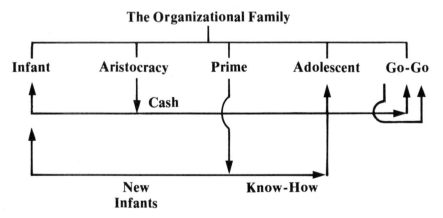

Figure 90: The Organizational Family

that is already dysfunctional or undesirable in the marketplace. To rejuvenate the Aristocracy, a **(PE)** is necessary.

A big **(E)** and a big **(I)** is needed to head Prime.

Now the organization has a portfolio of companies and a portfolio of leaders, a stable of horses for different races. There is somebody to take an organization from Infancy to Go-Go and, when it reaches Adolescence, he will either change his style or transfer the organization to a different type of leader, and he picks up another Infant. Somebody else will take the organization from Adolescence to Prime, and when he gets there, he will either transfer it to another leader, or change his style.

A large organization needs different leaders for different units. That's why a large, well-structured and staffed company with many different leadership styles can do better than a small company which can be vulnerable because it has only *one* style and *one* profit center.

A family structure should have not only different companies at different stages of the life cycle, i.e., a portfolio. Each unit should have different goals to deliver. An infant should try to break even; a Go-Go should seek market penetration, and an Aristocracy should deliver a return on investment. The goal of a Prime organization should be to produce new Infants.

Furthermore, different activities should be rewarded differently; each leadership style is motivated differently. This is called *organizational pluralism*. Good organizations are pluralistic. They not only allow the **(E)** to survive, but to thrive.

The repetitive mistake made, is in deciding who will be the head of the family. What is undesirable, but often happens, is that the leader comes from Aristocracy, the most established unit. When this happens, there is an identity problem. It is functional colonialism, not structural colonialism. It is functional colonialism due to the leader's style. Although we changed to a family structure, it

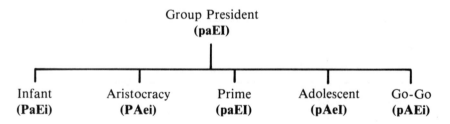

Group President
(paEI)

Infant	Aristocracy	Prime	Adolescent	Go-Go
(PaEi)	**(PAei)**	**(paEI)**	**(pAeI)**	**(pAEi)**

Figure 91: Leadership in the Organizational Family Structure

will not operate as designed in terms of behavior and expectations. The Aristocracy could still dominate through the behavior of the leadership. What is needed is someone with a big **(EI)** at the top, bigger than in Prime. Why? Because now he must integrate this pluralistic structure and direct it.

If structural pluralism (each unit has its different goals and leadership styles) is desired, an Aristocratic culture will be dysfunctional. Aristocracies, by and large, expect everybody to behave in the same way. To do this, they dress up a little baby like he is a grown-up, ready to go to a funeral. A baby is supposed to act like a baby. Adults shouldn't be expected to behave like babies, and babies shouldn't be expected to behave like adults. The leadership must recognize and legitimatize the differentiation in behavior in terms of predictability of outcomes, functionality of rules and how strictly the organization is expected to adhere to them.

Additionally, the organization must differentiate the kind of leadership that is put in this structure. Each individual and different style is rewarded for different things. Each unit is expected to perform, and achieve differently. Thus, the reward system should be different. The danger with colonialism is that there is one rule, one style, one behavior, and one incentive system. Sameness creates bureaucratization.

TREATING THE STABLE ORGANIZATION (PAeI)

What should be done in Stable? In Prime, the organization decentralized. In Stable, the organization should do the same therapy used in Aristocracy, except that it should be done with less time pressure. Stable is the beginning of the end, but the problems are not as pronounced as in Aristocracy. There is not as much pressure on the therapist to do fast interventions. What we have to watch out for in Stable is that the form is growing stronger than the function. *How* is becoming more important than *what*. How people appear, how they dress, and how they talk is emphasized. *How* they do things is more important than *what* they do. Note that the entrepreneurial spirit is starting to decline, and *CAPI* is being questioned, but this is all on the surface still. It is not strongly pronounced. What should be done?

Consciousness-raising is the most critical task for the Stable organization. Its members must realize that (E) has declined and (I) is growing. The members of the Stable organization agree on everything, and they are too close to everything that happens around them.

The assignments here are to forecast the future, analyze the environment, foresee the threats *and* opportunities, and to *stretch* when setting goals. Once the members of the Stable organization recapture a panoramic view of the future, the next step is to rapidly decentralize the company in order to stimulate and stabilize (E). If (E) is allowed to grow without disturbing (I) or affecting (A), then a (PAEI) organization can again be achieved.

The assignments in the Stable organization are given to a large group of people. Stringent deadlines are imposed in order to wake them up to the coming of age, and the group must be multidisciplinary in order to obtain the highest (E) possible.

For the Stable organization and organizations at later stages in the organizational Lifecycle, management transplantation becomes a problem. The Stable organization is set in its ways; a new style of management might be too trying. The older an organization becomes, the more it will resent different individual styles in managers. The Stable organization needs a capacity for (E). If a (paEi) manager is brought in from outside, he will most likely experience difficulties because he is different. The difficulties, however, are not so great as to preclude integration.

In getting to Stable, the factors that could be causing (E) to decline are: mental age, perceived relative market share, leadership style and structure.

If the cause for aging—and the loss of (E)—is mental age, we recommend restaffing top management positions with mentally younger people.

If the cause is perceived relative market share, the solution lies in mission definition (Phase IV), which should be redefined. If the organization has 35 percent of a certain market, all they need to do is redefine the market product scope. By moving the horizon to redefine their market, they can have only 3 percent of the market. This is analogous to climbing up a mountain. When a climber gets to the top of the mountain, he should look at the next ridge, and identify the next peak of another mountain. When he goes down it's not going down permanently, it's only going down to go up again. If they are in the paint business and have 35 percent of the paint business, they could redefine themselves as being in the wall protection decorative services market, and all of a sudden they will have 3 percent of the market because now it includes wallpaper.

The nature of a business must be continually redefined, so that the horizon is never reached.

If functionality of the organizational structure is the problem they must restructure the company in order to strengthen (E). That is done via decentralization into new profit centers, and correctly structuring of the staff units. If the decline in (E) is due to a leadership style, the organization requires change in its leadership style. Both these activities are discussed in detail in the following section.

TREATING THE ARISTOCRATIC ORGANIZATION (pAeI)

It is a bit more difficult to help the Aristocratic organization than to help organizations in other stages of the Lifecycle. The Aristocratic organization needs a real awakening from its "Finzi-Contini syndrome." The first step is to conduct a group diagnostic session, a methodology of synergetic participative diagnosis that the Adizes methodology calls Syndag. This diagnosis is a deep consciousness-raising session at which all participants share information about the problems the company is facing. Viewed in this way, the problems seem to be truly overpowering. The need for change becomes obvious. Diagnosis at many levels in the company is necessary to remind people of the present state of the organization, as opposed to the desired state. The therapist must constantly call attention to manifestations of the Finzi-Contini syndrome.

In attempting to treat Aristocratic organizations, consultants often say, "First, let's define your goals." If they define the goals without the organization feeling that they can achieve them, however, it's an exercise in futility. First, they have to feel they can make a change; they must feel they can work together; they must say, "Yes, we are potent." Then they can work on where they want to go.

In a Go-Go, Syndag does not have to be the first step. Go-Go organizations already have so much energy, that a diagnosis could be counterproductive; but in an Aristocracy, everyone is mild, relatively passive and complacent. By putting all the problems on the wall, the need to change is legitimatized and energy is created.

Once a strong commitment for change is established, the company can move promptly toward resolving the abnormal problems.

Mission definition (Phase IV) is essential for Aristocracies because it identifies new horizons. This mission definition must be done as a team process, focusing on divergent thinking. There is more than this company can do; there are more opportunities than it is presently exploring. The members are not really stuck, they can do something about their future. This process helps members of the group analyze the technological, political, economic, legal, social, and physical environments of the organization. It teaches them how to analyze their markets, product scope and values. All of this enables them to identify the opportunities and threats that face the organization. Identifying what they want the future to be, forces them to design a structure to realize that future.

A decentralized organizational structure is designed (Phase V) to implement the strategies discovered in mission. The organization pulls out any and all potential Infants and Go-Go organizations from the Aristocracy and restructure the Aristocracy horizontally into a family structure rather than the typical colonialistic structure.

Once the structure is completed, a redesign of information systems that support decentralized accountability is called for (Phase VI). This is followed by resource allocation (Phase VIII) and redesign of the incentive systems (Phase XI) to promote profitability and return to an achievement orientation.

A change in the leadership of the Aristocracy may also be required. However, prematurely bringing a person with a large (E) into an Aristocratic organization is not recommended. The members of such an organization constitute a mutual admiration society in which detail and maintenance, not growth, are the major attractions. In such a setting, a predominantly (E) person will experience difficulty in expressing himself and in exercising creative leadership. Success of such a transplantation would be more likely achieved after the restructuring is completed.

If (E) must be brought in before restructure is finished, or because it is needed for the restructure, the therapist must use the bypass system. If a person whose style alienates the organization is brought in, the Aristocratic organization will discourage his style. The (A) rejects the (E), since the latter injects turbulence which (A) cannot control. The outcome is that (E) is either rejected or absorbed into the organization as a benign substance. He loses effectiveness. In other words, the organization develops immunities to odd, strange or different substances, thereby rejecting qualities which may be significant and functional to its growth and survival.

To integrate (E) into an Aristocratic organization, the therapist begins by looking throughout the organization for anyone with an active (E). Such persons are easy to find; they are the ones who are complaining that one thing or another is not what it should be. They are also people the organization is usually trying to dump. The therapist insists that they be retained for a little longer. In a sense, this stops the bleeding of (E).

Next, the therapist establishes a task force to work on a new project that can be completed in a short period of time (such as a new product, market, or system). The therapist then recommends that the newly hired (E) lead this task force, which is composed of the organizational deviants. Since the latter are (E)s from several disciplines and levels of the organizations, they constitute a bypass of the (A) channels of the organization, with people who have already developed "arteriosclerosis." That is, they resent and reject change. As the task of the deviants is accomplished, (P) is created, which somewhat rejuvenates the organization. As several such teams are established, the outsider (E) soon begins to feel comfortable, especially as the structure changes, power centers shift, and expectations to produce results increase.

When an Early Bureaucracy develops, the task becomes much more difficult, since the (e) has been replaced by a blank, and there is a total rejection and resentment of change. Surgery, a change of management may be the only viable alternative for such an organization, since it is on the brink of bankruptcy. However, surgery in itself is not sufficient and recuperation, organizational therapy is needed later on.

TREATING EARLY BUREAUCRACY (pA-i)

The backbiting which characterizes this stage requires prompt surgical treatment. Several people whose attitudes are negative, who poison the climate, or who are totally ineffective must be replaced. This surgery should be done only once and very sparingly. If several surgical interventions are made in succession, it might paralyze the organization. Management's suspicion and paranoia, which are strong in this stage of the Lifecycle, might run rampant; in other words, the treatment might *reinforce*, rather than *treat* the neurosis.

Management should sell unprofitable units and stop the negative cash flow. Emphasis should be on survival. For that, *CAPI* must be together, usually in a single individual. In Aristocracy and Stable, *CAPI* is around teams, because there is time for teams. In Early Bureaucracy, there is no time. There must be one individual to bite the bullet and cut the company down to its profitable essence. The same treatment given to an Infant organization is recommended here: rolling 16 weeks cash flow projections, cost accounting be done to identify where the real leaks in profitability are, turnover of inventory and accounts receivable is done weekly.

After surgery, the same therapeutic treatment given to an Aristocracy is applied, except that the rate of intervention (the doses of treatment) is much higher. The emphasis is to cut down the *how* and pump up the *what*.

TREATING BUREAUCRACY (– – – A) AND DEAD (– – – –) ORGANIZATIONS

Adizes therapy is not applicable here because for therapy, time is of the essence and Early Bureaucracies have no time to spare.

Bureaucratic organizations usually prefer a system analyst to increase the (A) which they already have in overabundance. They usually hire computer consultants and auditors to solve their managerial problems. They ask for more (A) which they already have in abundance. Such organizations probably need surgery and a long period of rehabilitation. The surgery would be a type of bypass, an addition of (E). The (E) most likely, would have to be forced on the organization, which would probably fight it.

Rehabilitation is necessary in order to bring (P) back into action again. Shock treatment (threats of firing, unrealistic demands, and so on.) is inadvisable, because it would simply scare people, and make them go frantically through any steps required of them. The results would be short-lived, and eventually, the organization would fall back into apathy. In fact, a series of such treatments might spur the remaining good managers to leave, forcing the organization into a coma.

What is needed is multiple, simultaneous implementation of the eleven phases applied diagonally from top management to a work place, with close monitoring of the integration of the intervention.

As for restoring dead organizations to life, this is probably a capability reserved for saints.

Ill-Timed and Unnecessary Surgery

Surgery, changing top management is the fastest way to produce change, but it is also the most painful and dangerous treatment. It is often used because it can be done in a short time and is highly lucrative (to the executive search firm). Unfortunately, few organizational surgeons stay long enough to see the results of their surgery or accept the responsibility for post surgical complications.

What makes a successful surgeon is not how fast he cuts, but how well he monitors the post surgical complications that occur when the body is weak and vulnerable. Consultants who suggest a new organization chart, help in locating the people to fill in the boxes, collect their fee, and consider the task done, have not completed their job. When the new structure is put into effect, the *real* pain of adaptation starts. Although the pain may be acute, managers usually refuse to complain in public about any problems. They fear that if they point to some problems, another surgical treatment might follow. They would rather suffer quietly, or complain in dark rooms, than subject themselves to another surgery.

While organizational change is indispensable for long-run success, if it is induced as a cure at the wrong time, it may produce an almost permanent relapse; the organization may refuse to submit to it. If surgery has been painful and ineffective and exclusively applied as a cure, the organization may refuse to be operated on for preventive purposes, especially when a problem is not yet evident. Often, reorganization is attempted only when there is a crisis (for example, in Early Bureaucracy). At this stage surgery is inevitable. The treatment, however, should have occurred when its effect would not have been as painful—at the Prime stage of the organization's Lifecycle. At that time the organizational climate was conducive to change. Due to growth and positive expectations for the future, the perceived threats from change were much smaller and could have been minimized even further. In Early Bureaucracy, when the economic results are bad and the atmosphere is already suspicious, change reinforces fears rather than removing them.

If the organization is an Aristocracy, a *no firing* policy is recommended. There are many **(E)**s who act like **(A)**s to survive. For six months a change in the organizational climate to reflect expected opportunities for external growth will bring those **(E)**s to surface. There is no need to hire new **(E)** people that the organization needs. They are already there. Overall, such treatment has been successful.

Can An Internal Consultant Do The Job?

It has become fashionable for large organizations to develop their own consulting departments, often called *organizational development* (OD) departments.

Such departments can be functional during the early stages of the organizational Lifecycle. However, older organizations—Stable organizations and their successors—will have less success with OD departments. In a young organization, **(A)** and **(I)** are the necessary ingredients. These can be provided from within easily enough; the consultants would not have to fear losing their jobs. However, as an organization approaches its zenith, **(E)** is called for, and that requires insultants more than forsultants. An internal consultant might not be willing or able to make the necessary waves and create the consciousness and desire for change.

Organizational development specialists appear to have been trained and to be inclined to perform only the **(I)** role. Most frequently they are **(---I)**s. At *best*, they are **(paeI)**s. Such a style is of no use for an organization that requires serious therapy and rejuvenation. A **(paeI)** or **(---I)** style only maintains what exists. OD specialists operate more as establishment agents who make the existing fare seem palatable than as agents of change who create the necessary new dish.

Throughout the Adizes methodology of therapy as presented above, integrators who act as agents of change are trained and developed. For at least the beginning stages of therapy, I have found that external pacing is necessary to create the impetus and direction for change, and to buffer any negative short-term reactions that the organization may have. For organizations at a beyond the Stable stage, a more potent medication than simple advice is needed, and it usually must be administered externally.

LIFECYCLES REFERENCES

Chapter Reference	Source

Chapter 10
Page 269
Chandler, Alfred B.
Strategy and Structure: *Chapters in the History of the Industrial Enterprise*, (Cambridge: MIT. Press, 1962).

Chapter 7
Page 190
Djilas, Milovan.
The New Class: *An Analysis of the Communist System*, (San Diego: Harcourt Brace Jovanovich, 1983)

Chapter 11
Page 288
Shapiro, David.
Neurotic Styles: Forward by Robert P. Knight, (New York: Basic Books, 1983).

Chapter 13
Page 340
Samuelson, Paul A.
Economics: 12th Edition, (New York: McGraw-Hill, 1985), 950 pages.

Chapter 5
Page 145
Stigler, George Joseph.
The Theory of Price: (New York: MacMillian Company, 1966), p. 155.

Chapter 11
Page 291
"Who's Excellent Now": Business Week, (November 5, 1984), p. 76.

Chapter 3
Page 83
"Garden Of The Finzi Continis": (Warner Brothers: Italian, 1971).

Chapter 11
Page 291
Peters, Thomas J. and Waterman, Jr., Robert H. *In Search Of Excellence*: (New York: Harper & Row, 1982) 360 p.

Summary

This book presented a description, analysis, and prescriptive therapy of organizational cultures.

We have seen how organizational cultures change over the lifecycle. A theory of management was presented which enabled us to diagnose how and why a culture changes. We have proceeded to show how this theory can be used to change a location of an organization on its Lifecycle and how to change its culture.

The theory I presented is not "finished," however. I am still working out some of the theoretical parts of it in my mind, and I believe the reader should be aware of this. There is more work to be done in developing this theory.

No detailed description of the therapeutic part was provided in this book. No case studies have been included to show how the process works in action, to show its pitfalls. I tried to write both the therapy and the case studies in more detail. After much anguish over this, I decided to leave this material out. The book is too long as it is. Any short write ups, open more doors than they close windows. However, it simply could not get the right justifiable treatment in the available space. Obviously, a new book needs to be written.

Index